NATIONAL GEOGRAPHIC LEARNING | CENGAGE Learning

SO-CEJ-981

Life

2

John Hughes

Paul Dummett

Helen Stephenson

Life Level 2 Student Book

Helen Stephenson

Paul Dummett

John Hughes

Publisher: Sherrise Roehr

Executive Editor: Sarah T. Kenney

Associate Development Editor:
Nathan A. Gamache

Director of Global Marketing: Ian Martin

Senior Product Marketing Manager:
Caitlin Thomas

Director of Content and Media Production:
Michael Burggren

Senior Content Project Manager: Daisy Sosa

Senior Print Buyer: Mary Beth Hennebury

Cover Designers: Scott Baker and Alex Dull

Cover Image: © 2012 Pascal carrion / Getty Images

Compositor: MPS Limited

Cover image

A blanket of fog covers the Marina skyscrapers in Dubai.
Photo by Pascal Carrion.

© 2015 National Geographic Learning, a part of Cengage Learning

ALL RIGHTS RESERVED. No part of this work covered by the copyright herein may be reproduced, transmitted, stored or used in any form or by any means graphic, electronic, or mechanical, including but not limited to photocopying, recording, scanning, digitising, taping, Web distribution, information networks, or information storage and retrieval systems, except as permitted under Section 107 or 108 of the 1976 United States Copyright Act, or applicable copyright law of another jurisdiction, without the prior written permission of the publisher.

For permission to use material from this text or product, submit all requests online at **cengage.com/permissions**

Further permissions questions can be emailed to
permissionrequest@cengage.com.

Student Book
ISBN-13: 978-1-305-25577-7

Student Book + CD-ROM
ISBN-13: 978-1-305-25584-5

Student Book + PAC
ISBN-13: 978-1-305-26036-8

National Geographic Learning/Cengage Learning
20 Channel Center Street
Boston, MA 02210
USA

Cengage Learning is a leading provider of customised learning solutions with office locations around the globe, including Singapore, the United Kingdom, Australia, Mexico, Brazil and Japan.

Cengage Learning products are represented in Canada by Nelson Education Ltd.

Visit National Geographic Learning online at **ngl.cengage.com**

Visit our corporate website at **www.cengage.com**

Printed in the United States of America
3 4 5 6 7 8 19 18 17 16 15

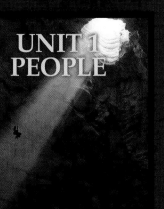

**UNIT 1
PEOPLE**

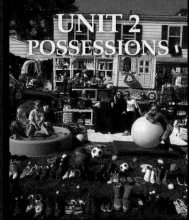

**UNIT 2
POSSESSIONS**

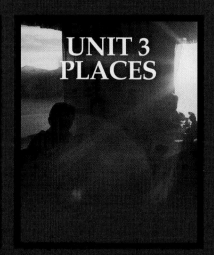

**UNIT 3
PLACES**

**UNIT 4
FREE TIME**

**UNIT 5
FOOD**

**UNIT 6
MONEY**

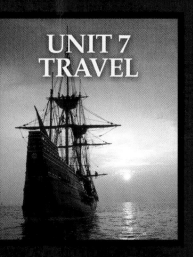

**UNIT 7
TRAVEL**

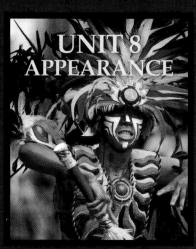

**UNIT 8
APPEARANCE**

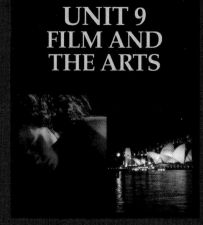

**UNIT 9
FILM AND
THE ARTS**

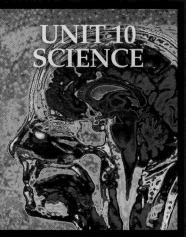

**UNIT 10
SCIENCE**

**UNIT 11
TOURISM**

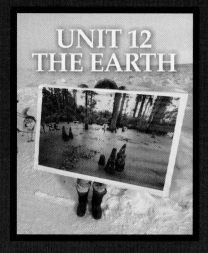

**UNIT 12
THE EARTH**

Contents

LISTENING	READING	CRITICAL THINKING	SPEAKING	WRITING
an interview with an explorer people at a conference	an article about a family of explorers an article about world population	the writer's purpose	asking questions friends and family facts about countries	text type: a personal description writing skill: *and, but*
an interview with Andy Torbet	an article about studio apartments an article about a global product	close reading	your objects and possessions a room in your home where things are from	a description of a room in your home text type: ads writing skill: describing objects with adjectives
someone talking about a 24-hour restaurant in Norway an interview with a student living in New York an interview with Frank Richards	an article about car-free zones an article about languages spoken around the world	making connections	your life exchanging information about a photographer favorite numbers and their relevance	text type: a travel website writing skill: capital letters
three people talking about their pastimes an interview with Paul Nicklen	an article about identical twins an article about a nature photographer an article about extreme sports an ad for volunteer work	fact or opinion	likes and dislikes daily life your abilities	text type: short emails writing skill: reference words
people describing famous dishes from their countries a conversation at a market	an article about food markets around the world an article about the Svalbard Global Seed Vault	summarizing	famous dishes from different countries planning a special meal buying food at a market summarizing an article	text type: instructions writing skill: punctuation
someone talking about street musicians an interview with two people at a museum people asking for money in different situations	an article about currency an article about a treasure an article about the history of money	relevance	someone's past life important years in your life a survey about money	a description of someone's life text type: thank you messages writing skill: formal and informal expressions

LISTENING	READING	CRITICAL THINKING	SPEAKING	WRITING
a radio show about journeys in history a program about animal migration	an article about a flight from the past an article about space travel	fact or opinion	a trip you made your opinion a general knowledge quiz	a general knowledge quiz text type: a travel blog writing skill: *so, because*
a conversation about masks at a festival	an article about a fashion photographer an article about tattoos a text about emoticons	close reading	people's appearance what people are wearing	text type: texts and online messages writing skill: textspeak
two people at a film festival an interview with a filmmaker two people discussing a Broadway show	an article about the Lights, Camera, Action! Film Festival an article about a wildlife filmmaker an article about nature in art	the writer's preferences	deciding which movies to see your future plans explaining preferences	text type: reviews and comments writing skill: giving your opinion with sense verbs
an interview with someone about technology a news report about a memory champion someone calling his office	a survey about outdated technology reading about memory an article about new inventions	the main argument and supporting information	experience with technology something you have learned	the main argument text type: a telephone message writing skill: imperatives
a podcast from a travel program two friends discussing a trip to South America	a quiz from a travel magazine a tourist information leaflet a travel article	arguments for and against	advice for a tourist rules what's important in a hotel	a description of a tourist destination text type: a feedback form writing skill: closed and open questions
an interview about movie director James Cameron and the Mariana Trench	maps showing climate change an article about unexplored places on Earth an article about a new planet an article about Earth Day	structuring an argument	your future places on Earth life on another planet	text type: a poster writing skill: important words and information

Life around the world

Unit 3

See the street life in Barcelona.

Unit 5 Gelato University

Learn how to make ice cream in Italy.

Unit 6 Bactrian treasure

Discover the history of an ancient civilization.

Unit 8 Festivals and special events

Visit some of the world's most colorful festivals.

Unit 1 World party

How big is seven billion?

Unit 7 Women in space

The story of the first female astronauts.

Unit 4 Urban Biking

Meet Danny MacAskill and learn about his unique style of bike riding.

Unit 12 Volcanoes

The science and history of Earth's most amazing places.

USA

UK

Spain Italy

Barcelona

Afghanistan

Saudi Arabia

India

Honduras

Australia

Unit 2 Coober Pedy's opals

Go under a town in Australia for opals.

Unit 9 Camera traps

How a director films the secret lives of animals.

Unit 10 Baby Math

Can babies do… math?

Unit 11 Mecca and the Hajj

Follow people who take religious vacations.

Unit 1 People

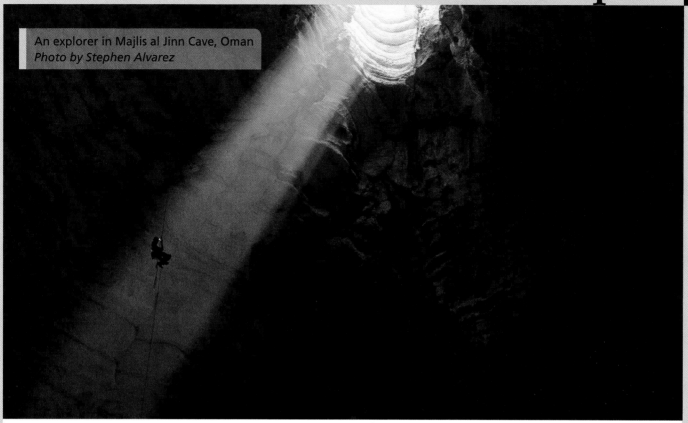

An explorer in Majlis al Jinn Cave, Oman
Photo by Stephen Alvarez

FEATURES

1 Look at the photo and the caption. Where is the explorer?
What is the photographer's name?

2 Talk to students in your class. Ask and answer these questions.

Hello. What's your name?

My name's …

Where are you from?

I'm from …

What's his/her name?

His/Her name's …

Where's he/she from?

He/She's from …

1a Explorers

Listening

1 Look at the photo of two explorers. Where are they from?

2 🎵 **1** Listen to the interview and mark the sentences true (T) or false (F).

1 His name's <u>Mike</u> <u>Burney</u>.
2 He's from <u>the US</u>.
3 He's <u>married</u>.
4 <u>Sally</u> Burney is his <u>wife</u>.
5 She's a <u>photographer</u>.
6 They're <u>twenty-six</u> years old.

Vocabulary personal information

3 Add the underlined words from the sentences in Exercise 2 to columns A and B.

	A	B	C
First name	....	....	
Last name	....		
Age	thirty-five	....	
Job/Occupation	explorer	....	
Country	Canada	....	
Marital status	married	....	
Relationship	wife	....	

4 Add information about yourself to column C in Exercise 3.

Grammar *be* (*am/is/are*)

5 🎵 **1** Listen again and read the interview with Mike Burney from Exercise 2. Circle the forms of *be* in each sentence.

I: Hello. What's your name?
M: My name's Mike Burney.
I: Are you from Great Britain?
M: Yes, I'm from the UK, but I travel all the time.
I: And are you married?
M: Yes, I am. My wife's name is Sally. She isn't at home at the moment.
I: Why? What's her job?
M: She's also an explorer and we often travel together.
I: Is she from the UK too?
M: No, she isn't. She's from Canada.
I: Are you the same age?
M: No, we aren't. I'm thirty-six and Sally is thirty-five.

6 Look at the forms you circled in Exercise 5. Which forms are (a) affirmative, (b) negative, (c) questions, and (d) short answers? Look at the grammar box and check your answers.

> ▶ **BE (AM/IS/ARE)**
>
> **Affirmative**
> I'm **(am)** a student.
> You/we/they're **(are)** married.
> He/she/it's **(is)** from Canada.
>
> **Negative**
> I'm not **(am not)** a teacher.
> You/we/they **aren't (are not)** married.
> He/she/it **isn't (is not)** from the US.
>
> **Questions and short answers**
> What's your name?
> Where **is** she from?
> **Are** you from Brazil? Yes, I **am**. / No, I'm **not**.
> **Is** she single? Yes, she **is**. / No, she **isn't**.
>
> For more information and practice, see page 157.

7 Mike Burney is at the airport. Complete the conversation with the correct form of *be*.

C = Customs officer, M = Mike Burney
C: Good afternoon. ¹_____ you in New Zealand for work or vacation?
M: For work. I ²_____ an explorer.
C: I see. What ³_____ your address in Auckland?
M: We ⁴_____ at 106a Eglinton Road.
C: We?
M: Yes, my wife and two children.
    They ⁵_____ with me.
C: ⁶_____ your wife an explorer?
M: Yes, she is, but she ⁷_____ in Auckland for work.
    She ⁸_____ on vacation.

8 Pronunciation contracted forms

a 🔊 **2** Listen and mark (✓) the form you hear.
1 'm ✓   am
2 're   are
3 'm not   am not
4 's   is
5 aren't   are not
6 're   are
7 isn't   is not
8 's   is

b 🔊 **2** Listen again and repeat the sentences.

Speaking

9 Work in pairs. Ask your partner about his/her:

- first and last names
- job/occupation
- country
- marital status

10 Introduce your partner to the class.

> *Rosana's from Chile. She's twenty-three.*
> *She's a teacher. She's single.*

1b A family in East Africa

Reading

1 Is your family big or small? Are you all from the same country?

2 Read about the Leakey family. Answer the questions.

1 Where are they from?
2 Are Louise and Maeve explorers?
3 What is Richard's job?
4 What is Colin's job?
5 Is Samira an explorer?
6 Is Philip married?

3 Read the article again and complete the family tree on page 13.

A family in EAST AFRICA

The Leakey family is very interesting. They live in East Africa, but the family is from England. Louise Leakey is an explorer, but for her family that's normal! Louise's mother is Maeve and she's also an explorer.

Her father is Richard Leakey. Richard is also in East Africa, but he's a farmer. Richard's half brother is Colin Leakey. Colin isn't in Africa, but he's an explorer and a scientist at Cambridge University in England.

Louise's grandparents (Louis and Mary) are dead, but they were also famous explorers. Louise's sister is Samira. She works for the World Bank. Their uncle and aunt are Phillip Leakey and his wife Katy. They have an international company.

dead (adj) /ded/ not living
were (v) /wɜr/ past tense of *are*

Louise Leakey and her mother, Maeve

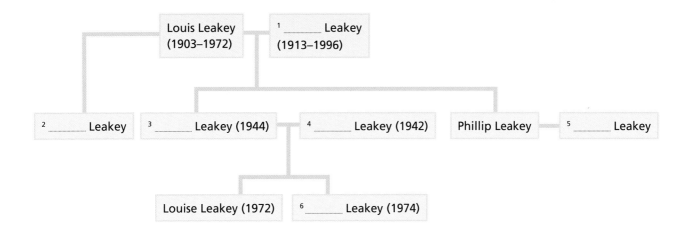

Louis Leakey
(1903–1972)

¹ _____ Leakey
(1913–1996)

² _____ Leakey

³ _____ Leakey (1944)

⁴ _____ Leakey (1942)

Phillip Leakey

⁵ _____ Leakey

Louise Leakey (1972)

⁶ _____ Leakey (1974)

Vocabulary family

4 Look at these family words. Which are men (M)? Which are women (W)? Which are both (B)?

mother	father	uncle	aunt
niece	nephew	cousin	mother-in-law
parent	stepbrother	half-brother	grandparent

5 Complete the phrases with words from Exercise 4.

1 your father's brother and sister _____ , _____
2 your brother's daughter and son _____ , _____
3 your uncle and aunt's son or daughter _____
4 a brother, but from one different parent _____
5 your husband or wife's mother _____
6 your mother or father _____
7 your parent's mother or father _____

> ▶ **WORDBUILDING word roots**
>
> You can make more words from a root word. For example:
> *mother* → *grandmother* → *stepmother* → *mother-in-law*

Grammar possessive 's and possessive adjectives

6 Look at the grammar box. Then find examples of the possessive 's and possessive adjectives in the article in Exercise 2.

> ▶ **POSSESSIVE 'S AND POSSESSIVE ADJECTIVES**
>
> **Possessive 's**
> Mike's wife is Sally. Mike and Sally's home is in Canada.
>
> **Possessive adjectives**
> She's **my** sister. What's **your** name? **His** name is Charlie.
>
> **Subject pronoun / Possessive adjective**
> I / my, you / your, he / his, she / her, it / its, we / our, they / their
>
> For more information and practice, see page 157.

7 Choose the correct word to complete the sentences.

1 *I / My* parents are Spanish.
2 *I / My* am the only boy in my family.
3 What's *you / your* name?
4 Where are *you / your* from?
5 *She / Her* is a photographer.
6 *He / His* uncle is in the US.
7 *We / Our* family is from Asia.
8 *They / Their* cousins are both girls.

8 **Pronunciation the same or different sounds**

🔊 **3** Listen to these pairs of words. Is the pronunciation of these words the same (✓) or different (✗)?

1 they're / their   4 are / our
2 he's / his   5 you're / your
3 its / it's

9 Say these sentences in a different way. Use the possessive adjective in parentheses.

My name's Fabien.

1 I'm Fabien. (my name)
2 Frank and Tony's cousin is Jane. (their)
3 Fritz's grandparents are dead. (his)
4 Are you Sylvain? (your name)
5 Helen is Peter's and my niece. (our niece)

Speaking

10 Write down five names of your friends and family. Introduce them to your partner.

Sandra is my best friend. She's from Colombia.

Nadia and Fatima are my two cousins in Morocco. They're my mother's nieces.

1c The face of seven billion people

Reading

1 There are seven billion people in the world. How many people are in your country?

2 Read the article and match the numbers in the box with the information (1–8).

51%	86	1 billion
1.2 billion	38%	21%
5 billion	2.5 billion	

1 the life expectancy of a Japanese woman
2 the population of India
3 the number of speakers of English as a second language
4 the percentage of Muslims
5 the percentage of workers in agriculture
6 the percentage of people in cities
7 the number of people who use the Internet
8 the number of people with cell phones

Critical thinking **the writer's purpose**

3 Read the article again. What is the writer's purpose? Choose the correct answer (a, b, or c).

He writes _____ .
a information
b an opinion
c a story

4 Which information in the article is new or surprising for you? Tell the class.

> *The information about the city and the countryside is new for me.*

Vocabulary **everyday verbs**

5 Find these verbs in the article. Then write them in the fact file.

| have | live | speak | use | work |

FACT FILE: China

* One point three billion people _____ in China.
* Seventy percent of the population _____ Mandarin.
* Over 1 billion Chinese people _____ a cell phone.
* Sixty-five percent of the population _____ in agriculture.
* Thirty-five percent of the Chinese population _____ the Internet.
(*statistics from 2012)

Word focus *in*

6 Look at the sentences in Exercise 5. Mark the correct information. We use *in*:

* with countries and cities
* with languages
* with areas of work or industry
* with the Internet

Speaking

7 Work in pairs. Student A: Turn to page 154. Student B: Turn to page 156. Read the information about both countries and prepare questions. Then ask and answer your questions to complete the tables.

THE FACE OF seven 7 billion people

There are seven billion people in the world and there are seven thousand people in this photo. Each person in the photo is equal to one million people. That's seven billion total!

A composite image of the world's most typical person: male, Chinese, 28 years old.

AGE
The average person in the world is 28 years old. In Japan, the average life expectancy for a woman is 86. In Afghanistan, it's 45.

POPULATION
Twenty percent of the world's population live in China. There are 1.2 billion people in India.

LANGUAGE
Thirteen percent of the world's population speak Mandarin as their first language. Five percent speak Spanish as their first language. Five percent also speak English as their first language; but English is the second language of 1 billion people.

RELIGION
Thirty-three percent of the world is Christian, 21 percent is Muslim, and 13 percent is Hindu.

JOBS
Forty percent of people work in a service industry (hotels, banks, etc.), 38 percent are in agriculture, and 22 percent are in manufacturing and production.

CITY AND COUNTRYSIDE
Fifty-one percent of the world's population live in cities and 49 percent live in the countryside.

INTERNET AND CELL PHONES
2.5 billion people use the Internet, and 5 billion people have a cell phone.

(is) equal (to) /ˈikwəl/ the same as (*2 + 2 = 4, two and two equals four*)
average (adj) /ˈævərɪdʒ/ usual, typical
life expectancy (n) /ˈlaɪf ɪkˌspektənsi/ the number of years you can expect to live

1d At a conference

Speaking

1 Pronunciation spelling

🔊 4 Listen and repeat the letters of the alphabet.

A B C D E F G H I J K L M N O P Q R S T U V W X Y Z

2 Work in pairs to spell these words. Check each other's spelling.

- your first name
- your last name
- your country
- your job

Listening

3 🔊 5 Listen to two conversations. Then choose the correct word to complete the sentences.

Conversation one
1 Gary is the *first* / *second* person at the conference.
2 Rita *is* / *isn't* the conference manager.
3 This is their *first* / *second* meeting.
4 Gary's last name is *Lawrence* / *Laurens*.

Conversation two
5 Valerie's last name is *Moore* / *Moreau*.
6 Valerie is from *France* / *New Caledonia*.
7 *Rita* / *Gary* says goodbye.

Real life meeting people for the first time

4 🔊 5 Look at the expressions for meeting people for the first time. Then listen again and mark the expressions you hear.

> ### ▶ MEETING PEOPLE
>
> **Introducing yourself**
> My name's … / I'm …
> I'm from …
> Nice to meet you.
> Nice to meet you too.
>
> **Introducing another person**
> I'd like to introduce you to …
> This is …
> He's from …
>
> **Saying good bye**
> Nice meeting you.
> Nice talking to you.
> See you later.
> Goodbye./Bye.

5 Work in groups of three: A, B, and C. Practice the conversation. Then change roles and repeat the conversation two more times.

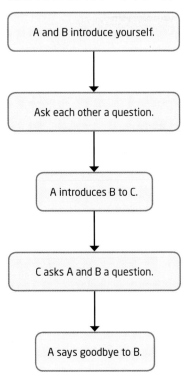

A and B introduce yourself.

↓

Ask each other a question.

↓

A introduces B to C.

↓

C asks A and B a question.

↓

A says goodbye to B.

1e Introduce yourself

Writing a personal description

1 Read the two online introductions. Look back at page 16. Where are Gary and Valerie at the moment?

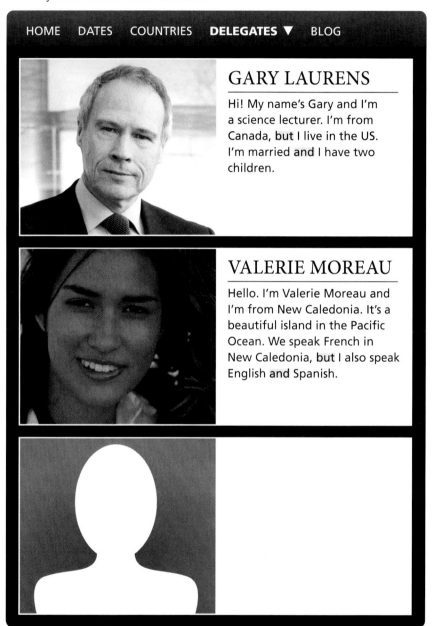

HOME   DATES   COUNTRIES   **DELEGATES** ▼   BLOG

GARY LAURENS

Hi! My name's Gary and I'm a science lecturer. I'm from Canada, but I live in the US. I'm married and I have two children.

VALERIE MOREAU

Hello. I'm Valerie Moreau and I'm from New Caledonia. It's a beautiful island in the Pacific Ocean. We speak French in New Caledonia, but I also speak English and Spanish.

2 Read the introductions again. Mark the information they give.

	Gary	Valerie
First name		
Last name		
Job		
Country		
Languages		
Other information		

3 Writing skill *and, but*

a Look at the words *and* and *but* in the introductions in Exercise 1. Which word is for extra information? Which word is for different information?

b Make one sentence from the two sentences with *and* or *but*.

1 I'm in Spain. I'm from Argentina.
I'm in Spain, but I'm from Argentina.

2 I'm 21. My sister is 21.
I'm 21 and my sister is 21.

3 I'm American. Spanish is my first language.

4 He's from Germany. He's in Vietnam at the moment.

5 My friend is 30. He's single.

6 I live in Mexico. I work in the United States.

7 She's a student. She's at Stanford University.

8 My family lives in the country. I live in the city.

4 Imagine you are going to the conference. Write an online introduction for yourself. Use the table in Exercise 2 to help you. Use *and* and *but*.

5 Exchange your introduction with your partner. Check your partner's text. Does he/she include all the information from Exercise 2? Does he/she use *and* and *but* correctly?

6 Display your introductions in the classroom. Walk around and read about each other.

World party

Street party in Bangkok for Chinese New Year

Before you watch

1 Work in groups. Look at the photo and answer the questions.

   1 Where is the party?
   2 Why are the people at this party?

2 Discuss these questions as a class.

   1 When do you have parties in your country?
   2 Where are these parties (e.g., in your house, in the street, in a restaurant, at your college)?

While you watch

3 The video is about a "World party" for seven billion people. Watch the video. Number the questions (a–c) in the order the video answers them.

   a How big is the place for a world party?
   b How big is seven billion?
   c Where is a good place for a world party?

4 Watch the video again. Match 1–8 with a–h.

   1 number of years to count from 1 to 7 billion
   2 number of stars you can see at night
   3 number of times around the Earth in seven billion steps
   4 number of text messages in the US every second
   5 the area for one person to stand in
   6 the area for one person at a party
   7 the area for seven billion people at a party
   8 the area for seven billion people in a photo

   a a thousand
   b six square feet
   c 1,500 square miles
   d three square feet
   e 200
   f 133
   g 65,000
   h 500 square miles

> 1 square foot = 0.9 square meter
> 1 square mile = 2.6 square kilometers
> 500 miles = 800 kilometers
> 1,500 miles = 2,400 kilometers

> **bit** /bɪt/ a small amount
> **about** (adv) /əˈbaʊt/ approximately
> **compare** (v) /kəmˈpeər/ to talk about the differences and similarities between one thing and another thing
> **correct** (adj) /kəˈrekt/ not wrong
> **takes** (two hundred years) (v) /teɪks/ lasts (two hundred years)

5 Number these sentences from the video in the correct order (1–9).

   a Don't count from 1 to 7 billion! ☐ *1*
   b There are seven billion stars. ☐
   c Or there's the state of Rhode Island. ☐
   d One person needs about three square feet. ☐
   e Walk around the Earth 133 times. ☐
   f People send seven billion texts every 30 hours in the US. ☐
   g So everyone needs about six square feet. ☐
   h The Juneau Icefield in Alaska is the correct size. But it's a bit cold. ☐
   i Los Angeles is 500 square miles. ☐

After you watch

6 Group discussion a party for your class

Work in groups. Discuss a party for your new English class. Think about these questions.

   1 How many people are in your class?
   2 Where is a good place for your party?
   3 What is important for a good party (e.g., food, music)?

7 Tell the class about the party.

> *Music is important for a good party.*

8 Class survey people in your class

Interview everyone in your class. Use these questions.

How many people …

• are in your class?
• are male or female?
• are under 30 or over 30?
• are students or have a job?
• speak two or more languages?
• are from this city?
• have a cell phone?
• use the Internet?

9 Write a short report about your class.

Example:
Fifteen people are in my class. Eight are male and seven are female.

UNIT 1 REVIEW

Grammar

1 Put the words in order to make questions.

1 your / name? / 's / what
2 from / are / Turkey? / you
3 are / you / where / from?
4 married? / you / are / single or
5 you / are / an explorer?

2 Work in pairs. Ask and answer the questions in Exercise 1.

3 Complete the conversation with *'s*, *isn't*, *are*, or *aren't*.

A: What ¹_____ his name?
B: His name ²_____ Felipe.
A: What ³_____ her name?
B: Camila.
A: ⁴_____ they married?
B: Yes, they ⁵_____ .
A: Are they from Mexico?
B: No, they ⁶_____ . They're from Brazil.
A: What ⁷_____ Felipe's job?
B: He ⁸_____ an explorer.
A: Is Camila a conservationist?
B: No, she ⁹_____ . She ¹⁰_____ an explorer too!

4 Choose the correct option to complete the sentences.

1 What's *you* / *your* name?
2 *He* / *His* aunt is American.
3 *They* / *Their* are my cousins.
4 The *photographer's* / *photographer is* wife is *my* / *I* best friend.
5 *She* / *Her* mother is from Germany, but *she's* / *she* from Switzerland.

I CAN

ask and answer questions with *what* and *where*

use the verb *to be* in sentences

talk about possession with possessive *'s* and possessive adjectives

Vocabulary

5 Match the words 1–6 with a–f.

1 last name   a 28
2 relationship   b single
3 age   c brother
4 job   d China
5 marital status   e teacher
6 country   f Obama

6 Complete the sentences with verbs.

1 Ninety percent of families h_____ a computer in their house.
2 Billions of people s_____ English.
3 More people l_____ in apartments than houses.
4 How many people w_____ in agriculture?

I CAN

talk about personal information

talk about everyday information

Real life

7 Put the conversation in the correct order (1–5).

☐ Sonia: Arnold is, but I'm not. I'm from Argentina.
☐ Arnold: Nice to meet you too, Rosa. I'm Arnold and this is my wife, Sonia.
☐ Rosa: I'm from Peru, but I live here. Are you and Arnold from the US?
☐ Rosa: Hi. I'm Rosa. Nice to meet you.
☐ Sonia: Hello, Rosa. Where are you from?

8 Work in groups of three. Practice a similar conversation to Exercise 7. Your names are Mike and Donna (married, from the US) and Lin (from China).

I CAN

introduce myself and other people

Speaking

9 Write three sentences (two true and one false) with personal information about yourself and / or your family.

10 Work in pairs. Take turns to read your sentences. Guess your partner's false sentence.

Unit 2 Possessions

A family with their plastic possessions
Photo by Sarah Leen

FEATURES

1 Look at the photo. How many people can you see in the photo? What are all the possessions made of?

2 Can you guess how many of these things are in the photo? Match the numbers with the words.

3	balls
7	shoes and boots
22	sofa
1	people
50	TVs

3 Work in pairs. Find these objects in the photo. What color are they?

| balls | boots | a chair | rollerblades | a sofa | shelves |
| shoes | a toy car | TVs | | | |

| black | blue | brown | gray | green | orange | pink |
| red | white | yellow | | | | |

The shoes are white.

4 Find three plastic objects in the class. What color are they?

2a My possessions

Vocabulary everyday objects

Kayaker

Diver

Climber

1 Look at the objects in Andy's backpack. Match the words with the objects.

boots camera compass
first-aid kit   gloves   hat
knife   map   cell phone
pens   flashlight

Grammar plural nouns

2 Look at the words in Exercise 1 again. Which nouns are plural? What is the extra letter for plural nouns?

> ### ▶ PLURAL NOUNS
>
> - Normally, add *-s*: *chair**s**, shoe**s***
> - Add *-es* to nouns ending in *-ch*, *-sh*, *-s*, *-ss* or *-x*: *bus – bus**es**, class – class**es***
> - Change nouns ending in *-y* after a consonant to *-ies*: *family – famil**ies***
> - Change nouns ending in *-f* and *-fe* to *-ves*: *shelf – shel**ves***
> - Some nouns are irregular: *man – m**e**n, person – **people**, child – **children***
>
> For more information and practice, see page 158.

3 Look at the grammar box. Then write the plural form of these nouns.

1 map ....
2 cell phone ....
3 compass ....
4 hat ....
5 camera ....
6 knife ....
7 country ....
8 box ....

Listening

4 💿 **6** Listen to an interview with Andy. Choose the correct answers.

1 Where are they?
  a by a mountain   b by the sea   c in a forest
2 Where is Andy from?
  a Canada   b The US   c Scotland
3 What is always in his backpack? Mark the objects.

> a hat   a laptop   a first-aid kit   pens
> a camera   gloves

Grammar *this, that, these, those*

5 💿 **7** Listen to the interview with Andy again. Choose the correct words.

I = Interviewer, A = Andy
I: I see. And what's ¹*this / that*?
A: It's a first-aid kit. It's always in my backpack.
I: Good idea. And what's ²*this / that*?
A: It's my camera. I take it everywhere. And ³*these / those* are my climbing boots.
I: Right. And over there. What are ⁴*these / those*?
A: My gloves.

> ### ▶ THIS, THAT, THESE, THOSE
>
> | Singular nouns | Plural nouns |
> |---|---|
>
>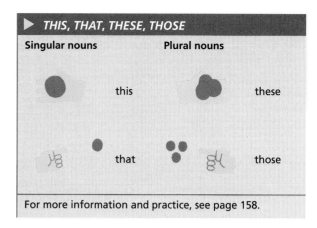
>
> For more information and practice, see page 158.

6 Look at the grammar box. Then complete the questions with *this, that, these,* or *those* and write the missing words in the answers.

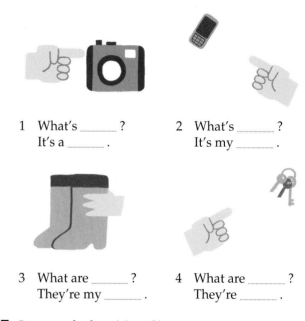

1 What's ....?
  It's a ....
2 What's ....?
  It's my ....

3 What are ....?
  They're my ....
4 What are ....?
  They're ....

7 Pronunciation /ɪ/ or /i/

Listen to these vowel sounds: /ɪ/ and /i/.

💿 **8** Listen to these words and write /ɪ/ or /i/. Then listen again and repeat.

1 this   5 pink
2 these   6 green
3 keys   7 big
4 it   8 read

Speaking

8 Work in pairs. Ask and answer questions about these things.

- objects in the classroom
- possessions in your bag or pocket

> *What's this/that?*
>
> *What are these/those?*

2b At home

Reading

1 Look at the four photos. What is the same? What is different?

2 Read the article. Are these things (1–5) the same (S) or different (D) for each photo?

1 the apartments
2 the number of rooms
3 the furniture
4 the pictures on the walls

Vocabulary furniture

3 Look at the furniture and other objects for apartment 1 in the chart. Find these things in the photo.

	1	2	3	4
sofa				
armchair				
chair	✓			
television (TV)				
desk				
lamp				
closet	✓			
pictures	✓			
blinds or curtains				
a bed	✓			
cupboards and drawers	✓			
rug or carpet				
table	✓			
plant	✓			

4 Look at apartments 2, 3, and 4 and complete the chart. Which furniture is in your living room at home? What about your bedroom? Tell your partner.

> --There is a sofa, TV, and lamp in my living room.

> --There is a TV in my living room too... and there is one in my bedroom!

A PLACE CALLED HOME

These four pictures are of studio apartments: apartments with only one room. There is a living space, a kitchen space, a sleeping space, and sometimes an office space, all in one open area. The bathroom is the only private area. There are many studio apartments in cities, where there are a lot of people but there isn't a lot of space. Would you like to live in a studio apartment?

Grammar *there is/are*, prepositions of place

5 Look at the sentence from the article. What form is the noun (singular or plural) after *there is* and *there are*?

There are many studio apartments in cities, where there are a lot of people but there isn't a lot of space.

> **▶ THERE IS/ARE**
>
> There's (is) a rug.
> There are two pictures.
>
> There isn't a table.
> There aren't any beds.
>
> Is there a TV? Yes, there is. / No, there isn't.
> Are there any books? Yes, there are. / No, there aren't.
> How many pictures are there? There are three.
>
> For more information and practice, see pages 158 and 159.

6 Look at the grammar box. Then complete the sentences with the correct form of *be*.

1 There 's a desk.
2 There _____ a rug, but there's a carpet.
3 There _____ three pictures on the wall.
4 There _____ any curtains.
5 _____ there a plant? Yes, there _____ .
6 _____ there any chairs? No, there _____ .
7 How many chairs _____ there? There _____ one.
8 _____ there any books? No, there _____ .

7 Work in pairs. Ask and answer questions about the apartments.

Student A: Choose one apartment and answer your partner's questions.

Student B: Ask your partner questions and guess the apartment.

Example:

Is there a TV?

No, there isn't.

Are there any blinds?

No, there aren't.

Is there a closet.

Yes, there is.

It's apartment 1.

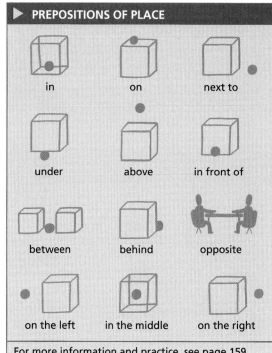

> **▶ PREPOSITIONS OF PLACE**
>
> in   on   next to
>
> under   above   in front of
>
> between   behind   opposite
>
> on the left   in the middle   on the right
>
> For more information and practice, see page 159.

8 Choose the correct prepositions to complete the description of apartment 4.

There is a picture [1] *in / on* the wall and the bed is [2] *under / next to* it. There's a TV [3] *opposite / between* the armchair and there's a window [4] *opposite / on the left of* the TV. There's a large rug [5] *on the right / in the middle* of the room. The chair is [6] *in front of / behind* the desk. There is a book [7] *in front of / on* the desk.

9 Complete the description about apartment 1.

The bed is [1] _____ of the room. The table and chairs are [2] _____ the closet and the bed. There isn't a rug in this apartment. There's a picture [3] _____ the wall on the right and the bed is [4] _____ it. The cupboards are [5] _____ the bed and there's a plant [6] _____ to the bed.

10 Work in pairs. Turn to page 154 and follow the instructions.

Writing and speaking

11 Write a description of a room in your home. Then work in pairs and read your description to your partner. What is the same about your and your partner's rooms? What is different?

2c Global objects

Reading

1 Look at the photo of the Mini on page 27. Is this car famous in your country? What are popular cars in your country?

2 Read the article on page 27. Choose the correct answer (A–C) for the questions.

A Germany B Britain C Many different countries

1 Which country is BMW from?
2 Where are the parts for a Mini from?
3 Where is the factory for the Mini?

Critical thinking close reading

3 Read sentences 1–8. Write answers T, F, or 0.

T = True
F = False
0 = The information isn't in the article.

1 In the past, the Mini was a British car.
2 Some parts are from Asia.
3 The Mini is a global product.
4 The Mini is famous in Brazil.
5 The two types of engine are from two different countries.
6 The seats are made in America.
7 The windows are from a factory in France.
8 The mirrors are from a Canadian company with a factory in Germany.

Vocabulary countries and nationalities

4 Write the missing names for the countries and nationalities.

Country	Nationality
1 *Britain*	British
2 Germany	
3 Austria	
4	Dutch
5 Canada	
6 Italy	
7 Japan	
8	Belgian
9 Brazil	
10	English
11 Spain	
12	French

> **WORDBUILDING suffixes (1)**
>
> Add a suffix *-ish*, *-n*, *-an*, *-ian*, or *-ese* to countries to say the nationality:
> *Poland – Polish, Turkey – Turkish*
> *Australia – Australian, Mexico – Mexican*
> *Vietnam – Vietnamese, China – Chinese*
> Some nationalities are irregular:
> *France – French, Thailand – Thai*

5 Pronunciation word stress

🔊 **9** Listen to these nationalities. Underline the main stress in each word. Listen again and repeat.

Example:
British

1. Mexican	5. Spanish
2. Chinese	6. Brazilian
3. Chilean	7. Turkish
4. Egyptian	8. Portuguese

6 Work in pairs. Answer the questions about the continents in the box.

Africa	Asia	Europe
North America		South America

1 Which continents are in the article?
2 Name two countries for each continent in the box.

Speaking

7 Work in pairs. Which country or continent are these objects from?

- your shoes
- your bag
- your cell phone
- your car
- this book
- classroom objects

My bag is from China.

My car is German.

I don't know where my ... is from.

GLOBAL OBJECTS

The Mini was a British car until 2000. Now BMW, a German company, is the producer of the Mini, but the car factory for the Mini is still in Oxford, England. There are 2,500 parts in the Mini and they are from countries and continents all over the world, including the Americas and Europe. So, what nationality is a car produced by a German company, with international parts and a factory in Britain? It's a global product.

Hood
This is from a factory in the Netherlands, but the company is Austrian.

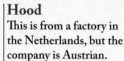

The roof
Part of the roof is from England, but the company is Spanish.

Mirrors
These are from a factory in Germany, but the headquarters is in Canada.

Seats
Johnson Controls is an American company. They make the car seats in a factory in Britain.

Front and back bumper
These are from Britain, but the company's headquarters is Canadian.

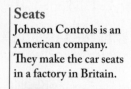

Engine
The Mini has two different engines. There's a gas engine and a diesel engine. The gas engine is Brazilian and the diesel engine is Japanese.

Windows
The glass in the windows is from a company in France, but the factory is in Belgium.

Wheels
The wheels aren't from one country; they're from two! There are different parts and Italian and German companies produce them.

factory (n) /ˈfæktəri/ where the company produces the object
headquarters (n) /ˈhedˌkwɔrtərz/ main office of a company

2d Shopping

Real life shopping

1 🔊 **10** Listen to conversations in three shops. Match the conversation with the item and the price.

Conversation 1	purses	$21.00
Conversation 2	coffee	$19.35
Conversation 3	a soccer ball	$3.50

2 Read these sentences from the conversations. Who says them: the customer (C) or the salesperson (S)?

> ▶ SHOPPING

Can I help you?	*S*
I'd like a coffee, please.	*C*
Large or small?	
Large, please.	
Is there a size medium?	
Are there other colors?	
These ones are red.	
Those are nice!	
How much are they?	
They're nineteen dollars and thirty-five cents.	
Are they all black and white?	
This one's red, white, and blue.	
OK, that one, please.	
How much is it?	
It's twenty-one dollars.	

3 Work in pairs. Use the prompts to make a conversation between a salesperson (S) and a customer (C). Then change roles and repeat the conversation.

S: Hi. Can / help?
C: I'd / T-shirt
S: Large / Medium?
C: Medium. / other colors?
S: These / green and blue
C: How much / they?
S: $7.50

Word focus *one/ones*

4 Complete these sentences with *one* or *ones*.

1 I'd like a glass of water, please. A small _____ .
2 I'd like two T-shirts. Small _____ , please.
3 This ball is nice, but that _____ is horrible!

5 Pronunciation **contrastive stress**

🔊 **11** Listen to sentence 3 in Exercise 4. Note the stress on *this* and *that*. Listen again and repeat.

6 Work in pairs. Practice two conversations between a customer and a salesperson in the tourist shop.

Student A: Turn to page 154.
Student B: Turn to page 155.

2e For sale

Writing ads

1a Read these ads. What is for sale in each one?

COMPUTER DESK AND CHAIR

Useful, modern, white desk and chair. Cheap at only $5!

☎ Call **206-685-6978** today.

Car for sale

Gray 2006 Jeep Cherokee with fast, new engine.

☎ Call **209-671-3360** today.

BACKPACK FOR SALE

Large, green backpack. Good for camping. Never used.

Email **l.taylor@gmail.com**

1b **Vocabulary adjectives**

Find the opposite of these adjectives in the ads above.

1 old	*modern* , _____	4 slow	_____
2 bad	_____	5 small	_____
3 useless	_____	6 expensive	_____

2 Writing skill describing objects with adjectives

We can describe objects with adjectives in two ways. Look at the example. Then rewrite sentences 1–4.

The desk is modern. = It's a modern desk.

1 The car is old.
It _____ .
2 The computers are modern.
They _____ .
3 The sofa is brown.
It _____ .
4 The rollerblades are fast.
They _____ .

3 Read the ads again. Write in the adjectives before the nouns.

Opinion	Size	Age	Color	Noun
useful		*modern*	*white*	desk
				Jeep
				engine
				backpack

4 Write the adjectives in the correct order to make sentences from ads. Use the table in Exercise 3 to help you.

1 It's a (Japanese / new / fast) car.
It's a fast, new, Japanese car.
2 They're (red / lovely) gloves.
3 There are two (Italian / beautiful / old) chairs for sale.
4 A (nice / gray / small) computer desk for sale.
5 For sale. A (large / modern / white) house.

5 Write an ad for an object in your house.

6 Display your ads around the classroom. Read them. Are the adjectives in the right order?

Coober Pedy's opals

Opals

Before you watch

1 Look at the photo of the opals. What colors are in the opals?

2 Work in pairs. Answer these questions about opals with *Yes, No,* or *Don't know.*

   1 Are opals expensive?
   2 Are most opals from Australia?
   3 Is the color important?

While you watch

3 Watch the video. Check your answers in Exercise 2.

4 Number these things in the order you see them.

   a a home in a tunnel
   b opal shops in Coober Pedy
   c one opal
   d five opals

5 Choose the correct word to complete these sentences.

   1 The video is in *northern / southern* Australia.
   2 Coober Pedy is famous for its *opals / miners*.
   3 *All / Red* opals are very expensive.
   4 There are a lot of *tunnels / shops* under the ground in the town.
   5 There's *an office / a house* in one tunnel.
   6 A lot of miners *find opals everyday / don't find opals*.

6 Complete the sentences from the video with these words.

113	3,000	300,000	90	95	millions

   1 In the summer, the temperature is over .... degrees.
   2 About .... % of the world's opals are from Australia.
   3 About .... people live here.
   4 These opals are worth about .... dollars.
   5 .... % of opals have no color.
   6 They always believe they are near opals in the ground. And that these opals are worth .... of dollars.

> **(be) worth** /wɜrθ/ the cost in money
> **mine** (n) /maɪn/ to dig a tunnel under the ground and take something (e.g., gold, silver, opals)
> **miner** (n) /'maɪnər/ a person who works in a mine

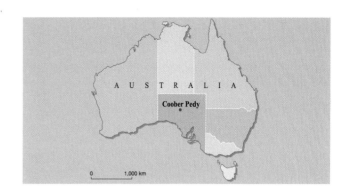

After you watch

7 Role play shopping for opals in Coober Pedy

Work in pairs.

Student A: You are a customer in an opal shop in Coober Pedy. Ask the salesperson about the different colors and sizes of opals. Then, buy an opal in the photo on page 30 for a good price.

Student B: You are a salesperson in an opal shop in Coober Pedy. Answer the customer's questions about opals. Then, sell an opal in the photo on page 30 for a good price.

8 These things are also from under the ground. Match the words with the photos (1–5).

coal	diamonds	gas	gold	oil

1 ....   2 ....   3 ....

4 ....   5 ....

9 Work in groups. Discuss these questions.

   1 Are there mines in your country?
   2 What is in them (e.g., coal, gold)?

UNIT 2 REVIEW

Grammar

1 Write the singular form of these nouns.

1	classes	*class*	5	knives
2	shelves		6	children
3	families		7	boots
4	women		8	shoes

2 Complete the questions with *this, that, these,* or *those*.

1 Who's _____ ?

2 Is _____ your pen?

3 Are _____ your rollerblades?

4 Are _____ your boots?

3 Look at the photo. Choose the correct options.

Concordia Hotel

1 There *is / isn't* a sofa.
2 There *are some / aren't any* flowers.
3 There *is / isn't* a picture.
4 There *is a / aren't any* rugs.
5 The desk and chair are *in front of / between* the window.
6 The red shoes are *in / on* the floor.
7 The sofa is *between / opposite* the table and the bed.
8 The bed is *under / behind* the sofa.

I CAN	
talk about everyday objects and their location	
ask where objects are	

Vocabulary

4 Cross out the incorrect word in each group.

1	COLORS	red gray white ~~chair~~
2	FURNITURE	sofa desk map chair
3	COUNTRY	Peru Thai Japan China
4	ON YOUR FEET	shoes rollerblades hat boots
5	ON THE FLOOR	carpet blinds rug
6	NATIONALITY	Turkey British Brazilian Spanish
7	ADJECTIVES	slow age useless large

5 Complete the sentences with one word from each group in Exercise 4.

1 Stop the car at a *red* light.
2 The computer is on my _____ .
3 _____ is a country in South America.
4 Are these _____ fast?
5 There's a _____ next to the bed.
6 _____ people speak Portuguese.
7 The opposite of "fast" is _____ .

I CAN	
talk about everyday objects, countries, and nationalities	
describe objects with different adjectives	

Real life

6 Match the questions with the correct response.

1 Can I help you?
2 Large or small?
3 Is there a medium size?
4 Are there other colors?
5 How much are they?
6 Are they all black and white?

a A small one, please.
b No, there are also blue and gray.
c Yes, please. I'd like a coffee.
d Three dollars and fifty cents.
e I'm sorry, but there isn't.
f Yes, there's also blue and gray.

7 Work in pairs. Practice a conversation in a store. The customer asks for an object on page 22.

I CAN	
ask about and buy objects in a store	

Speaking

8 Work in pairs. Describe your favorite object at home.

The Midnight Sun restaurant, Norway
Photo by Marvin E. Newman

FEATURES

1 Look at the photo and caption. Where is it? Is it day or night?

2 🔊 **12** Listen to part of a TV program about restaurants in different places. Answer the questions.

1 What time is it?
2 Where is the TV presenter?
3 Why is the restaurant popular?
4 How many hours a day is the restaurant open in the summer?

3 🔊 **13** Complete the times. Then listen, check, and repeat.

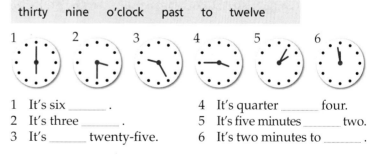

thirty	nine	o'clock	past	to	twelve

1 It's six _____ .
2 It's three _____ .
3 It's _____ twenty-five.
4 It's quarter _____ four.
5 It's five minutes _____ two.
6 It's two minutes to _____ .

4 Work in pairs. Ask and answer questions. What time is …

- it now?
- sunrise and sunset?
- noon?
- your English class?

3a Car-free zones

Reading

1 Read the article and match the cities with the photos (1–4).

2 Answer the questions.

1 What is a problem in many cities?
2 Why is it a problem?
3 How many people live in downtown London?
4 What is beautiful in downtown London?
5 What are popular in Tokyo?
6 How many people take the bus to work in Bogotá?
7 Why is Bourke Street popular?

Vocabulary adjectives about cities

3 Underline all the adjectives in the article in Exercise 1.

Which adjective means:
1 doesn't cost money ....
2 lots of people? ....
3 has bad air? ....
4 many people like it? ....
5 very good? ....

Which adjective means the opposite of:
6 quiet ....
7 ugly ....
8 dirty ....
9 cheap ....
10 big ....
11 old ....

4 Work in pairs. Which places in a city you know are:

- free or cheap?
- small and crowded?
- polluted and noisy?
- modern and popular?
- beautiful and relaxing?

CAR-FREE ZONES

Many people have cars in the city. But pollution is a problem because of the traffic. Nowadays some downtown areas around the world don't have cars. These car-free zones are areas for people, bicycles, and public transportation only.

London
Eight million people live in the center of London and another two million people go to work there every day. The downtown area is very noisy with hundreds of cars, buses, and taxis, but there are also a lot of beautiful parks with free music concerts. At lunchtime and after work, many people go there for a break.

Tokyo
Parts of Tokyo are always crowded with hundreds of people—but no cars! These modern car-free zones are very popular and people like shopping there.

Bogotá
In the past, Bogotá was polluted because there were lots of cars and traffic. Now the downtown area is a car-free zone and the air is clean! Many people don't have a car and half a million people take the bus to work.

Melbourne
In many cities, people don't like to shop downtown. But in Melbourne, Bourke Street is popular because there are lots of great stores and no cars. It's expensive, but lots of people eat lunch in the small cafés.

Grammar simple present (*I/you/we/they*)

5 Look at the two sentences from the article. What is the main verb? What verb do you add for a negative sentence?

Many people have cars.
Some downtown areas around the world don't have cars.

> **SIMPLE PRESENT (*I/YOU/WE/THEY*)**
>
> I **live** in Tokyo.
> You **don't live** in London.
>
> We **eat** in cafés.
> They **don't take** the bus to work.
>
> For more information and practice, see page 159.

6 Choose the correct form to make these sentences true for you.

1 I *live / don't live* downtown.
2 I *have / don't have* a car.
3 I *take / don't take* the bus to work.
4 I *meet / don't meet* friends downtown after work.
5 I *like / don't like* shopping downtown.

7 Make more sentences about life in the city with these phrases.

eat lunch	go to work	have a car
like shopping	live	work

Most people work downtown. They have cars, but they don't drive to work.

Listening

8 🎵 **14** Listen to a reporter interview a student about living in New York City. Complete his notes with adjectives.

DOWNTOWN LIVING
- The stores are ¹ _____ .
- There are lots of ² _____ places like art galleries and museums.
- The city has ³ _____ theaters.
- The restaurant is ⁴ _____ with tourists and is ⁵ _____ at lunchtime.
- Central Park is beautiful and ⁶ _____ .

9 🎵 **14** Match the reporter's questions with the student's answers. Then listen again and check.

1 Do you have a car in New York? *b*
2 Where do you live?
3 Do you like art?
4 What do you do?
5 What time do you get off work?

a I'm a student and I work in a restaurant at lunchtime.
b No, I don't. I go everywhere by bike.
c At about three o'clock.
d Yes, I do. And I like the theater.
e Downtown, in Manhattan.

Grammar simple present questions

10 Answer these questions about items 1–5 in Exercise 9.

1 What is the main verb in each question?
2 What extra verb do you add?
3 Which questions have yes/no answers?

> **SIMPLE PRESENT QUESTIONS (*I/YOU/WE/THEY*)**
>
> **Do** you **like** shopping? Yes, I **do**. / No, I **don't**.
> **Do** they **live** in New York? Yes, they **do**. / No, they **don't**.
>
> What **do** you **do**?
> Where **do** you **live**?
> What time **do** we **have** lunch?
>
> For more information and practice, see pages 159 and 160.

11 Write *do* in the correct place in these questions.

1 What you do?
2 Where you live?
3 You like shopping?
4 What time you get off work?
5 You have a car?
6 You eat in cafés at lunchtime?

Speaking

12 Work in pairs. Ask and answer the questions in Exercise 11.

What do you do?

I'm a website designer.

3b Working underwater

Vocabulary workplaces

1 Match these jobs with the workplace (1–8).

a doctor	a photographer	a pilot
a sailor	a student	a teacher
a waiter	an accountant	

1	in an office	5	in a hospital
2	on a ship or a boat	6	in a restaurant
3	in a studio	7	in a classroom
4	on a plane	8	in a university

2 Where do you work or study? Tell your partner.

Listening

3 Look at the photo and caption. What does Frank Richards do? Where does he work?

4 🔊 **15** Listen to an interview with Frank Richards. Number the questions in the correct order (1–5).

- a Do you work late?
- b Where do you work?
- c What do you do? *1*
- d Do you have a family?
- e What time do you start work?

5 🔊 **15** Listen again and choose the correct words to complete the sentences.

1 I study places *on land / under the sea*.
2 I *work / don't work* in an office very often.
3 On the boat, I get up just after *five / six* o'clock.
4 I meet my team for breakfast at about *seven / six*.
5 I *finish / don't finish* work late when I'm at home.
6 I live with my wife and my *son / children*.

Word focus *work*

6 Complete the sentences from the interview with Frank with *for* or *with*.

1 I work _____ National Geographic.
2 I work _____ a team of marine biologists.

7 Work in pairs. Make the sentences in Exercise 6 true about you. Tell your partner.

Grammar simple present (*he/she/it*)

8 Underline all the verbs in this text about Frank. Then answer the questions.

1 In affirmative sentences, how does the verb change for *he/she/it* forms?
2 In negative sentences, what verb do you add?

Frank Richards studies places under water. He has an office, but he doesn't work there very often. He's usually on a boat or under the sea. On the boat, he gets up early and he meets his team for breakfast. He starts work after breakfast and he finishes late. At home, he doesn't finish work late. He lives with his wife and son.

> **SIMPLE PRESENT (*HE/SHE/IT*)**
>
> He **works** in an office.
> She **goes** to work every day.
> He **studies** archaeology at a university.
> She **doesn't work** in an office.
>
> For more information and practice, see page 160.

9 Complete the text about another archaeologist with the simple present form of the verbs.

Dr. James E. Campbell [1] _____ (come) from England and he's an archaeologist. He [2] _____ (study) the ancient pyramids in Egypt. James [3] _____ (speak) three languages. He [4] _____ (have) an office, but he [5] _____ (prefer) to work in the pyramids. He [6] _____ (not / have) much free time because he [7] _____ (travel) all over the world. He [8] _____ (not / get) bored in his job!

10 Pronunciation *-s* endings

16 Listen to the third person form of the verbs. Do you hear the sound /s/, /z/ or /ɪz/? Listen again and repeat.

1	works	/s/	7	starts	
2	lives	/z/	8	loves	
3	finishes	/ɪz/	9	speaks	
4	studies		10	teaches	
5	gets		11	goes	
6	meets		12	travels	

11 **17** Match these questions about Frank and James with the answers.

1 What does Frank do?
2 Where does James come from?
3 When does Frank start work?
4 Does James have an office?
5 Does Frank finish work early?

a Yes, he does.
b No, he doesn't.
c After breakfast.
d He's a marine archaeologist.
e England.

> **SIMPLE PRESENT QUESTIONS (*HE/SHE/IT*)**
>
> What **does** he **do**? He's a doctor.
> **Does** she **have** children? Yes, she **does**. / No, she **doesn't**.
>
> For more information and practice, see page 160.

Speaking

12 Work in pairs. Exchange information to complete a fact file about Joel Sartore, pictured below.

Student A: Turn to page 153.
Student B: Turn to page 154.

3c Places and languages

Reading and vocabulary

1 How many languages do you speak? Which language(s) do you speak in different places (e.g., at home, at school, at work)?

2 Read the article. What is it about? Choose the correct answer (a–c).

   a   The languages people speak in different places
   b   Places with new languages
   c   Why English is important in different places

3 Read the article again. What do these numbers refer to?

   1   over 190   *countries in the world*
   2   about 7,000
   3   over 1 billion .... and
      ....
   4   380 million
   5   400 million
   6   80%
   7   65
   8   109
   9   1

4 Find these words in the article and match them with the definitions (1–4).

ancient   first   official   second

   1   the language you learn after your first language
   2   the main language that people in a place speak
   3   the language of the government
   4   a very old language

   > ▶ **WORDBUILDING collocations**
   >
   > We use certain words together. These are called *collocations*. Many nouns have adjective and noun collocations: *first language, official language*.

5 Discuss these questions as a class.

   1   What is your first language? Is English your second language?
   2   Does your country have an official language?
   3   What languages do people normally learn at school? Why do they learn these languages?

Critical thinking making connections

6 Read the article again. Add these sentences (a–d) to the end of each paragraph.

   Paragraph 1: ....
   Paragraph 2: ....
   Paragraph 3: ....
   Paragraph 4: ....

   a   English is the world's biggest second language.
   b   That's one point five languages for every island.
   c   When he dies, his language dies.
   d   Many people there speak Spanish as their first language.

Vocabulary cardinal and ordinal numbers

7 Look at these two sentences from the article. Which says how many and which says the order?

   1   In first place is China.
   2   There are over one billion speakers of Mandarin Chinese.

8 Work in pairs. Complete the sequence of numbers. Then tell your partner the numbers. Check your answers with your instructor.

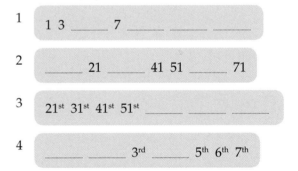

   1   1 3 .... 7 ....
   2   .... 21 .... 41 51 71
   3   21st 31st 41st 51st ....
   4   .... 3rd 5th 6th 7th

9 Pronunciation saying numbers

   🔊 **18** Listen and check your answers in Exercise 8. Then listen again and repeat.

Speaking

10 Write down three favorite numbers. Tell your partner why they're your favorites.

   > *My birthday is on June third.*

PLACES AND LANGUAGES

First place and first languages

There are over one hundred and ninety countries in the world and about seven thousand languages. In first place is China. Over one billion people speak Mandarin Chinese as a first language. In second place is India with speakers of Hindi. And in third place is Spanish. Spain isn't a big country, but there are over four hundred million Spanish speakers around the world, especially in Latin America.

English as a global language

As a first language, English is in fourth place. About three hundred and eighty million people are native English speakers. But English is in first place as a second language. Over a billion people speak English for doing business, reading the news, or studying science and medicine. In some countries, English is not the native language but it is the official language for the government and in schools.

The other 6,996 languages

Chinese, Hindi, Spanish, and English are the "big" languages. About eighty percent of the world's population speak them. But what about the other 6,996 languages? Many countries have lots of different languages. For example, the sixty-five islands of Vanuatu in the South Pacific Ocean have one hundred and nine different languages!

The last speakers

Finally, there are some languages with only one speaker. They are old people and they speak the language of their parents and grandparents. For example, Charlie Muldunga lives in Australia. He speaks English but his native language is Amurdag. It's an ancient Aboriginal language and he is its last speaker.

ancient (adj) /ˈeɪnʃənt/ very old
last (adj) /læst/ final
over (adv) /ˈoʊvər/ more than
about (adv) /əˈbaʊt/ approximately

新幹線
Shinkanse

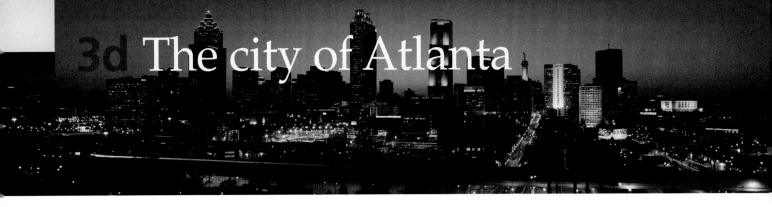

3d The city of Atlanta

Vocabulary places in a city

1 Look at the map of Atlanta. Where do you do these things?

1 get tourist information
2 learn about history
3 relax outside
4 see a play or a musical
5 park your car
6 read a book
7 meet clients and colleagues
8 look at marine life

Real life giving and getting directions

2 🔘 **19** Listen to a conversation at the visitors' center. What places on the map do they talk about?

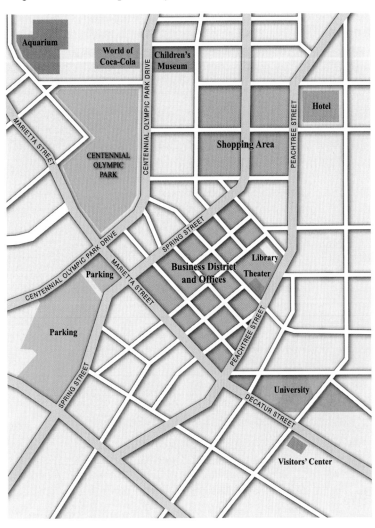

3 🔘 **19** Look at the expressions for giving directions. Listen again and complete the conversation at the visitors' center.

T = Tourist, G = Guide

T: Hi, we'd like to go to the aquarium. Is it ¹ _____ _____ ?

G: It's ² _____ fifteen minutes _____ , but you go past some interesting places on the way. Here's a map. Go ³ _____ Decatur Street and continue on Marietta Street. ⁴ _____ Spring Street and ⁵ _____ _____ _____ Centennial Olympic Park Drive. The park is on your left. It's very nice. Go ⁶ _____ _____ the top of the park and on the right there's the World of Coca-Cola.

T: Oh, that sounds interesting.

G: Yes, it is. Go past it and the aquarium is opposite.

T: Great. Thanks a lot.

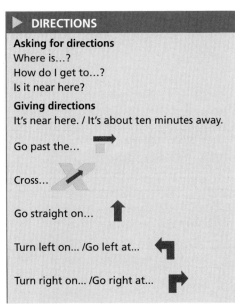

> **DIRECTIONS**

Asking for directions
Where is…?
How do I get to…?
Is it near here?

Giving directions
It's near here. / It's about ten minutes away.

Go past the… ➡

Cross… ✖

Go straight on… ⬆

Turn left on… /Go left at… ⬅

Turn right on… /Go right at… ➡

4 Work in pairs. Ask for and give directions to different places on the map of Atlanta.

3e Describing a place

Writing a travel website

1 Bella Potachouck writes for a travel website. Read about her favorite city. Mark the items she describes (1–6).

1 the name of her city
2 good places to visit
3 her favorite time of day, month, or season
4 places to meet friends
5 her favorite cafés and restaurants
6 good ways to travel around the city

WHY I LOVE MOSCOW

My favorite place in Russia is Red Square in Moscow because there are interesting museums and art galleries. But I also like other parts of Moscow. Krasnaya Presnya Park is great. On Saturdays in the summer, I meet friends there in the afternoon. We relax and play sports. Summer is between May and September, but I love winter. December is my favorite month because the snow is beautiful and we go ice-skating.

2 Writing skill **capital letters**

a Read the website in Exercise 1 again. Which one of these things 1–7 does not have a capital letter?

1 the word at the beginning of a sentence
2 the pronoun *I*
3 names of people, cities, or places
4 countries, nationalities, or languages
5 days and months
6 seasons and parts of the day
7 streets, roads, parks, and squares

b Rewrite this description with capital letters.

i'm from australia and i love sydney! there are over four million people here, but it's never crowded. that's because there's the harbor with the famous sydney opera house and there are beautiful beaches. my favorite season is summer because of the surfing. lots of people go to bondi beach, but on saturdays i go with my friends to narabeen beach. it's quiet and relaxed. afterwards we go downtown. there are over 3,000 restaurants with every type of food, from japanese to lebanese.

3 Write a description of your favorite town or city for a website.

4 Display the descriptions around the classroom. Read each other's descriptions and check the capital letters.

Las Ramblas in Barcelona, Spain.

Before you watch

1 Look at the photo and read the caption. With a partner, describe what you see using the appropriate words from the list.

noisy	modern
polluted	small
beautiful	quiet
crowded	big
ugly	relaxing

2 In the video, people talk about the Ramblas, an important street in Barcelona, Spain. Look at the list of words in Exercise 1. Which words do you think describe the Ramblas?

3 Look at the word box below. Listen and repeat the words after your instructor.

While you watch

4 As you watch the video, check the people and things that you see.

- ☐ hospital
- ☐ musicians
- ☐ people dancing
- ☐ singers
- ☐ people sleeping
- ☐ buses
- ☐ flowers
- ☐ people in costumes
- ☐ museum
- ☐ trees
- ☐ performers
- ☐ outdoor café
- ☐ books
- ☐ paintings

5 Watch the video again. Complete the quotes with the missing words.

friend	living
lively	inspiring
music	entertained
street	way

a "There is always something going on. You can always find a ＿＿＿＿ on the street. It's where ＿＿＿＿ is."

b "You can go out in the street at night. It's always ＿＿＿＿."

c "I felt somehow better than in Amsterdam, more alive… vital. That makes it very enjoyable… ＿＿＿＿, too."

d "In the Ramblas you can find theater, ＿＿＿＿ from Argentina, from Spain, from Africa…"

e "The Ramblas is the street in Barcelona, in Europe, and I think, in the world, that you're going to be ＿＿＿＿."

f "Even the ＿＿＿＿ is decorated."

g "It's a ＿＿＿＿ of life."

6 Match the quotes from Exercise 5 with the person. Two of the people have two quotes.

1

2

3

4

5

After you watch

7 Work with a partner. Compare the Ramblas to a street in your city or town.

The Ramblas is crowded…

8 Your friend is traveling to Spain. Write an email to your friend. Explain why he/she should visit the Ramblas when he/she is there. Be sure to mention:

- where it is
- things to buy
- things to see or do during the day
- when to visit
- where to eat
- things to see or do at night

When you are in Spain, you can visit Barcelona. There is a very interesting street there …

decorate (v) /ˈdekəˌreɪt/ to make an object attractive by putting something on it

enjoyable (adj) /enˈdʒɔɪəbəl/ something that is fun, nice, or pleasant

entertain (v) /ˌentərˈteɪn/ to amuse someone by singing, dancing, etc.

inspiring (adj) /ɪnˈspaɪərɪŋ/ causing people to want to do or make something

lively (adj) /ˈlaɪvli/ with a lot of movement and activity

performer (n) /pərˈfɔrmər/ a person who acts, sings, dances, etc., for a crowd

vital (adj) /ˈvaɪt(ə)l/ with a lot of energy

way of life (n) /ˈweɪ əv ˈlaɪf/ the habits and customs of a person or group of people

UNIT 3 REVIEW

Grammar

1 Complete the sentences with these verbs.

eat	have	like	live	take	work

1 I _____ with my family in Dubai.
2 We _____ in a restaurant near my house.
3 I don't _____ to shop downtown.
4 They _____ in an office.
5 I don't _____ a car so I _____ the bus to work.

2 Complete the conversation with *do* or *don't*.

A: Where [1] _____ you live?
B: In New York.
A: [2] _____ you like it?
B: Yes, it's great. There are lots of places to go.
A: [3] _____ you have a car?
B: No, I [4] _____ . And I [5] _____ take public transportation because I have a bike.

3 Choose the correct option to complete the sentences.

1 I *come / comes* from Egypt.
2 He *live / lives* in Santo Domingo.
3 My friend *speak / speaks* four languages!
4 We *don't / doesn't* have much free time.
5 She *don't / doesn't* work in an office.
6 What *do / does* your husband do?

I CAN	
talk about my daily life	
ask people about their lives	

Vocabulary

4 Say these times.

1 5:56   3 11:45
2 7:15   4 1:03

5 Match the words with the sentences.

parking lot	hospital	hotel	library
museum	office	park	restaurant

1 There are waiters here. _____
2 People read books here. _____
3 Doctors work in this place. _____
4 People stay the night here. _____
5 An accountant works here. _____
6 People relax here at lunchtime. _____
7 You park your car here. _____
8 You can learn about history here. _____

6 Complete the adjectives in the article.

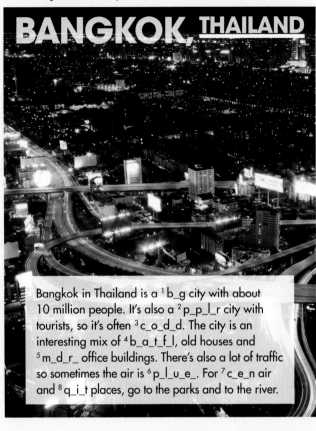

BANGKOK, THAILAND

Bangkok in Thailand is a [1] b_g city with about 10 million people. It's also a [2] p_p_l_r city with tourists, so it's often [3] c_o_d_d. The city is an interesting mix of [4] b_a_t_f_l, old houses and [5] m_d_r_ office buildings. There's also a lot of traffic so sometimes the air is [6] p_l_u_e_. For [7] c_e_n air and [8] q_i_t places, go to the parks and to the river.

I CAN	
say the time	
describe a town or city	
talk about places of work	

Real life

7 Complete the word in each sentence.

1 W_____ is the museum?
2 Is it n_____ here?
3 It's about ten minutes a_____ .
4 C_____ this street because it's on the other side of the road.
5 T_____ right then go straight.

I CAN	
ask for places in a city	
give directions	

Speaking

8 Work in pairs. Describe six actions in your normal day and what time you do each action.

> *I get up at six o'clock.*

Unit 4 Free time

Early morning fishing in Ontario, Canada.
Photo by Mary Ellen McQuay

FEATURES

1 🔊 **20** Listen to three people talking about their pastimes. Which one (1, 2, or 3) is in the photo?

2 🔊 **20** Listen again. Match the information to each person.

	Activity?	When?	Who with?	Why?
Person 1	go fishing	after work	my brother	It's quiet and relaxing.
Person 2	go shopping	every Saturday	friends	It's good for you.
Person 3	go to the gym	early in the morning	on my own	It's fun!

3 Think about your free time. Write notes about:
- what activity? (go running? watch TV?)
- when? (morning? evening? on the weekend?)
- who with? (friends? family? on your own?)
- why? (fun? good for you? relaxing?)

4 Work in groups. Talk about your free time.

> *I get together with friends on the weekend and we play video games. It's fun.*

4a 100% identical?

100% IDENTICAL?

Identical twins look the same, but do they do the same things?

The Mulgray Twins

Morna and Helen Mulgray are 73 years old. They love books and they write books together. They live in the same house and they like gardening. On the weekend, they take walks together.

The Kitt Twins

Camille and Kennerly Kitt are musicians and actors. They both play the harp. They don't have much free time, but they do Tae Kwon Do and they like swimming—together, of course.

The Bryan Twins

Mike and Bob love playing tennis. They are professional players and they play tennis all over the world. In their free time, they watch movies and play video games. But they don't do everything together. On their days off, Bob likes going to the gym, but Mike doesn't. He likes meeting friends at the beach.

> **identical** (adj) /aɪˈdentɪkəl/ exactly the same
> **twins** (n pl) /twɪnz/ two children born at the same time by the same mother
> **days off** (n) /ˈdeɪz ˈɔf/ free days from work

Reading

1 Discuss these questions.

  1 Do you know any twins? Do they do the same job? Do they have the same hobbies and interests?

  2 Do you have any brothers or sisters? Do you spend your free time together?

2 Read the article. Is it about work, free time, or both?

3 Read the article again and complete the table.

	The Mulgray Twins	The Kitt Twins	The Bryan Twins
Job?	*writers*		
Free-time activity?			*Bob goes to the gym.*
Who with?			

Vocabulary pastimes

4 Match the verbs with the nouns to make pastimes. Then check your answers in the article.

1	take	video games
2	play	movies
3	do	friends
4	play	the gym
5	watch	a walk/walks
6	play	Tae Kwon Do
7	go to	a musical instrument
8	meet	tennis

> ▶ **WORDBUILDING verb + noun collocations**
>
> We use certain verbs with certain nouns. For example: *play golf, do yoga, go biking, go running, watch TV, play video games, play music, go camping, play soccer, read a magazine*

5 Write questions about free time to complete the questionnaire.

Example:
In your free time, do you <u>go fishing</u>?

In your free time, do you ...

- _____ ? ☐
- _____ ? ☐
- _____ ? ☐
- _____ ? ☐
- _____ ? ☐

6 Work in pairs. Interview your partner with your questionnaire.

> *Do you go fishing?*

> *Yes, I do. / No, I don't.*

Grammar *like/love + -ing*

7 Look at the underlined words in these sentences from the article in Exercise 2. Which two sentences have (a) *like/love + noun*? (b) *like/love + verb + -ing*?

1 They <u>love</u> <u>books</u>.
2 They <u>like</u> the same <u>activities.</u>
3 Mike and Bob <u>love</u> <u>playing</u> tennis.
4 Bob <u>likes</u> <u>going</u> to the gym.

> ▶ **LIKE/LOVE + -ING**
>
> I like/love swimming.
> He likes singing.
>
> I don't like gardening.
> She doesn't like dancing.
>
> Do you like shopping?
> Does he like shopping?
>
> For more information and practice, see page 160.

8 Pronunciation /ŋ/

💿 **21** Listen and repeat.

| playing | listening | singing | watching |
| going | doing | dancing | shopping |

Speaking

9 Write three sentences (two true and one false) about your interests and hobbies. Use *love, like,* or *don't like*.

Example:
I love playing the guitar. (true)
I don't like going out to dinner. (false)
I like watching soccer. (true)

10 Work in pairs. Read your three sentences to your partner. He/She guesses which one is false.

11 Ask you partner more questions about his/her likes and dislikes. Ask about these topics:

- books and movies
- music
- sports
- food and shopping
- video games

> *What's your favorite book?*

> *What kinds of music do you like?*

> *Why do you like tennis?*

4b Free time at work

Reading

1 Which of these activities do you do when you take a break at work?

> send emails to friends
> visit social networking sites
> make a phone call   read a book
> take a walk   shop online
> play video games   have coffee
> surf the Internet   watch videos

2 Paul Nicklen is a nature photographer. Discuss these questions.

1 Do you think he works long hours?
2 Do you think he has a lot of free time?
3 What do you think he does in his free time?

3 Read about Nicklen. Answer these questions with *Yes, No,* or *Don't know.*

1 Does Nicklen come from Germany?
2 Are his hobby and his job different?
3 Are his photos in lots of different magazines?
4 Does he photograph people?
5 Does he like the Arctic?
6 In the Arctic, does he often work during the day?

Paul Nicklen comes from Canada. His hobby is photography, but his hobby is also his job. He's a professional photographer and his photos are often in *National Geographic* magazine. He does a lot of work in the national parks in North America because he only photographs nature and animals. He usually goes to the Arctic. In the summer, the sun shines twenty-four hours a day; it never gets dark. He loves it there and his photos of polar bears are famous. When he takes photos of them, he sometimes waits hours for the perfect one. In the end, he always gets the perfect shot.

Polar bear in the Arctic
Photo by Paul Nicklen

Grammar adverbs of frequency

4 Look at the adverbs of frequency in these sentences and answer the questions.

His photos are often in *National Geographic* magazine.

When he takes photos of them, he sometimes waits for hours.

1 Do adverbs of frequency come before or after the verb *to be*?
2 Do they come before or after other verbs?
3 Underline more adverbs of frequency in the article and write them on this scale.

100% ◄———————————————► 0%
always ¹   ²   ³   not often   ⁴

> **► ADVERBS OF FREQUENCY**
>
> *I'm **often** away on the weekend.*
> *I **sometimes** watch TV.*
> *I **never** play video games.*
>
> For more information and practice, see pages 160 and 161.

5 Make these sentences true for you. Add an adverb of frequency to each sentence.

1 I work eight hours a day.
2 I'm late for work.
3 I take a long lunch break at work.
4 I leave work early.
5 I travel to other countries on vacation.
6 I work at night.

Listening

6 🔵 **22** Listen to this description of Paul Nicklen's work. Choose the correct option.

1 Paul Nicklen *always / usually* works in the Arctic.
2 He *never / sometimes* travels to warm climates.
3 He *often / not often* works in cold places.
4 He is *always / sometimes* at home on Vancouver Island.
5 He *sometimes / never* takes photos of manatees.

7 Do you think Paul Nicklen has a good job? Why? Discuss with a partner.

> *His job is cool... he travels a lot.*

> *Yeah, but usually in cold places!*

Grammar expressions of frequency

8 Where do expressions of frequency (e.g., *once a year*) usually go in a sentence?

Interviewer:	How often do you go to the Arctic?
Nicklen:	I go once a year.
Interviewer:	How often do you see polar bears?
Nicklen:	Between August and November, you see polar bears every day.

> **► EXPRESSIONS OF FREQUENCY**
>
> *I read a newspaper **every morning**.*
> *We have our English lesson **twice a week**.*
>
> For more information and practice, see page 161.

9 Match the words in the box to replace the underlined words in the sentences with an expression of frequency.

every	day
once a	week
twice a	month
three times a	year

1 I go to the gym on <u>Tuesdays, Thursdays, and Saturdays</u>.
   I go to the gym three times a week.
2 My family goes on vacation <u>in April and in September</u>.
3 I drink a cup of coffee <u>in the morning, at eleven, and after lunch</u>.
4 At work, we have a team meeting <u>on the first day of the month</u>.

10 Pronunciation linking

🔵 **23** Listen and repeat these sentences. The words ending with a consonant link with the word starting with a vowel.

1 I'm_always late for work.
2 We don't_often take breaks.
3 How_often do you go there?
4 I go to the gym twice_a week.

Speaking

11 Choose one topic below and prepare five *How often* questions. Then take turns asking and answering your questions.

- sports and exercise
- work and travel
- vacations and time off
- evenings and weekends

4c Extreme sports

Vocabulary sports

1 In pairs, look at these sports and answer the questions.

baseball	basketball	biking	boxing	football
hockey	running	sailing	skiing	soccer
surfing	swimming	tennis		

1 Which sports do you play? Which sports do you like watching on TV?

2 Which sports:
   a need a ball?
   b are in water?
   c are on snow or ice?
   d are between two teams?
   e use the verb *play*?
   f use the verb *go*?
   g have a verb form?

3 Which of these adjectives describe each sport?

boring	dangerous	exciting	fast	relaxing	slow

Reading

2 Look at the photos of four extreme sports on page 51. Which adjective from Exercise 1 describes each sport?

3 Read the article. Match the sentences (1–5) to the sports (A–D). More than one answer is possible for some sentences.

This extreme sport:
1 is usually in different places.
2 is in the air.
3 is on a mountain.
4 needs water.
5 is usually in very high places.

Critical thinking fact or opinion

4 Look at these sentences and decide if they are fact (F) or someone's opinion (O).

1 Lots of people play sports in their free time, but these people do extreme sports!
2 Cliff diving is a very exciting extreme sport.
3 Highlining is a great adventure.
4 The landscape is perfect.
5 Extreme paragliders can fly up to 10,000 feet.

5 Find another fact and another opinion in the article.

Grammar *can/can't*

6 Look at the sentences about ability (a–c) from the article. Answer the questions (1–4).

   a He **can** jump between 65 and 100 feet.
   b It's early evening so he **can't** see well.
   c How well **can** you bike across the top of a mountain?

1 *Can* is a modal verb. Does it come before or after the main verb?
2 Do we add *-s* to *can* for *he/she/it* forms?
3 Do we need *don't* in a negative sentence?
4 What is the adverb in sentence b?

> ▶ **CAN/CAN'T (+ ADVERB)**
>
> I **can** swim.
> I **can't** play tennis.
> **Can** you play the piano?
>
> Use an adverb to say how well/fast/high, etc.
> I can play **very well**.
> I can speak French **a little**.
> I **can't** jump **very high**.
> How **well** can you play the piano?
>
> For more information and practice, see page 161.

7 Complete the sentences with *can* or *can't*. Which sentences contain adverbs?

1 I _____ swim well.
2 How well _____ you play tennis?
3 _____ you bike up a mountain? No, I _____ .
4 I _____ play the guitar well.
5 How many languages _____ you speak?
6 I _____ speak French very well and Chinese a little.

Speaking

8 Write down a sport, a musical instrument, and a language. Ask a classmate *Can you …?* questions with your words.

Can you play/speak …?

Yes, I can … very well.

EXTREME SPORTS

Lots of people do sports in their free time, but these people do extreme sports!

A Cliff diving

Cliff diving is a very exciting extreme sport and Cyrille Oumedjkane is an expert cliff diver. In this photo, he is in Kragero, Norway, at the cliff diving world series. He can jump between 65 and 100 feet (20–30 meters) into the water feet first. Normal divers jump from 30 feet (10 meters) into the water head first. "I cliff dive because I don't like soccer. I like the adrenaline," he says.

B Highlining

You can "highline" in a lot of places, but mountains are popular. You put a line between two high places and walk across. In this photo, American Andy Lewis walks above a canyon in Utah, US. It's early evening so he can't see well. Also, the wind is strong so he can't walk fast, but highlining is a great adventure.

C Mountain biking

Perhaps you go biking often, but how well can you bike across the top of a 3,000-foot (100-meter) mountain? Professional mountain biker Kenny Belaey bikes across South Africa's Table Mountain in this photo. "The landscape is perfect," he says.

D Paragliding

In this photo Justin Ferrar flies above Fronalpstock in the Swiss mountains. The weather is perfect. But paragliding isn't usually relaxing! Extreme paragliders can fly up to 10,000 feet (3,000 meters) for more than 200 miles (300 kilometers).

adrenaline (n) /əˈdrenəlɪn/ a chemical in your body. Humans produce the chemical when they are excited (often in sports).

4d In your year off

Reading

1 Read the website. What does it offer? What are the top three volunteer jobs?

GAP YEAR VOLUNTEER WORK

Do you need a break from your everyday work? Do you want to travel and live in other countries? Take a year off between school and college!

We have hundreds of volunteer jobs for your year off. This week, our TOP THREE volunteer jobs are:

1 Help the lions: Volunteer in Zambia to help care for orphaned lion cubs.

2 Write for a newspaper: An English newspaper in Bolivia needs young, enthusiastic journalists.

3 Teach English: Work with young children in schools all over the world.

Call **800-678-5847** now and ask for more information.

---

orphaned (adj) /ˈɔːfənd/ having no parents

---

2 Do people take a year off, or "gap year," in your country? What do they do during that time? Do you do any volunteer work?

Real life talking about abilities and interests

3 🎧 **24** Listen to the conversation. Which volunteer job is the caller interested in?

4 🎧 **24** Listen again. Mark the expressions you hear.

> ▶ **TALKING ABOUT ABILITIES AND INTERESTS**
>
> Are you good at teaching?
> How well can you speak English?
> Can you teach?
> Do you like animals?
>
> I can speak English well.
> I can't go for eighteen months.
> I'm not very good at writing.
> I don't like animals.
> I love them!

5 Pronunciation **sentence stress**

🎧 **25** Listen to these sentences. Notice the stressed words. Then listen again and repeat.

1 Are you <u>good</u> at <u>teaching</u>?
2 I'm not very <u>good</u> at <u>writing</u>.
3 <u>Can</u> you <u>write</u>?
4 I <u>can</u> speak <u>English</u> <u>well</u>.
5 Do you <u>like</u> <u>animals</u>?
6 Yes, I <u>love</u> <u>them</u>!

6 Work in pairs. Look at the website in Exercise 1 again and role play this telephone conversation.

Student A: You work for the Gap Year Volunteer Work company. Ask Student B about his/her abilities and interests.

Student B: You want to take a year off. Answer questions about your abilities and interests.

Afterwards, change roles.

4e You have an email

Writing short emails

1 How do you communicate with people in other places (by phone, by email, etc.)? Is it different at work and in your free time? Why?

2 Read these short emails. Which are about work and which are about free time?

1
> Do you want to see the new Spielberg movie? It starts at 8.

2
> Dear Sandy,
>
> The receptionist is very busy today. Do you have any free time? Can you help her?
>
> Regards,
>
> Molly

3
> Ray—The party's at 8 p.m. on Friday. Omar thinks it's on Saturday. Can you tell him?

4
> Hi. I'm at work until six so do you want to eat out tonight? The new restaurant on Main Street does sushi. Do you like it? We can go there.

5
> Are you any good at fixing photocopiers? The one in my office doesn't work. Please help!

6
> Hi Enrique,
>
> I can't understand this email from two customers in Quito. You can speak Spanish so can you translate it for me and reply to them? Thanks.

3 Writing skill reference words

a Look at email 1 in Exercise 2. The writer doesn't repeat information because he uses "it." What does "it" refer back to?

b Look at these words from emails 2–6. What do they refer back to?

2 her ....   5 one ....
3 it .... him   6 it .... them ....
4 it .... there

4 Remove the repetition from the sentences by replacing the underlined words with these words.

here	him	it	one	them	there

1 I like Joe's café. Can we meet at Joe's café?
   there
2 I have your letter. Can you come and get the letter?
3 Olav can't finish his work. Can you help Olav?
4 Matt and Suki are late. Please call Matt and Suki.
5 I like the new nightclub. Can we go to the new nightclub?
6 Can you buy a new computer? This computer is very old.

5 Write two short emails to your partner. Use reference words to avoid repetition.

Message 1: Ask for help with something at work.

Message 2: Invite your partner somewhere.

6 Work in pairs. Exchange emails with your partner. Write a reply to each message.

The city is a playground.

Before you watch

1 Work with a partner. Look at the photo and answer the questions.

1 How do you think they play this sport?
2 What equipment do they use?

2 In pairs, make a simple drawing or give an example for each word in the box. Then share your drawings and examples with another pair.

3 In the video, you will see stunt rider Danny MacAskill riding his bicycle. What do you think the stunts are like? Write down three adjectives.

While you watch

4 As you watch the video, check the places where you see Danny MacAskill do stunts on his bicycle.

☐ walls

☐ handrails

☐ recycling bins
☐ inside a house
☐ a bridge
☐ a car
☐ subway station

☐ ramp

5 Watch the video again. Complete the description with the missing words.

backward	balance	can	flip
loves	top	wall	

Danny MacAskill _____ doing stunts on his bicycle. He rides all over the city of Edinburgh. Here are the stunts Danny _____ do: he can _____ his bike on one wheel, _____ on a ramp, ride _____ down the street, and jump from one _____ to another. Danny can even ride across the _____ of a bridge. He's great!

6 Riding across the bridge is a challenge for Danny. In pairs, answer these questions.

1 According to Danny, what is easy about this challenge?
2 What is difficult?
3 Why do you think it is difficult?

After you watch

7 Danny MacAskill is coming to your city or town. He needs a new challenge! In pairs, come up with a new stunt for Danny to conquer on his bicycle, in your neighborhood. Then describe the stunt to the class.

8 What extreme sports do people like to do in your area? Make a list. Then survey your classmates to find out who likes to do them.

backward (adv) /'bækwərd/ toward the back, toward what is behind
balance (v) /'bæləns/ to hold your body in position by keeping your weight the same on all sides
challenge (n) /'tʃælənʤ/ something that is hard to do
conquer (v) /'kɑŋkər/ to become successful at something through a lot of effort
flip (v) /flɪp/ to turn over quickly in the air
handrail (n) /'hænd,reɪl/
narrow (adj) /'næroʊ/ small from one side to the other
ramp (n) /ræmp/
slippery (adj) /'slɪpəri/ difficult to stand or move on because it is smooth or wet
stunt (n) /stʌnt/ a difficult and dangerous action

UNIT 4 REVIEW

Grammar

1 Complete the sentences with the *-ing* form of these verbs.

> go   listen   play   swim   watch

1 I love _____ . It's great exercise!
2 He likes _____ tennis.
3 She doesn't like _____ to the gym.
4 They love _____ to jazz music.
5 We don't like _____ soccer on TV.

2 Write sentences about these people's free time.

1 Shelly / watch TV (never)
   Shelly never watches TV.
2 Chris / watch TV (often)
3 Annette / go to the movies (once a month)
4 Shelly / play video games (sometimes)
5 Chris / play video games (every day)
6 Chris / go to the movies (sometimes)
7 Annette / play video games (not often)
8 Shelly / go to the gym on the weekend (usually)

3 Match the questions with the answers.

1 Can you speak Italian?
2 Can you swim fast?
3 I can't sing very well. Can you?
4 How high can you jump?

a No, I can't, but my friend can sing very well.
b No, but I can run fast.
c Yes, I can, but not very well.
d Not very high.

I CAN	
talk about likes and dislikes	☐
talk about frequency	☐
talk about ability	☐

Vocabulary

4 Which words cannot follow the verb in CAPITAL letters? Cross out the incorrect word.

1 PLAY   tennis   golf   running
2 DO   yoga   camping   exercise
3 GO   fishing   biking   soccer
4 WATCH   the guitar   videos   a movie
5 READ   a book   a magazine   a harp
6 GO TO   the movies   the theater   TV
7 LISTEN TO   the gym   the radio   music
8 MEET   friends   family   sports

5 Complete the sentences with these words.

> ice   mountain   skis   sky   teams   water

1 The people in the photo use _____ .
2 The sports of surfing, swimming, and sailing are in _____ .
3 You can play hockey on _____ .
4 Two _____ play soccer and baseball.
5 You can go climbing and biking on a _____ .
6 Paragliding is high up in the _____ .

I CAN	
talk about hobbies	☐
talk about different sports	☐

Real life

6 Choose the correct options to complete the conversation.

A: I'd like a job for the summer.
B: OK. Are you good ¹*on / at* English? I have a job for an English teacher.
A: I can speak English ²*good / well*, but I don't like teaching. Is there anything else?
B: How well can you ³*do / play* tennis?
A: Not ⁴*very well / a little*. And I don't like tennis.
B: ⁵*Can / Do* you like animals?
A: Yes, I love them!

7 Complete these sentences about yourself. Then compare with a partner.

1 I'm good at …, but I'm not good at …
2 I can … well, but I can't … well.
3 I love …, but I don't like …

I CAN	
talk and ask about abilities and interests	☐

Speaking

8 Work in pairs. Complete these questions for your partner. Then take turns to ask and answer.

Do you like …?   How well can you …?
How often do you …?   Are you good at …?

A noodle chef at a street café in Chinatown, Thailand
Photo by Dean McCartney

FEATURES

1 Look at the photo and caption. What is the man's job? What
food does he cook? Where does he work?

2 Complete the sentences about Chinatown in Bangkok
with these food verbs. Then check your answers with your
instructor.

cook	eat	~~make~~	serve	smell	taste

1 All the street chefs *make* the food by hand.
2 Then they _____ it on a real fire.
3 So when you walk up the street, you can _____ the food in
  the distance.
4 The chefs _____ the noodles with a hot sauce.
5 They _____ delicious.
6 I can _____ them at any time of day—for breakfast, lunch
  or dinner!

3 Work in pairs. Tell your partner about your favorite dish.

5a Famous for food

Vocabulary food

1 Match the words to the pictures 1–20.

cheese	chicken	eggs	fish	French fries	juice	lamb
lemons	lentils	nuts	onions	oranges	pasta	pepper
peppers	potatoes	raisins	rice	salt	shrimp	

2 Work in pairs. Complete these sentences about yourself with the food in Exercise 1. Compare sentences with your partner.

1 I eat _____ , but I never eat _____ .
2 I cook _____ . I never cook _____ .
3 I grow _____ at home, but I buy _____ from a store.
4 I know what _____ tastes like, but I've never had _____ .

3 Pronunciation /tʃ/ or /dʒ/

🔊 **26** Listen to these words. Do you hear /tʃ/ or /dʒ/? Listen again and repeat.

1 **ch**icken   3 **ch**eese
2 **j**uice   4 orange

Speaking and listening famous for food

4 Many countries are famous for a type of food or a special dish. Match the dishes (1–6) with the countries (a–f). Check your answers on page 153.

1 pizza   a Italy
2 ceviche   b Indonesia
3 satay   c Peru
4 kabsa   d Poland
5 pierogi   e India
6 curry   f Saudi Arabia

5 Tell the class what people eat in your country.

6 🔊 **27** Listen to three people describing a dish from their country. Match each person to a photo (A–C) on page 59.

1: _____   2: _____   3: _____

7 🔊 **27** Listen again. Match the dishes with the sentences. Write *B*, *K*, or *C*. More than one answer is possible.

1 It's popular in other countries.
   B, K, C
2 You make it with meat.
3 You make it with fish.
4 You can also add different vegetables.
5 You cook it.
6 You serve it with rice.
7 You serve it with salad.
8 You eat it hot.

Grammar count and noncount nouns (*a*, *some*, and *any*)

8 Look at the highlighted words. Which nouns can you count? Which nouns can't you count?

Cook the chicken with an onion.
You put some juice on the fish.
I don't use any carrots.
You always need some meat, onions, and tomatoes.

A

B

C

9 Look at the grammar box and check your answers in Exercise 8.

> ▶ **COUNT AND NONCOUNT NOUNS**
>
> **Count nouns**
> You can say a number before these nouns (which have a plural form): *one banana, two bananas.* You can also use *a/an: a banana, an orange.*
>
> **Noncount nouns**
> You can't say a number or *a/an* before these nouns (which don't have a plural form): *a pasta, three bread.*
>
> **some/any**
> You can use *some* or *any* with count and noncount nouns:
> *I'd like some bananas/bread.*
> *I don't need any bananas/bread.*
> *Do you have any bananas/bread?*
>
> For more information and practice, see pages 161 and 162.

10 Choose the correct options to complete the conversation. Check your answers with your instructor.

A: To make satay we need [1]*any / some* chicken. Can you buy [2]*a / some* pound when you go to the supermarket?
B: Sure.
A: And we need [3]*a / an* onion.
B: There are [4]*any / some* onions in the fridge. Can we have a salad with it?
A: Good idea.
B: We need [5]*a / some* tomatoes.
A: And I'd like [6]*a / some* olive oil as well. There isn't [7]*any / some* left.
B: OK. So we need [8]*any / some* chicken, tomatoes, and olive oil. Anything else?

11 Work in pairs. You and your partner have two recipes you want to make and some food in the kitchen. Find out what you need from the supermarket.

Student A: Turn to page 154.
Student B: Turn to page 156.

Speaking

12 Work in pairs. Plan a special meal for six people with different dishes. Then make a list of the food you need.

> *We need some …*

> *And we also need a …*

> *Do we need any …?*

13 Tell the class about your meal and the food you need.

5b Food markets

Reading

1 Where do you like shopping for food? Choose an answer (a–d).

  a at a supermarket
  b at a market
  c from different specialty stores
  d I don't like shopping!

2 Read the article about markets around the world. Answer the questions.

  1 What's good about supermarkets?
  2 Why does the writer like food markets?
  3 How old is the St. Lawrence market?
  4 What is hot in Castries Market?
  5 What is upstairs at Kreta Ayer Wet Market?
  6 What can you hear in La Vucciria?
  7 When is Haymarket open?

3 Discuss these questions as a class.

  1 Do you have a food market in your town or city? What days is it open?
  2 Can you buy fresh food and local dishes there? What kind?
  3 What other street markets are in your town or city? What do they sell?

Grammar *a lot of* and *not much / not many*

4 Look at these sentences. Then complete the rules (1–3) with *a lot of*, *not much*, and *not many*.

There's a lot of different food …
There are a lot of shops here.
There aren't many markets …
There isn't much food for sale late in the day.

  1 Use .... with count or noncount nouns.
  2 Use .... with count nouns.
  3 Use .... with noncount nouns.

> ▶ **A LOT OF** and **NOT MUCH / NOT MANY**

Count	**Noncount**
There are **a lot of** apples.	There's **a lot of** cheese.
I **don't** eat **many** apples.	I **don't** eat **much** cheese.
I **don't** eat **a lot of** apples.	I **don't** eat **a lot of** cheese.
Do you eat a lot of / many apples?	Do you eat a lot of / much cheese?
Yes, I do. / No, not many.	No, I don't. / No, not much.

For more information and practice, see page 162.

My Top ⑤ | Food markets

Supermarkets are good for everyday shopping. But food markets are great for fresh food and local dishes. Here are my top five markets from around the world.

① St. Lawrence Market, Toronto, Canada

This food market, in downtown Toronto, is 200 years old. It has well over 100 shops with every kind of meat and seafood. Shoppers visit from all over the world.

② Castries Market, St. Lucia

Naturally, this island in the Caribbean has a market famous for fish and fruit. Buy some bananas for lunch and some fish for dinner. And try the local sauce—it's very hot!

③ Kreta Ayer Wet Market, Singapore

There's a lot of different food here and there's also a great restaurant upstairs. Go at around 6 a.m. and have some tasty noodles for breakfast.

④ La Vucciria, Palermo, Italy

There aren't many markets in the world with live music. But in Palermo, musicians play and sing for shoppers. It's a great atmosphere!

⑤ Haymarket, Boston, US

This market is almost 200 years old and famous with food lovers. It's open during daylight hours every Friday and Saturday and it's good to go early. There isn't much food for sale late in the day!

5 Rewrite the sentences with *much* or *many* where possible.

1 I don't eat ~~a lot of~~ fast food.
   I don't eat much fast food.
2 He eats a lot of fresh fruit and vegetables.
   not possible
3 There aren't a lot of local markets in my region.
4 Do you buy a lot of candy for the children?
5 There isn't a lot of milk in the fridge.
6 My family buys a lot of food.
7 She doesn't put a lot of salt on her food.
8 Do you eat a lot of strawberries in the summer?

6 Work in pairs. Make true sentences about yourself with these expressions and tell your partner.

I eat a lot of …
I don't eat many …
I don't eat much …

Listening and vocabulary quantities and containers

7 🔊 **28** Listen and answer the questions.

1 How many bananas does he buy?
2 How many pounds of rice does he buy?
3 How many bottles of sauce does he buy?

St. Lawrence food market

8 Match these quantities and containers to the noncount nouns (1–8).

| bag | bottle | can | glass | package |
| piece | pound | slice | | |

1 **2** **3** **4**

5 **6** **7** **8**

1 a _____ of sauce
2 a _____ of chocolate
3 a _____ of bread
4 a _____ of water
5 a _____ of pasta
6 a _____ of tuna
7 a _____ of flour
8 a _____ of rice

Grammar *how many / how much*

9 Look at the questions in the two excerpts from the conversation in Exercise 7. Which question asks about count nouns? Which asks about noncount nouns?

A: I'd like some bananas, please.
B: How many do you want?
A: Six, please.

A: Some rice, please.
B: How much do you want?

> ▶ **HOW MANY / HOW MUCH**
>
> Count: How many (apples) do you want?
> Noncount: How much (rice) do you want?
>
> For more information and practice, see page 162.

Speaking

10 Work in pairs. Role play four conversations at a food market about this food. Take turns being the shopper.

Conversation 1: five apples and some rice
Conversation 2: some bread and a bottle of sauce
Conversation 3: four cans of tuna and a slice of cake
Conversation 4: a package of pasta and six eggs

5c The seed vault

Reading

1 Do you ever grow plants from seeds? Do you ever grow your own food? Why? / Why not?

2 Read the article on page 63. Is it about growing, storing, or buying seeds?

3 Read the article again. Answer the questions.

   1 Why don't plants grow sometimes?
   2 Who needs new seeds?
   3 Do seeds grow in the vault?
   4 Where is the biggest seed vault in the world?
   5 Is the seed vault at the North Pole or in Norway?
   6 Is the seed vault above or below the ground?
   7 How many varieties of seeds are in the vault?
   8 How many seeds can be put in the vault?

Word focus *of*

4 Look at the underlined phrases in these sentences from the article. Notice the position of *of*. Now write *of* in sentences 1–6.

<u>A lot of countries</u> need different <u>types of seeds</u>. The vault is on <u>the island of Spitsbergen</u>.

   1 A lot people in Brazil eat fruit for breakfast.
   2 I live in the United States America.
   3 I'd like a bottle water, please.
   4 A friend mine is vegetarian.
   5 I eat my main meal in the middle the day.
   6 There are many varieties potato.

5 Pronunciation linking *of*

🔊 **29** Listen to the completed sentences in Exercise 4. Notice the link between *of* and the word before each time. Listen again and repeat.

A lot‿of people in Brazil eat fruit for breakfast.

Critical thinking **summarizing**

6 Match these summary sentences with the paragraphs (1–5) in the article.

   a A seed vault is a place to store different types of seeds.
   b There are many different seeds from all over the world in the vault.
   c Most of the Svalbard Global Seed Vault is underground.
   d The seed vault is important to humans.
   e It's important to have new seeds.

Speaking

7 Work in pairs. Summarize the main points of the article. Use all these phrases.

store different types of seed	cold place
Svalbard Global Seed Vault	three large areas
island of Spitsbergen	thousands of years
half a million varieties	

The SEED VAULT

1 Why are new seeds important?
A lot of countries need different types of seeds so they can plant them again. There is an important reason for this. Sometimes plants don't grow in a country because of bad weather or disease, so farmers need new seeds.

2 Where can countries store the seeds?
You can store seeds in a "seed vault." It's a place that's kept at a special temperature. The seeds don't grow, but they can live for a long time. Norway has the biggest seed vault in the world: the Svalbard Global Seed Vault. It has seeds from a lot of different countries.

3 Where is the Svalbard Global Seed Vault?
The vault is on the island of Spitsbergen. The island is about 600 miles (1,000km) from the North Pole. It's a very cold place so it's good for seeds. Above the ground, the doorway is small, but inside, the building is huge. You walk down a long corridor that goes 430 feet (30m) into a mountain. At the end, there are three large areas with seeds.

4 How many varieties of seeds are there?
There are about half a million varieties of seeds inside the vault. For example, there are varieties of rice seeds from Asia and Africa, 32 varieties of potato seeds from Ireland, and seeds for different chili peppers from the US.

5 How long can the seeds live?
The seed vault has space for a lot more seeds. In total, you can put about 2.2 billion seeds inside. The seeds can live here for thousands of years because of the cold temperature of −0.4°F (−18°C). So in the future, humans can grow any seed they want. In other words, the seed vault may be the difference between life and death.

disease (n) /dɪˈziz/ an illness in people, animals, or plants
seed (n) /sid/ we grow plants from these
store (v) /stɔr/ to keep or save in something
vault (n) /vɔlt/ place, usually below the ground, for storing things
variety (n) /vəˈraɪəti/ type of something (e.g., different types of potato)

5d At the restaurant

Speaking and vocabulary

1 What are common appetizers, main courses, and desserts on a menu in your country? What about your favorite restaurant?

2 Look at the parts of the menu. What dishes would you order? Tell your partner.

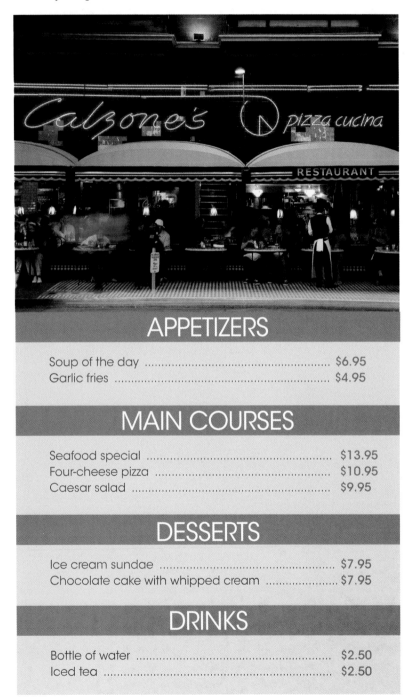

APPETIZERS

Soup of the day	$6.95
Garlic fries	$4.95

MAIN COURSES

Seafood special	$13.95
Four-cheese pizza	$10.95
Caesar salad	$9.95

DESSERTS

Ice cream sundae	$7.95
Chocolate cake with whipped cream	$7.95

DRINKS

Bottle of water	$2.50
Iced tea	$2.50

Real life ordering a meal

3 🔊 **30** Listen to the conversation. Look at these phrases for ordering a meal. Who says them: a customer (C) or a waiter (W)? Listen again and check. Two items are not in the conversation; can you guess who would say them?

> **▶ ORDERING A MEAL**
>
> Here is the menu.
> Can I get you anything to drink first?
> I'd like a bottle of water, please.
> I don't want an appetizer.
> I'll have the seafood special.
> I'd also like dessert.
> Are you ready to order?
> I'd like a four-cheese pizza.
> How is/was everything?
> That was delicious.
> Can I get you anything else?
> Could we have the check, please?
> Keep the change.
> The tip is included.

4 Pronunciation **contracted forms**

🔊 **31** Listen and repeat these contracted forms.

I'd   *I'd like a bottle of water, please.*
       I'd also like dessert.
       I'd like the seafood special.
       I'd like a four-cheese pizza.
I'll   *I'll have the seafood special.*

5 Work in groups of three. One person is the waiter, two people are customers. Practice a conversation at Calzone's restaurant. Use the menu in Exercise 2. Then change roles.

5e What do I do next?

Writing instructions

1 Read the three instructions (1–3). Match the texts to where you read them (a–c).

a   inside a box
b   in a cookbook
c   on a food label

1 You can make this cake in about fifteen minutes. First, heat the oven to 350°F. Put the flour in a bowl and add the milk, eggs, butter, and salt.

2 Thank you for buying this Home Barbecue Grill. Please follow these instructions:
1   Do not use the barbecue inside a building.
2   Never leave children with the barbecue.

3 Store this bottle of sauce in a cool, dry place. After you open the bottle, use the sauce within three months.

2   Writing skill punctuation

a Match these types of punctuation to their uses by finding examples in the instructions.

. (period)   , (comma)
: (colon)

1   between words in a list
    comma (milk, eggs, butter, and salt)
2   at the end of a sentence
3   between two or more adjectives
4   to introduce a list of instructions
5   after a sequence word (e.g., *First*)
6   between two clauses in one sentence

b Add the missing punctuation to the recipe.

Fortune cookies are easy to make
You need the following pieces of paper three eggs sugar salt and flour
First write your messages on the pieces of paper After you mix the eggs sugar salt and flour pour the mixture onto a tray

3 Work in pairs. Write instructions to make your favorite type of dish, sandwich, or salad. Use some of these verbs in your instructions.

mix   chop   pour

spread   put   slice

4 Exchange your instructions with another pair. Check the punctuation. Would you like to make the food?

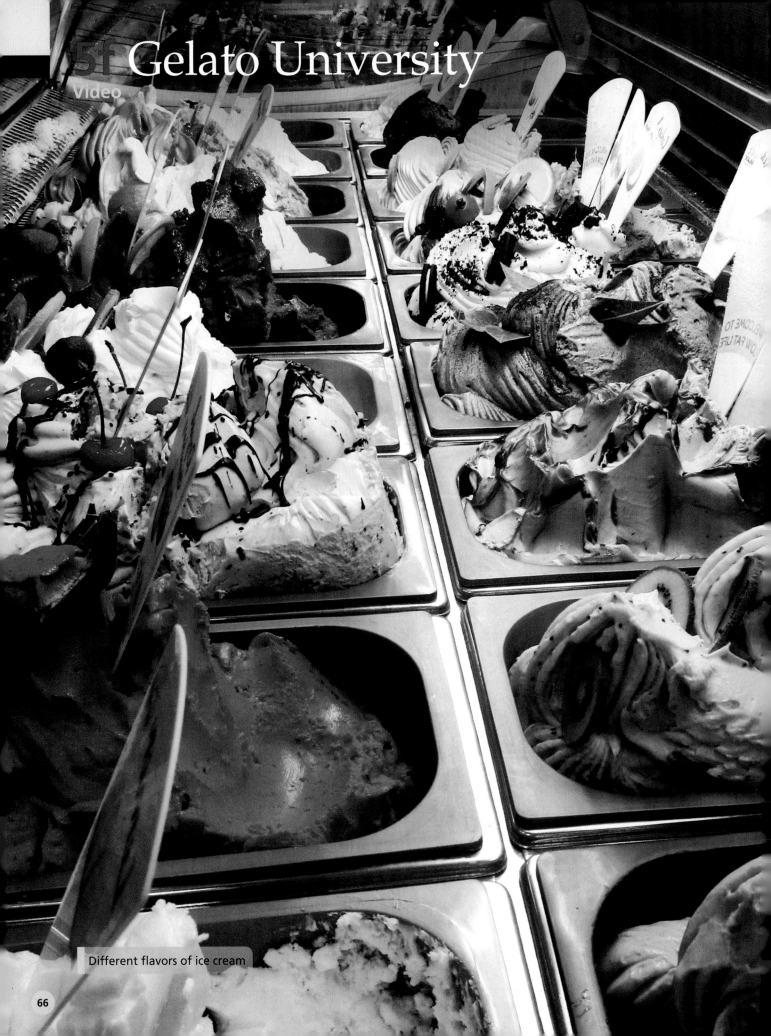

Gelato University

Different flavors of ice cream

Before you watch

1 Look at the photo and read the caption. Do you like ice cream? Which flavor is your favorite?

2 Match these flavors (1–7) to the ice creams (A–G).

1 chocolate   5 banana
2 orange   6 lime
3 coffee   7 vanilla
4 strawberry

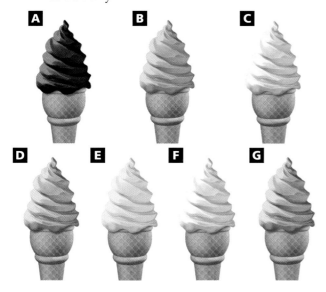

While you watch

3 Watch the video. Number the topics in the order you learn about them (1–3).

a where students come from
b the cost and the profit of a gelato business
c why students come

4 Watch the video again. Answer these questions.

1 Where is the university?

2 Where are the students from?

3 What do they learn?

4 What is the average age of a student?

5 Where is Holly from?

6 How much is the course per week?

7 They learn about making gelato, but what else do they learn about?

8 How much does the equipment cost?

After you watch

5 Match the people from the video (1–3) with what they say (a–c).

1 Kaori Ito (first woman)
2 Holly (second woman)
3 Kevin Koh

a I want to open an Italian Gelato parlor in Antananarivo, the capital of Madagascar. The shop is for a certain class of people. It isn't for everyone.
b They're ready to stop doing their old jobs and to open a new chapter in their lives.
c There's actually a lot about the ingredients, a lot about understanding the building blocks, about what goes in the gelato.

6 Match the highlighted expressions (a–c) in Exercise 5 with these definitions (1–3).

1 people with a lot of money
2 basic information
3 to start something new

7 Role play **a conversation with a student at Gelato University**

Work in pairs.

Student A: You are a new student at Gelato University. Answer a reporter's questions about the course. Think about:

• why you are taking the course
• what you learn in the course
• your plans for the future

Student B: You are a reporter. Prepare questions to ask a new student at the university. Ask about:

• his/her age
• his/her country
• why he/she is taking the course
• what he/she learns in the course
• what his/her plans are for the future

8 Work in groups. Discuss these questions.

1 Why do students often study at universities in other countries?
2 Do a lot of students in your country study abroad? Why? What do they study?

---

gelato (n) /dʒəˈlɑtoʊ/ Italian word for ice cream
ice cream parlor (n) /ˈaɪs ˌkrim ˌpɑrlər/ a store which only sells ice cream

UNIT 5 REVIEW

Grammar

1 Match the beginnings (1–6) with the endings (a–f).

1 We need	a banana, please.
2 Are there any	b pounds.
3 Please buy two	c some chicken.
4 Chop an	d onions?
5 I'd like a	e onion.
6 Do we need a	f lemon?

2 Choose the correct options to complete the conversation. In two items, both words are correct.

A: Do you want an apple?
B: No, thanks. I don't eat ¹*many / much* fruit.
A: Why not? ²*A lot of / Much* fruit is good for you.
B: I know, but I prefer other food. And I eat ³*many /a lot of* pasta and pizza. Do you eat ⁴*a lot of / much* Italian food?
A: Yes, I do. It's delicious. Are there ⁵*a lot of / many* Italian restaurants in your town?
B: No, ⁶*not a lot of / not many.*

3 Complete the table with these words.

eggs	oranges	rice	soup	bottles of water

How much …?	How many …?

I CAN	
use count and noncount nouns	
talk and ask about quantities of food	

Vocabulary

4 Complete the categories with these words.

bag	can	chicken	curry	juice	lamb
milk	oranges	peppers	potatoes	raisins	satay

1 fruit .... , ...
2 vegetables .... , ...
3 meat .... , ...
4 drinks .... , ...
5 a dish .... , ...
6 a container .... , ...

5 Work in pairs. Think of one more word for each category in Exercise 4.

6 Complete the text with these verbs.

make	mixes	pour	put	tastes

This photo is from Morocco. Moroccans
¹ .... a lot of mint tea. On a hot day, it ² ....
delicious! You need a tall glass with a lot of mint
leaves. Also, you need to ³ .... some sugar in
the glass. Boil some water and ⁴ .... it slowly
into the glass. Wait for five minutes so the sugar
⁵ .... with the mint. Then drink!

I CAN	
talk about different types of food	
describe how to make a drink or a recipe	

Real life

7 Replace the words in bold with these phrases.

Are you ready to	I'd like	Can we have
Would you like		

1 **Can I get you** anything to drink? ....
2 **I'll have** a bottle of water. ....
3 **Would you like to** order? ....
4 **We'd like** the check, please. ....

I CAN	
order a meal in a restaurant	

Speaking

8 Work in pairs. Describe your favorite café or restaurant. What do you normally order?

Unit 6 Money

A mariachi band plays in the street.

FEATURES

1 Look at the photo and caption. How do these men earn money? Who gives them money?

2 🔘 **32** Listen to someone talking about street musicians. Which verb + *money* collocations do you hear?

change	earn	give	save	spend

3 Match the collocations in Exercise 2 with these places.

in a bank	at a currency exchange	in stores
in the street	at work	

You save money in a bank.

4 How often do you give money to street musicians? How much money do you give?

6a The face of money

Reading

1 Match a country with the currency. Check your answers on page 154. Do you know other countries with these currencies?

dollar	euro	peso	pound
renminbi	riyal	rouble	rupee
yen			

Canada	China	Egypt
France	Japan	Mexico
Pakistan	Russia	Saudi Arabia

2 Look at the pictures in the article below. Which people's faces are on the money in your country:

- kings or queens?
- presidents or politicians?
- scientist or artists?
- other people?

3 Read the article. Which countries have Queen Elizabeth's face on their money?

A FACE ON MONEY

The faces of kings and queens are everywhere—on TV, in newspapers, and even on money. For example, Queen Elizabeth II's face is on money all over the world. There are coins and bills with her face in over thirty countries.

In 1936, Princess Elizabeth was ten years old and her parents were king and queen. Her face was on this Canadian twenty-dollar bill.

In her mid-twenties, her face was on money in Bermuda and Cyprus.

In 1953, she was the queen and there were nine countries with her face on their money.

Surprisingly, there weren't any pound bills in the UK with her face before this one in 1960.

In 1977, after twenty-five years as queen, she appeared on new pound bills with this picture in eight countries.

In the past, pictures of the queen were formal. But in her late fifties, she appeared on this Canadian bill informally.

In 1992, the Queen was on money in Fiji, Guernsey, Bermuda, and the Bahamas. She was formal again, but smiling!

In the past, there weren't any happy faces of the queen, but finally, in her seventies, she was happy on this Scottish bill in 2002!

formal (adj) /ˈfɔrməl/ official, more serious

4 Read the article again. Fill in the years.

Born: ¹ _1926_
Face on Canadian twenty-dollar bill:
² _____
Face on pound bills in the UK: ³ _____
Twenty-five years as Queen: ⁴ _____
Face on money in Fiji, Guernsey, Bermuda, and the Bahamas: ⁵ _____
Happy face on Scottish bill ⁶ _____

Vocabulary age

5 Read the article again and complete 1–3.

1 Underline any words about the age of the Queen. For example: *ten years old.*
2 We also talk about age in general with the words *early, mid, late*. For example: *early thirties, mid twenties, late fifties.* What are these ages in general?

29	35	41	55	61	89

3 Discuss these questions in pairs.

- What age is young, middle-aged, or old?
- What is a good age to be a student? Get married? Start a company? Be president?

Grammar *was/were*

6 Look at the simple past form of *be* in this sentence. Then find more examples of the simple past form of *be* in the article. What is the negative form?

In 1936, Princess Elizabeth was ten years old and her parents were king and queen.

> ▶ **WAS/WERE**
>
> I/he/she/it **was** ten years old.
> You/we/they **were** young.
>
> I/he/she/it **wasn't** middle-aged.
> You/we/they **weren't** old.
>
> There **was** a coin.
> There **were** bills.
>
> Was I/he/she/it on the bill?
> Yes, I/he/she/it was. / No, I/he/she/it wasn't.
> Were you/we/they young?
> Yes, you/we/they were. / No, you/we/they weren't.
>
> For more information and practice, see pages 162 and 163.

7 Choose the correct form to complete the texts about other people and places on currencies.

In 1789, George Washington ¹ *was / were* the first president of the United States of America. However, his face ² *wasn't / weren't* on the US dollar. In 1869, he ³ *was / were* on the dollar and he's still there today.

Frida Kahlo and Diego Rivera ⁴ *was / were* famous artists in the twentieth century and you can see their faces on both sides of a Mexican 500-peso bill. For the first time, there ⁵ *was / were* two people on one bill.

On January 1, 2002, the euro ⁶ *was / were* the new currency for fifteen countries. There ⁷ *wasn't / weren't* famous people on the coins and bills. Instead, there ⁸ *was / were* historical buildings and a map of Europe.

8 Work in pairs. Ask and answer questions to complete texts about other people on currencies.

Student A: Turn to page 153.
Student B: Turn to page 155.

Writing and speaking

9 Write five sentences about someone's life.

Examples:
He was born in Italy, but he was British.
In their mid twenties, they weren't rich.

10 Work in pairs. Take turns to read your sentences. Ask questions about your partner's person.

> *Where was he born?*

> *Was she British?*

6b Discover the past

Listening

1 Read the text and answer the questions.

1 What is the building? Where is it? Why do visitors go there?
2 Do you have museums in your town or city? Do you visit them? Why? / Why not?

Birmingham Museum and Art Gallery is a famous museum in central England with lots of different exhibitions. Visitors can learn about local history and see archeological objects over a thousand years old. At the moment, there is a special exhibition of objects from the Anglo-Saxons.

Anglo-Saxons (n pl) /ˈæŋgloʊˈsæksənz/ people living in England a thousand years ago
exhibition (n) /ˌeksɪˈbɪʃən/ when a museum or gallery shows objects or paintings to visitors

2 🎵 **33** Listen to an interview with two visitors to the museum. Answer the questions.

1 Why does he ask visitors about their experience at the museum?
2 Does the woman visit all of the museum or one exhibition?
3 How does she know about the exhibition?
4 Why is the man at the museum?
5 Does he often visit museums?

Vocabulary -ed/-ing adjectives

3 🎵 **33** Listen again and choose the adjective you hear in these sentences.

1 I'm *interested* / *interesting* in the exhibition of Anglo-Saxon objects.
2 It's very *excited* / *exciting*.
3 Is it *interested* / *interesting*?
4 I think history's *bored* / *boring*.
5 My children are *excited* / *exciting*.

4 In Exercise 3, which adjectives ending in *-ed* and *-ing* describe how the person feels? Which describe a thing or situation?

5 Complete the sentences with the correct adjectives.

interested / interesting
1 Old Roman coins are very _____ .
2 I'm not very _____ in history.

bored / boring
3 TV shows about history are very _____ .
4 The children are _____ . Let's go home.

excited / exciting
5 I'm going to Egypt and I'm very _____ .
6 Modern history is _____ .

6 Do you think history is boring / interesting / exciting? Discuss the question as a class.

Reading

7 Read the article about the Anglo-Saxon objects at the Birmingham Museum. Answer the questions.

1 When were the Anglo-Saxons in England?
2 What were they famous for?
3 Where were the metal objects?
4 How many objects were there?
5 Were people interested in them?
6 What was the final value of the objects?

Anglo-Saxon gold under the ground

The Anglo-Saxon people **lived** in England one thousand years ago. They **worked** in the fields and they were also famous for their metal work and jewelry. They **made** beautiful objects from gold and silver.

In 2009, the Birmingham Museum **received** a phone call about some gold and silver objects under a field near Birmingham. The next day, archaeologists **studied** the objects. They were from the Anglo-Saxon period. In the end, the archaeologists **found** 1,500 objects there.

The Birmingham museum **showed** the objects in 2009, and thousands of visitors came. In fact, the museum **moved** the exhibition to a bigger building because so many people **wanted** to see them. The final value of the objects was over five million dollars, but for many archaeologists, they are priceless.

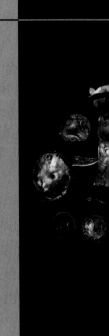

Grammar simple past (affirmative): regular and irregular verbs

8 Read the first paragraph of the article again. Answer the questions.

1 Is the paragraph about the past or the present?
2 Underline the past form of these verbs: *live, work, make*. Which two verbs are regular? Which is irregular?

> **SIMPLE PAST (AFFIRMATIVE): REGULAR AND IRREGULAR VERBS**
>
> We talk about finished actions and events in the past with verbs in the simple past tense.
>
> **Regular verbs**
> We add -*ed* or -*d*: *play – played, die – died.*
>
> **Irregular verbs**
> We use irregular forms: *become – became, get – got, go – went, meet – met.*
>
> For more information and practice, see page 163.

9 Look at the other simple past verbs in the newspaper article. Which are regular and which are irregular?

priceless (adj) /ˈpraɪslɪs/ to describe an object with no price because it is so important.
value (n) /ˈvælju/ the cost or price of something

10 Complete this text with the simple past form of the verbs.

THE FACE MASK OF TUTANKHAMEN

Howard Carter was born in 1874. His family ¹ _____ (live) in London, but in 1891 Carter ² _____ (go) to Egypt and ³ _____ (work) there as an archaeologist. On Novermber 4, 1922, Carter ⁴ _____ (discover) the tomb of Tutankhamen. Tutankhamen ⁵ _____ (become) a King when he was nine years old and he ⁶ _____ (die) when he was nineteen. The Egyptians ⁷ _____ (make) his face mask of gold and the tomb ⁸ _____ (have) 50,000 gold and silver objects inside.

tomb (n) /tum/ place with a dead body inside

11 Pronunciation -*ed* endings

a 🔊 **34** Sometimes -*ed* adds an extra syllable to verbs in the simple past. Listen and write the number of syllables.

1	live *1*	lived *1*		5	start	started
2	decide *2*	decided *3*		6	play	played
3	like	liked		7	visit	visited
4	want	wanted		8	travel	traveled

b 🔊 **34** Listen again and repeat.

Speaking

12 Think of five important years in your life and the reason why they are important (e.g., *In 2001, I went to New York.*). Next, write down the five years but do not write down the reason.

13 Work in pairs. Show the years to your partner and he/she guesses why the years are important to you.

1995.   *You went to college in 1995.*

You started your first job.   *Yes, correct.*

6c A cashless world?

Reading

1 Discuss these questions as a class.

1 Do you usually pay for things:
    a with cash (coins and bills)?
    b by credit card?
    c online?
    d with a check?
2 Where do you usually keep
    your money?
    a in a purse or wallet
    b in a bank account
    c under your bed!
    d in your pocket

2 Read the article and put these
methods of payment on the
timeline.

animals	checkbook
credit card	metal coins
cell phone	paper money
seashells	

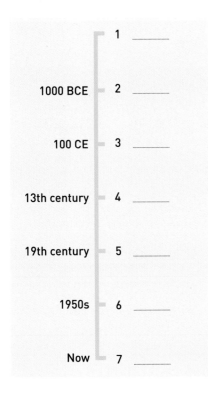

```
                    1  ..............

    1000 BCE        2  ..............

    100 CE          3  ..............

    13th century    4  ..............

    19th century    5  ..............

    1950s           6  ..............

    Now             7  ..............
```

> ▶ **WORDBUILDING compound nouns**
>
> We make compound nouns with two nouns. For example: *credit + card = credit card.*

Critical thinking **relevance**

3 These are the last sentences for each paragraph in the article. Match the sentences with the paragraphs.

a They also put the head of their emperor on them.
b The total transaction time took sixteen seconds.   *1*
c And personally, I still prefer real cash in my pocket to numbers in a bank account.
d It was also easy to carry.
e Over 180 million people in the US have more than one credit card.
f But is that really possible?

Speaking

4 Work in pairs. Ask and answer the questions in the survey. Write your partner's answers.

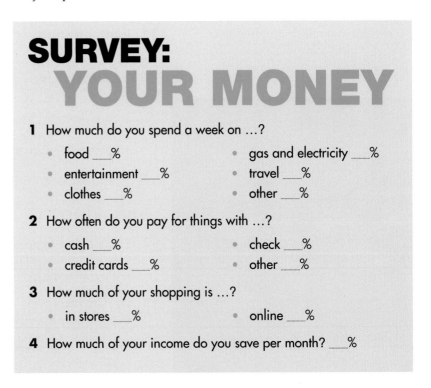

SURVEY:
YOUR MONEY

1 How much do you spend a week on ...?

- food ____%
- entertainment ____%
- clothes ____%
- gas and electricity ____%
- travel ____%
- other ____%

2 How often do you pay for things with ...?

- cash ____%
- credit cards ____%
- check ____%
- other ____%

3 How much of your shopping is ...?

- in stores ____%
- online ____%

4 How much of your income do you save per month? ____%

5 Join another pair. Present and compare your answers. Are your answers similar or different? Why?

A CASHLESS WORLD?

A bank of stone money on the island of Yap

It's midnight in Buenos Aires and I need money quickly. The banks are closed, but outside there's an ATM (cash machine). I put in my ATM or debit card, enter my PIN (personal identification number), and ask for 500 pesos. The ATM sends a message to my bank in Washington, D.C. My bank replies to the message and says I have the money in my bank account. After a few short moments, I receive my cash.

Nowadays, we move money around the world at high speed. I can get money from a bank anywhere in the world or I can pay my hotel bill with a credit card. In fact, some people think we don't need money at all.

Before money, people bought and sold goods with animals. But you can't carry animals around your neck or in a bag so people needed something small. About three thousand years ago, the Chinese used seashells and later they used metal coins. The Romans also bought and sold objects with metal coins.

In the thirteenth century, the explorer Marco Polo traveled to China. He saw paper money for the first time. A century later, countries in Europe used paper money too. One reason was that it was good for paying large amounts.

Like paper money, checks were also practical and the Bank of England made the first checkbook in the nineteenth century. Then, in the early nineteen fifties, the US introduced credit cards or "plastic money." This form of payment is still popular today.

For the first time since humans used animals for payment, we can now buy and sell with no coins, bills, or checks. You can even pay for things with a cell phone. In Africa, around six million people already use cell phones instead of cash. So do we live in a cashless world? Not quite. Every day, we usually still need some cash for a coffee or a subway ticket.

6d Help!

Listening

1 Do you know these international charities? Who do they help? Check your answers on page 156.

 International Federation of Red Cross and Red Crescent Societies

2 💿 **35** Listen to three conversations about money. Match the conversations to the topics.

Conversation 1   a   It's for someone at work.
Conversation 2   b   It's for charity.
Conversation 3   c   It's for parking.

Real life requesting

3 💿 **35** Listen again. Complete the sentences with these words.

Can I (x2)	Could you (x2)	I'm afraid
I'm sorry	OK	Yes, of course

Conversation 1
A: It's for poor children in different countries. We use the money for food and hospitals and also for new schools. So ¹＿＿＿ give us something?
B: ²＿＿＿ . Here you are.

Conversation 2
A: Hey. ³＿＿＿ ask you something?
B: ⁴＿＿＿ . What is it?
A: Well, I don't have any money until tomorrow. ⁵＿＿＿ lend me some money?
B: ⁶＿＿＿ , but I can't.
A: Don't worry. I can ask someone else.
B: OK. Sorry.

Conversation 3
A: The machine only takes coins. You can't use bills. ⁷＿＿＿ borrow some money?
B: Actually, I don't have any coins.

4 Complete the list of useful phrases with requests and responses from the conversations in Exercise 3.

> **▶ REQUESTING**
>
> **Requests**
> 1   Could you give us something?
> 2   ＿＿＿＿＿＿＿＿＿＿
> 3   ＿＿＿＿＿＿＿＿＿＿
> 4   ＿＿＿＿＿＿＿＿＿＿
>
> **Responses**
> Yes, certainly.
>
> ＿＿＿＿＿＿＿＿＿＿
> ＿＿＿＿＿＿＿＿＿＿

> **lend** (v) /lend/ you give the money to someone and they return the money later
> **borrow** (v) /'barou/ you receive the money from someone and you return the money later

5 Pronunciation **stress in questions**

💿 **36** Listen to the four requests (1–4) in Exercise 4. Notice the stressed words. Listen again and repeat.

Could you <u>give</u> us <u>something</u>?

6 Work in pairs. Practice the three conversations in the recording. Take turns to request and respond with "yes" or "no." Then practice your own conversation. Ask your partner for money or help.

6e Thanks!

Writing thank you messages

1 Do you ever write a "thank you" note, email, or letter to people? If yes, is it for any of these reasons?

- after a meal at their house
- when they give you a present
- for their help
- to a client or customer at work
- after you stay with someone

2 Read the card, email, and letter. Why does the writer say "thank you" each time?

 A

Hi!

Thanks for my graduation present!
I spent it on some new clothes.
See you soon!

Love,
Ginny

B

Subject: Conference in Rio

Dear Nadia,

Thank you for your work in Rio. We were pleased with the conference. It was very successful. In particular, we enjoyed the dinner on the last night!

Everyone in the team sends their thanks.

See you again next year.

Best,
Sanjit

C

Dear Mr. Keeping,

Thank you very much for your interest in our products. Enclosed is our catalog for this year with prices.

I look forward to hearing from you in the future.

Yours sincerely,

AM Freeman

Arnold M. Freeman

3 Writing skill formal and informal expressions

a Complete the table with expressions from the thank you messages in Exercise 2.

	A	B	C
introduction	*Hi!*		
thank the person			*Thank you very much for …*
talk about future contact		*See you again next year.*	
end the writing			

b Which message (A–C) uses very formal expressions? Which message uses very informal expressions?

4 Choose a situation (1–3) and write to the person. Use formal or informal expressions.

1. You borrowed money from a friend. You want to return it. Write and send a check.
2. You were on a business trip Singapore. Your client there helped you on the trip and showed you around the city.
3. A customer emailed you and asked for information about your company.

5 Work in pairs. Exchange your messages. Does your partner use the correct formal or informal expressions for the situation?

Bactrian treasure

Ancient treasure from Bactria

Before you watch

1 Work in pairs. Look at the photo and read the caption. Then complete the text about Bactria with the simple past form of these verbs.

> be   become   buy and sell   call   discover
> make   travel

Over two thousand years ago, Bactria ¹ _____ a region between the Mediterranean Sea and China and India. Many traders ² _____ across the region and they ³ _____ goods from different countries. As a result, the people of Bactria ⁴ _____ rich and powerful and they ⁵ _____ beautiful objects with gold, silver, and stone. In 1978, a group of archaeologists ⁶ _____ more than 20,000 Bactrian objects. They ⁷ _____ it the "Bactrian Treasure."

2 Work in groups. Look at these photos of the Bactrian treasure. What do you think the objects are? Use phrases like "I think/Maybe it's/they're…" to talk about the objects.

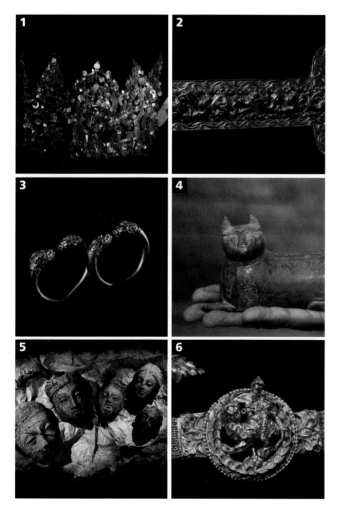

While you watch

3 Watch the video. Match these descriptions to the photos in Exercise 2.

- _____ a belt
- _____ faces of people from Bactria
- _____ a cat
- _____ gold bracelets with lion heads on them
- _____ a beautiful gold crown
- _____ He doesn't say.

4 Watch the video again. Choose the correct option (a–c) to complete these sentences.

1. Over two thousand years ago, the northern part of _____ was called Bactria.
   a India
   b China
   c Afghanistan
2. It became a rich region and famous for its _____, their palaces, and gold.
   a kings and queens
   b people
   c presidents
3. The archaeologists moved the treasure to the national _____ in Kabul.
   a palace   b museum   c castle
4. Then, in 2004, archaeologists discovered six underground _____ in Kabul.
   a vaults   b museums   c palaces
5. The statue of the cat tells us that _____ were important in Bactrian culture.
   a crowns   b people   c animals
6. Now the Bactrian treasure is traveling to museums all around _____.
   a America
   b Asia
   c the world

After you watch

5 Discussion **important objects in history**

Work in groups.

You want to make a short video called *The World in the Early 21st Century*. In your video, you can show seven photos of important objects from this period of history. Choose seven objects for your video. Discuss why they are important for the video. What do they tell people about the early 21st century?

6 Present your seven objects to the class. Explain to the class why you chose them.

UNIT 6 REVIEW

Grammar

1 Complete the text with the simple past of the verbs.

In 1801, Thomas Jefferson [1] _____ (become) the president of the United States. At this time, there [2] _____ (be) no route from the east coast to the west coast of North America, but Jefferson [3] _____ (want) one. In 1804, he [4] _____ (send) a group of 30 men across the United States. Meriwether Lewis and William Clark [5] _____ (be) the two leaders of the group and there was a woman with them. Sacagawea [6] _____ (be) a Native American and she [7] _____ (work) for Lewis and Clark as a guide and a translator. In 1806, they [8] _____ (discover) a route to the Pacific coast. Nowadays, Sacagawea is famous in the United States. Her face [9] _____ (be) on the US gold dollar coin in 2000.

2 Complete the questions about the text in Exercise 1.

1 _____ between the coasts?
No, there wasn't.
2 _____ the leaders of the group?
Yes, they were.
3 _____ with them?
Yes, there was. Her name was Sacagawea.
4 _____ a Native American?
Yes, she was.
5 _____ on a U.S. dollar bill?
No, it was on a gold coin.

I CAN	
talk about past events with the simple past tense	
ask about the past	

Vocabulary

3 Make five sentences with the words in the table.

We	change earn spend give keep	money	to charity. at a currency exchange. in a purse or wallet. in stores. at work.

4 Complete the words.

1 Can I pay by credit c_____ or check?
2 Turn off your cell p_____ in class.
3 You can find sea s_____ on a beach.
4 How much money is in your bank a_____?

5 Complete the adjectives with -ed or -ing.

1 We're interest_____ in history.
2 The story is very excit_____.
3 This movie is a bit bor_____.
4 I'm tir_____ and I need to go to bed.

6 Work in pairs. Say the name of a famous person and guess how old he or she is (e.g., Do you think the person is in his mid or late forties?).

I CAN	
talk about money	
use -ed/-ing adjectives	
talk about age	

Real life

7 Put the words in order to make requests.

1 me / a / could / you / give / dollar?
_____
2 ask / something? / you / can / I
_____
3 you / lend / your / phone? / me / could
_____
4 borrow / car? / can / I / your
_____

8 Work in pairs. Take turns to say the requests in Exercise 7. Your partner responds to the requests.

I CAN	
request things and respond to requests	

Speaking

9 Work in pairs. Talk about a time when you:

- were excited about something
- visited an interesting place
- asked someone for help

Unit 7 Travel

The *Mayflower II* sets sail.

FEATURES

1 Look at the photo and the caption. What mode of transportation do you see? Is this the first *Mayflower* ship or the second? What do you know about the *Mayflower*?

2 Choose the correct travel verbs to complete the text.

The *Mayflower II* is a copy of the 17th century ship, the *Mayflower*. The original Mayflower ¹*sailed / flew* from England to North America in 1620. It ²*arrived in / left* England with 102 passengers on board. The journey was ten weeks long. It ³*arrived in / left* North America on November 9, 1620. In 1957, the *Mayflower II* traveled from England to the US. When it arrived, hundreds of people ⁴*traveled / drove* by sea and air to meet the ship. Today, you can see the *Mayflower II* in Plymouth Harbor, Massachusetts, in the US.

3 Work in pairs. Ask and answer the questions. Use these verbs.

cycle	drive	fly
sail	take (public transportation)	travel by (car/train/ship, etc.)

1 How do you normally travel to work (or school)?
2 What's your favorite way to travel? Why?
3 What's your favorite trip? Why?

7a Flight of the *Silver Queen*

Reading

1 Look at the photo and map of a journey. Where was the flight from and to?

2 The article is in the wrong order. Number the paragraphs 1 to 4.

3 Mark the sentences true (T) or false (F).

1 The trip was in 1920.
2 All the airplanes landed in Cape Town.
3 The first part of the trip was from England to Italy.
4 Van Ryneveld and Brand stopped between Italy and Cairo.
5 They didn't have any problems with the engine.
6 They left Bulawayo in the *Silver Queen*.
7 The trip took 44 days.
8 They received $10,000 from the newspaper.

4 Discuss as a class why you think these pilots went on these trips. For money? Something else? Would you take a similar trip?

Grammar **simple past: negatives**

5 Look at these two sentences from the article. Answer the questions.

Four airplanes didn't finish the journey.
The newspaper didn't give them $16,000.

1 What auxiliary verb do you use in simple past negative sentences?
2 Does the negative auxiliary verb change for *I/you/we/they* and *he/she/it*?
3 What form of the verb is after the negative auxiliary?

Flight of the SILVER QUEEN

A ☐
It was a long, dangerous journey. The pilots Pierre Van Ryneveld and Quintin Brand flew in a plane called the *Silver Queen*. They traveled from England to Italy. A few days later, they took off again for Egypt. They didn't stop over the Mediterranean Sea and landed the next day in Cairo.

B ☐
Eventually, 44 days later, they landed in Cape Town and won. However, the newspaper only gave them $8,000 because they didn't use the same plane for the whole trip. It was still an incredible journey!

C ☐
In 1920, a British newspaper offered $16,000 to fly from England to South Africa. Five airplanes entered the competition, but four didn't finish the journey.

D ☐
Through Africa, they had a lot of mechanical problems with the plane and its engine. The worst problem was in Bulawayo. The *Silver Queen* couldn't take off, so in the end they changed their plane for a different one.

take off (v) /'teɪk 'ɒf/ to leave the ground (for airplanes)
land (v) /lænd/ to return to the ground (for airplanes)

> **SIMPLE PAST: NEGATIVES**
>
> I/you/he/she/it/we/they **didn't** fly. (not: *They didn't flew.*)
>
> For more information and practice, see pages 163 and 164.

6 Work in pairs. Make true sentences about the 1920s with the words in this table. Use the simple past.

In the 1920s, people		travel pay	into space by train by credit card with cash games computer games maps satellite navigation
	didn't	play use	

Example:

In the 1920s, people didn't travel into space / traveled by train.

7 Write down three things you didn't do ten years ago, but you do now. Tell your partner.

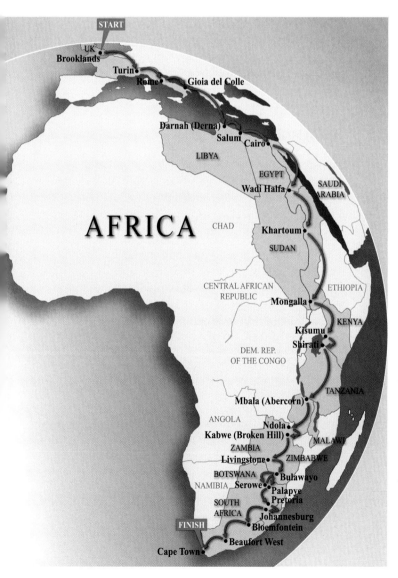

Listening

8 🎧 **37** Listen to part of a radio show and number the topics discussed in order from 1 to 3.

   a   the reasons why they traveled
   b   where the *Silver Queen* traveled
   c   who the pilots were

9 🎧 **37** Listen again and choose the correct options to complete the sentences.

   1   Pierre Van Ryneveld and Quintin Brand *had / didn't have* maps for Europe, Egypt, and South Africa.
   2   They *had / didn't have* maps for other parts of Africa.
   3   Van Ryneveld and Brand *went / didn't go* for the money.
   4   They *wanted / didn't want* to be the first.

Grammar simple past: questions and short answers

10 Look at the two questions. What is the auxiliary verb in simple past questions?

Did Van Ryneveld and Brand have maps? Why did they go on this trip?

> **SIMPLE PAST: QUESTIONS AND SHORT ANSWERS**
>
> ***Yes/No* questions and short answers**
> Did they go to Lima?
> Yes, they did. / No, they didn't.
> ***Wh-* questions**
> When did they go? Why did they go?
>
> For more information and practice, see pages 163 and 164.

11 Work in pairs. In 1999, three modern pilots went on a similar trip.

Student A: Turn to page 155.
Student B: Turn to page 156.

Speaking

12 Think about a trip you took in the past. Answer these questions.

   • Where, why, and how did you go?
   • Did you have any problems?
   • How long did the journey take?

13 Work in pairs. Talk about your journey.

7b Animal migrations

Vocabulary travel adjectives

Every year, animals around the world go on long and difficult journeys. Sea animals swim across oceans and birds fly north and south with the seasons. Land animals, such as the wildebeest (below), go on slow and dangerous migrations for food and water like this one, from the Serengeti into Kenya.

migration (n) /maɪˈɡreɪʃən/ when an animal travels from one place to another at different times of the year

1 Find the opposite of these travel adjectives in the text.

> easy   fast   safe   short

2 Work in pairs. Describe these trips to and from your home with adjectives from Exercise 1.

1 My trip to work is …
2 The trip home at night is …
3 The bus downtown is very …

Listening

3 🔊 **38** Look at the animals on page 85 and listen. Match the animals (1–3) with the distances (a–c).

1 saiga
2 loggerhead turtle
3 tree frog
a 100 feet (30m)
b 22 miles (35km) a day
c 9,000 miles (14,000km) in fifteen years

male (n/adj) /meɪl/ ♂
female (n/adj) /ˈfiːmeɪl/ ♀
calf (n) /kæf/ a baby saiga
lay eggs /ˈleɪ ˈegz/ when a female animal leaves eggs outside its body

4 🔊 **38** Listen again. Answer the questions.

1 Where does the saiga live?
2 What does the female saiga have in the spring?
3 Where does a loggerhead's migration begin?
4 Where does the female lay her eggs?
5 Where does the tree frog lay its eggs?

Grammar comparative adjectives

5 We use comparative adjectives to compare two things. Look at the comparative adjectives in these sentences. Answer the questions.

The male saiga is **faster** than the female.
The journey is **more difficult** for a female saiga.

1 What two letters do you add to short adjectives?
2 What word comes before long adjectives?

> ▶ **COMPARATIVE ADJECTIVES**
>
> One-syllable adjectives: *It's a warm country.* → *It's warmer than other countries.*
> Adjectives ending in one vowel + one consonant: *It's a big animal.* → *It's bigger than a saiga.*
> Two-syllable adjectives ending in -y: *It's an easy journey.* → *It's an easier journey.*
> Two-syllable (or more) adjectives: *It's a difficult job.* → *It's more difficult than other jobs.*
>
> There are some irregular adjectives: *good* → *better, bad* → *worse*
>
> For more information and practice, see page 164.

1 saiga

2 loggerhead turtle

3 tree frog

6 Complete the table with comparative adjectives.

Adjective	Comparative adjective
cold	1 ....
hot	2 ....
dangerous	3 ....
cheap	4 ....
expensive	5 ....
long	6 ....
interesting	7 ....
high	8 ....

Word focus *than*

7 When we compare two things, we often use *than* after the comparative adjective: *Africa is hotter <u>than</u> Europe.* Make similar sentences about these pairs with a comparative adjective + *than*.

1 Australia / Antarctica
2 rock-climbing / surfing
3 travel by air / by sea
4 an elephant / a lion
5 Paris / New York
6 train journeys / plane journeys

8 Pronunciation stressed and weak syllables /ə/

🔊 **39** Listen to the stressed and weak syllables in these sentences. Then listen again and repeat.

              /ə/ /ə/
1 <u>A</u>frica is <u>hotter</u> than <u>Eu</u>rope.
             /ə/ /ə/
2 Aus<u>tra</u>lia isn't <u>colder</u> than Ant<u>arc</u>tica.

Speaking

9 Which of these sentences is a fact and which is opinion? Repeat the opinion with these phrases.

Antarctica is colder than Australia.
Rock-climbing is more dangerous than surfing.

> I think …   In my opinion …

10 Write sentences with your opinion. Compare two:

- places or cities
- sports or free-time activities
- types of travel or vacations
- places in the city
- types of transport
- famous people

11 Work in pairs. Take turns reading your opinions. Do you agree with your partner?

> I think Hong Kong is more expensive than Dubai.

> I agree! / I don't agree!

7c The longest journey in space

Reading

1 Do you think it's important to travel in space?

2 Look at the photos and read the caption on page 87. What is the name of the spacecraft? What did it take photos of?

3 Read the article on page 87 and answer the questions.

1 Which planets did Voyager 1 visit?
2 Which planets did Voyager 2 visit?
3 Where are the Voyager spacecraft now?

4 Replace the underlined words with these words.

> Florida   Jupiter   Neptune
> outside the solar system   Saturn   Uranus
> Voyager 1   Voyager 2

1 NASA sent Voyager 1 and 2 from <u>here</u>.
2 <u>It</u> had a mechanical problem with its camera.
3 <u>This planet</u> is famous for its rings.
4 <u>It</u> sent the best pictures of <u>this planet</u>.
5 Voyager 2 went to <u>this planet</u> last.
6 <u>This planet</u> is very cold and has lots of ice.
7 Voyager 1 and 2 are on a journey <u>there</u> now.

Critical thinking fact or opinion

5 Look at the first two sentences in paragraph 1 of the article. Which sentence is a fact? Which sentence includes the writer's opinion?

6 Find more sentences in paragraphs 2, 3, and 4 with the writer's opinion.

Grammar superlative adjectives

7 Look at these two sentences. Which sentence compares more than two things in a group?

a Saturn is smaller than Jupiter.
b Jupiter is the largest planet in the solar system.

> ▶ **SUPERLATIVE ADJECTIVES**
>
> It's the largest planet.
> It's the most dangerous place.
>
> For more information and practice, see pages 164 and 165.

8 Underline the superlative form of these adjectives in the article.

> good   famous   cold   far   amazing

9 Complete the quiz about the planets in our solar system with the superlative form of the adjectives. Then answer the questions. Check your answers on page 155.

> ❶ Which planet is _____ (near) to the Sun?
> ❷ Which planet is _____ (easy) to see in the sky?
> ❸ Which planet is _____ (far) from Earth?
> ❹ Which planet is the _____ (good) for human life?
> ❺ Which planet is the _____ (hot)?

Writing and speaking

10 Work in groups. Follow the instructions.

1 Write another general-knowledge quiz on different subjects. Write five quiz questions with superlatives.
2 Compete with another group. Ask and answer your questions.

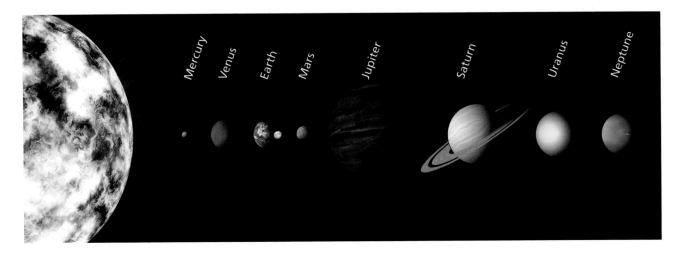
Mercury   Venus   Earth   Mars   Jupiter   Saturn   Uranus   Neptune

Voyager 1 photographed these planets and moons on its journey through our solar system.

The LONGEST
JOURNEY IN SPACE

On August 20 and September 5, 1977, two spacecraft took off from Florida, U.S. Voyager 1 and Voyager 2 started a long and difficult journey to the end of the solar system. They flew past new places in our solar system and sent photos of planets and moons to NASA (National Aeronautics and Space Administration).

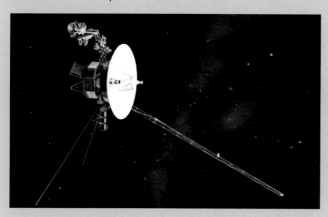

Voyager 1's Journey
Voyager 1 arrived at Jupiter, the largest planet in the solar system. At a distance of 480 million miles from Earth, Voyager 1 sent scientists the best photographs of the planet, and they discovered a lot about the planet's weather from them. They studied the clouds, lightning, and strong winds of about 180 miles per hour. Jupiter also has a moon with volcanoes. Voyager 1's next stop was Saturn. Saturn is smaller than Jupiter and it's most famous for its rings. From Voyager 1's photographs, scientists discovered the rings are mostly water and ice.

Voyager 2's Journey
Voyager 2 also visited Jupiter and Saturn, but it continued to Uranus, the coldest planet in the solar system. It has a lot of ice on its surface. During its journey around Uranus, Voyager 2's camera had mechanical problems. Eventually, scientists fixed it and Voyager 2 traveled to Neptune, the farthest planet from the Sun (2.8 billion miles). It was the last planet on Voyager 2's journey.

The Journey Continues
The two Voyagers finished their official journeys in 1989, but they continued traveling. Now they are at the end of our solar system and scientists think the two spacecraft can travel until 2025 on their most amazing journey: into space outside our solar system.

7d How was your trip?

Vocabulary *journey*, *travel*, or *trip*?

1 Look at the sentences (1–3). Then match the nouns *journey, travel,* and *trip* to the definitions (a–c).

1 My **journey,** through the Gobi desert was amazing!
2 **Travel** is good for you because you learn a lot.
3 I had a business **trip** to Berlin for two days.

a the activity of going from one place to another place
b when you travel a long distance or a long time
c when you travel somewhere for a short time and return to the same place

2 Look at the pictures from a work trip. Which of these words can you use to describe each part of the trip?

> comfortable   delicious   really useful   tiring   terrible
> very interesting

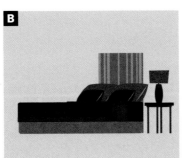

> **WORDBUILDING** *really/very* + adjective

You can make some adjectives stronger with *really* and *very*. For example:
The journey was tiring. → *The journey was* **very** *tiring /* **really** *tiring.*

Real life asking about a trip

3 🔊 **40** Listen to two conversations about a trip. For each conversation, answer these questions.

1 Is Dr. Egan still on the trip or is he back in his own country?
2 What parts of the trip does the other person ask about?
3 What is Dr. Egan's answer? What adjectives does he use?

4 🔊 **40** Listen again and complete the questions from the conversations.

> ▶ **ASKING ABOUT A TRIP**
>
> 1 _____ your flight?
> 2 _____ comfortable?
> 3 _____ try the local food?
> What ⁴_____ the weather _____?
> Why? What ⁵_____?

5 **Pronunciation intonation in questions**

🔊 **41** Listen to the questions in Exercise 4. Notice the intonation in the questions. Repeat with the same intonation.

6 Work in pairs. Act out the trip in Exercise 2.

Student A: Answer Student B's questions about the trip.

Student B: Ask Student A questions about his/her trip.

7 Change roles and act out the trip on page 155.

7e The digital nomad

Vocabulary online writing

1 Discuss these questions as a class.

1 Do you read blogs? Which ones?
2 Do you write a blog? What is it about?

2 Read about Andrew Evans. Why is his blog called "Digital Nomad"?

Travel Home | Top 10 | Destinations A-Z | Trip Ideas |

Andrew Evans is a **blogger** for National Geographic's **website**. He's called "The Digital Nomad" because he travels all the time and he's always **online**. Every day he **blogs** about his journeys. He writes **posts** from different countries and **uploads** videos of amazing places. Readers can also leave Andrew a **comment** on his articles.

His **homepage** is
http://digitalnomad.nationalgeographic.com/

3 Match the highlighted words in Exercise 2 with the definitions.

1 a destination on the Internet
2 writes an online diary
3 connected to and using the Internet
4 the first page of a website
5 person who writes for a blog or blogs
6 adds content to a website or blog
7 a reply or opinion from a reader
8 articles on a blog

Writing a travel blog

4 Read the post and answer the questions.

1 Where is the blogger and how long is his journey?
2 What can he see?
3 What happened to the bus?
4 Why did he feel sorry for the bus driver?
5 Why did he walk to the border?

5 Writing skill *so, because*

a Look at *so* and *because* in the third paragraph of the blog in Exercise 4. Which word is about (a) the reason for something and (b) the result of, or response to, something?

b Complete the sentences with *so* or *because*.

1 We stopped at a restaurant _____ I was hungry.
2 The train was late _____ we waited for it.
3 We put on sunscreen _____ the weather was hot.
4 It started raining _____ we bought an umbrella.
5 We rented a car _____ there were no trains or buses.

6 Write a short travel blog about a journey or place you visited. Think about these questions. Use *so* and *because*.

- Where were you?
- When was it?
- Who was there?
- What happened?

7 Work in pairs. Exchange blogs. Check that your partner (a) answered the questions in Exercise 6 and (b) used *so* and *because*.

Today was the final day of my bus journey from Lhasa to Kodari, at the border with Nepal. It's the highest road in the world. It's also a very long journey. You travel for three days through the Himalayas and you can see the north side of Everest.

This afternoon, we were only ten miles from Kodari and suddenly the bus stopped. The driver got out and looked at the engine. For the next three hours, he tried to fix it, but it didn't start.

Finally, a lot of the passengers got out and started walking to the border. I felt sorry for the bus driver because he looked a little sad. However, I also wanted a good hotel and a hot meal so I left the bus and walked to Kodari too.

Sally Ride, an astronaut with NASA

Before you watch

1 Look at the photo of Sally Ride and read the caption. Discuss the questions.

1 What is her job?
2 Would you like to do this job? Why? / Why not?

2 Work in pairs. Read the sentences and choose the option you think is correct.

1 Sally Ride was the first *woman in space* / *American woman in space*.
2 She spent six *days* / *months* in space.
3 She *traveled* / *never traveled* into space again.
4 After Sally's journey, *other women* / *no other woman* went into space.

While you watch

3 Watch the video and check your answers in Exercise 2.

4 Watch the video again. Match the years with the events.

| 1 1958 | 3 1983 | 5 1984 | 7 1995 |
| 2 1969 | 4 1963 | 6 1992 | 8 2005 |

.... the first Russian woman in space
.... Sally Ride's second journey into space
.... the first female pilot of a space shuttle
.... the first man on the Moon
.... Eileen Collins' third flight
.... the first American woman in space
.... NASA began
.... the first African-American woman in space

5 Watch the video again. Choose the correct answers (a–c) for each question. Some questions have more than one answer.

1 What does the phrase "space was a man's world" mean?
   a All the US astronauts were men.
   b Only men worked for NASA.
   c American women didn't want to go into space.
2 How many women were in the group of candidates to be the first female astronaut?
   a two   b six   c ten
3 What did Sally do in space?
   a She helped to launch two satellites.
   b She did scientific experiments.
   c She flew the Challenger space shuttle.
4 What did she do after she returned from space?
   a She left NASA.
   b She gave talks across the US.
   c She trained other female astronauts.

5 What was Mae Jamison's job before she became an astronaut?
   a She was a doctor of physics.
   b She was a physician.
   c She didn't have a job.
6 At the end of the video we hear: "Young women—as well as young men—now dream of becoming astronauts and making a journey into space." Why do young women now dream of this?
   a Because of the space shuttle.
   b Because of NASA.
   c Because of female astronauts.

After you watch

6 **Role play** an interview with Sally Ride

Work in pairs.

Student A: You are Sally Ride. Answer a reporter's questions about your journey into space. Use the information in the video and prepare notes about:
- what you did before you were an astronaut
- the first flight on the Challenger space shuttle
- what you did in space
- what you did after you returned
- why you think your journey was important

Student B: You are a reporter. Interview Sally Ride. Use the information in the video and prepare questions about:
- what she did before she was an astronaut
- the first flight on the Challenger space shuttle
- what she did in space
- what she did after she returned
- why she thinks her journey was important

When you finish, switch roles and repeat the conversation.

7 Work in pairs. We can call Sally Ride a role model for young women. This is someone we admire and try to copy. Think of a role model in your life or for other people. Think about these questions.

1 Who is this person?
2 Is it someone in your family? In sports? On TV?
3 Why is he/she a role model?

Tell your partner about your role model.

---

experiment (n) /ɪkˈsperɪmənt/ scientific tests
launch (v) /lɔntʃ/ to send a rocket or space vehicle from the ground into the air or into space
pilot (n) /ˈpaɪlət/ person who controls and flies an airplane or space vehicle

UNIT 7 REVIEW

Grammar

1 Complete the text with the simple past form of the verbs.

Marco Polo ¹_____ (begin) his famous journey to China when he was seventeen years old. He ²_____ (travel) from Venice to Persia to Afghanistan and along the Silk Road to Cambulac (now Beijing). The journey ³_____ (take) three years. Polo ⁴_____ (not return) to Venice for seventeen years because he ⁵_____ (stay) in China and he ⁶_____ (work) for the Khan (or Emperor).

Marco Polo returned to Venice in 1295 and he ⁷_____ (not travel) to Asia again. But his book about the journeys in Asia called *Miracles of the World* ⁸_____ (become) famous across Europe. People ⁹_____ (not believe) everything in the book, but they loved the stories. Before Marco Polo died in 1324, he ¹⁰_____ (say) everything in the book was true.

2 Write questions about Marco Polo. Then ask and answer them with a partner.

1 When / Marco Polo / his journey to China?
  When did Marco Polo begin his journey to China?
2 Where / he / from?
3 How long / the journey / ?
4 How long / he / in China?
5 After 1295 / he / to Asia again?

3 Read the information. Then write two comparative sentences using the adjectives.

1 The summer temperature in Qatar is 104°F. It's 68°F in Berlin. (hot / cold)
  Qatar is hotter than Berlin. Berlin is colder than Qatar.
2 A Porsche can travel at 190 mph. A Mini can travel at 140 mph. (fast / slow)
3 This house costs $1,000,000. This apartment costs $250,000. (cheap / expensive)
4 Seoul has a population of 10 million. Havana has a population of 2 million. (big / small)
5 The Nile River is 4,132 miles long. The Amazon River is 4,170 miles long. (long / short)

4 Complete the superlative sentences by comparing each sentence to the information in Exercise 3.

1 The summer temperature in Anchorage is 64°F. Anchorage is *the coldest* city.
2 A Bugatti Veyron can travel at 270 mph. It's _____ car.
3 This castle costs $10 million. It's _____ home.
4 Delhi has a population of 12 million. It's _____ capital city.
5 The Mississippi River is 2,320 miles. It's _____ river.

I CAN	
talk about the past with the simple past tense	☐
ask questions about the past	☐
compare people and things	☐

Vocabulary

5 Write one type of transportation you can:

1 ride   2 fly   3 sail   4 drive

6 Choose the correct options. In one sentence, both answers are correct.

1 We went on a long *travel / journey*.
2 How was your business *trip / journey*?
3 I always *take / go* the bus to work.
4 My friend *writes / blogs* about his travels.

I CAN	
talk about transportation and travel	☐

Real life

7 Complete the questions with these words.

flight   hotel   meal   weather

1 How was the _____? Delicious!
2 How was the _____? It rained every day.
3 How was the _____? Very comfortable.
4 How was the _____? Tiring. It was six hours!

I CAN	
ask about a trip	☐
talk about a trip	☐

Speaking

8 Work in pairs. How much can you remember about these journeys from Unit 7?

The *Mayflower*   The Flight of the *Silver Queen*
The Journeys of Voyager 1 and 2

Unit 8 Appearance

The Dinagyang Festival in the Philippines. Locals dress up and dance through the streets.
Photo by Mario Babiera

FEATURES

1   Look at the photo and read the caption. Where is the festival? Which adjectives describe it?

| boring | colorful | crowded | exciting | fun |
| loud | popular | quiet | relaxing | noisy |

2   Discuss these questions using the adjectives.

1   What is an important day or festival in your town or city? When is it?
2   Do people change their appearance?
3   What do people do on that day? Do they eat special food?

... is a popular festival in my country. There's music and dancing.

Listening

1 🔊 **42** Listen to a conversation and number the children in the photo in the order they are discussed.

2 🔊 **42** Listen again. Answer the questions.

1 What and when is the festival?
2 Who is in the masks?
3 Why do people travel there?
4 Does the woman think the masks are beautiful or ugly?
5 What does the man think is "amazing"?
6 Why is the girl similar to the man's daughter?

3 What do you think about the masks? Do you think they are ugly or beautiful?

Grammar *be* vs. *have*

4 We use two verbs frequently to talk about appearance. How are they used?

a The masks are a bit ugly.
b She has these great big blue eyes.

> ▶ **IS VS. HAS**
>
> We use *be* + adjective to describe appearance (inherent qualities).
> - *She is pretty.*
> - *They are tall.*
> - *We are Vietnamese.*
>
> We use *have* + adjective + noun to describe specific attributes.
> - *He has blue eyes.*
> - *I have long hair.*
> - *You have a great sense of humor!*
>
> For more information and practice, see page 165.

5 Complete the description of a different festival with the correct form of *be* or *have*.

FACE AT A FESTIVAL

This Polga tribesman ¹ _____ a dancer at a festival in Papua New Guinea. All the men ² _____ tall and handsome and they ³ _____ colorful clothes with red hats over their short, dark hair. They ⁴ _____ white faces and black lines around their brown eyes, on their eyebrows, and on their cheeks. The man in the photo ⁵ _____ red paint on his lips and nose, and he ⁶ _____ black paint on his chin and a string of seashells around his neck.

Vocabulary face and appearance

6 Look at the highlighted words in the text in Exercise 5. Point at these parts of the face on the photo or on your own face.

7 Find one more word in the text for each category in the table.

General appearance	Height
beautiful (usually women) _____ (usually men) ugly	short / _____
Hair	**Eyes**
long / _____ straight / curly _____ / fair / blonde	blue green _____

8 Work in pairs. Make true sentences about your classmates.

He She They	is / are have / has don't have / doesn't have	handsome big heads brown hair a white face red cheeks curly hair glasses beautiful	a hat red lips tall brown eyes

9 Write a short description of your appearance. Use words from this page. Then read your description to your partner. Does your partner think it's accurate?

Speaking

10 Work in pairs. Play this game. Then change roles and play the game again.

Student A: Choose a person in the class. Answer Student B's questions.
Student B: Ask Student A questions and guess the person.

Does he have …?

Yes, he does. / No, he doesn't.

Is she …?

Yes, she is. / No, she isn't.

8b Global fashion

Reading

1 How often do you buy new clothes? Which of these is most important to you: the price, the size, the color, or the brand?

2 Read the article and answer the questions.

1 What type of photographer is Gillian?
2 Where does she normally work?
3 Where is she at the moment?

3 Choose the correct answer (a or b).

1 Where can you see her photographs?
   a in shops   b in magazines
2 Who does she work for?
   a a clothing company   b different companies
3 What does the writer think about global fashion?
   a It's the same.   b It's different.
4 Does Gillian agree with this opinion?
   a Yes, in some places.
   b No, she doesn't.

GLOBAL FASHION

Gillian Turner-Niles is a fashion photographer. She lives in New York and works in the fashion capitals of the world. You can see her photographs on the pages of fashion magazines across the world. Her clients include Gucci, Dior, Ferragamo, even the sports clothing company Nike. But today she's calling me from the middle of Sudan. So, what is she doing there?

"I'm taking photographs, of course!" She explains, "I'm not taking photographs for *Vogue* or anyone else. It's like a vacation. In my business, it's easy to forget there's another world out there. And I like looking at clothes in a different way when I travel."

But in this world of global fashion, people all over the world wear the same clothes. A business suit in Beijing is like a business suit in Berlin. And jeans and T-shirts are almost a uniform these days.

"Yes, I think that's true in the big international cities," Gillian says. "But I'm visiting regions in the world with their own traditional clothes and their own fashions. That's especially true in this part of Africa."

suit (n) /sut/ clothes (jacket and pants/skirt) made from the same material, often for work.
uniform (n) /ˈjunɪˌfɔrm/ the same clothes for a group of people (e.g., in the army or in school)

Word focus *like*

4 Look at the sentences with the verb *like*. In which sentence does *like* mean "similar to"? Find another sentence in the article with this meaning of *like*.

1 It's like a vacation.
2 I like looking at clothes.

5 Work in pairs and discuss.

1 Do you like fashion? Is it important to you?
2 Do you wear clothes like your friends, or like famous people in magazines?

Grammar present continuous

6 Look at these two sentences and answer the questions.

a She lives in New York and works in fashion.
b Today she's calling me.

1 Which sentence describes an action now or around the time of speaking?
2 Which sentence describes a permanent state or routine? What tense is the verb?

> ### ▶ PRESENT CONTINUOUS
>
> I'm (am) working.
> You/we/they're (are) working.
> He/she/it's (is) working.
>
> I'm not (am not) working.
> You/we/they aren't (are not) working.
> He/she/it isn't (is not) working.
>
> Are you/they/we working?
> What is he/she/it doing?
> Where are you/they/we working?
>
> For more information and practice, see pages 165 and 166.

7 Find examples of the present continuous form in the article in Exercise 2.

8 Complete the telephone conversation using the present continuous. Then listen and check.

S = Sam, G = Gillian
S: Hello?
G: Hi Sam. I ¹_____ (call) from Tokyo.
S: Excuse me, but who ²_____ (call)?
G: Sam. It's me. Gillian.
S: Oh sorry, Gillian. It's a really bad line. Give me the number of your hotel and I can call you back.
G: No, I ³_____ (not stay) in Tokyo. I ⁴_____ (wait) for my flight at the airport.
S: Where ⁵_____ (you / go) now?
G: To Vietnam. Ho Chi Minh City.
S: Oh, I see. ⁶_____ (you / travel) by yourself?
G: No, Jess is with me. We ⁷_____ (work) on a project together. It's about fashion in Asia.
S: Great! Can you email me some of your photographs?
G: Sure, but my email ⁸_____ (not / work) at the moment.
S: OK, send them tomorrow … Bye.

9 Choose the correct form to complete these sentences about Gillian.

1 At the moment, she *travels / is traveling* in Asia.
2 Now *she visits / she's visiting* different parts of the world.
3 She *likes / is liking* clothes and fashions.
4 Currently she *takes / is taking* photos for a project.
5 She *doesn't go / isn't going* on vacation very often.
6 *Does she have / Is she having* a house in New York?

Vocabulary clothes

10 Match these words with the clothes (1–10).

belt   dress   skirt   hat   sweater   shirt   shoes   socks   tie   pants

Speaking

11 Work in pairs. Take turns describing what you, your partner, and your instructor are wearing today.

I'm wearing a red T-shirt.

8c In fashion or for life?

Reading

1 Discuss as a class what is currently in fashion (popular at the moment) and what is now out of fashion (not popular anymore). Talk about clothes, music, technology, and what's on TV or the Internet.

2 Look at the photos of the two men on this page and the next. Which tattoos are fashion and which are tradition?

3 Read the article. Which paragraph (1–4) talks about:

a tattoos in Polynesian culture?
b why modern societies have tattoos?
c tattoos in ancient cultures?
d tattoos in the US?

Critical thinking close reading

4 Read the article again and mark the sentences true (T), false (F), or don't know (DK).

1 Some famous people have tattoos.
2 In the US, more women go to tattoo parlors than men.
3 Before 5,000 years ago, nobody had a tattoo.
4 Different ancient cultures had tattoos.
5 There weren't tattoos in ancient China.
6 In Polynesia, people don't have tattoos anymore.
7 Chris Rainier says tattoos are a type of fashion.
8 The writer doesn't like tattoos.

> ▶ **WORDBUILDING** phrasal verbs
>
> A phrasal verb is a verb with a particle. English has many phrasal verbs. For example: *Every morning I **put on** my coat and go to work.*

Vocabulary parts of the body

5 Underline parts of the body in the article. Then label these pictures. Two body parts are not in the article. Do you know what they are called?

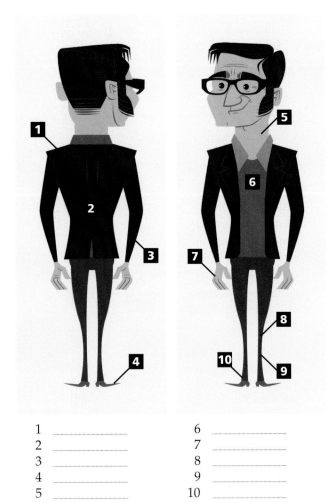

1	6 ....
2	7 ....
3	8 ....
4	9 ....
5	10 ....

Speaking

6 Discuss the questions in pairs.

1 In your country, are tattoos in fashion? Out of fashion? Traditional? Not part of the culture?
2 Do you like tattoos on other people? Why? / Why not?

In many countries, tattoos are in fashion. On TV you can often see a famous actor or musician with a tattoo on her arm or foot. Many athletes have them, too. In the U.S., tattoos are very popular. Forty percent of Americans aged between 26 and 40 have a tattoo, and 60 percent of customers in U.S. tattoo parlors are women. These people are often professional people like doctors, teachers, and lawyers.

However, tattoos are not modern. In fact, they are very old in human history. For example, archaeologists found a human in ice from 5,000 years ago. He had 57 tattoos on his back, ankles, legs, knees, and feet. Tattoos were used for many different reasons. In ancient Egypt, people got tattoos because they were "beautiful." But in ancient Rome, tattoos were negative and put on criminals and prisoners. In India, tattoos were religious.

In the 16th and 17th century, European sailors arrived on the islands of Polynesia. They saw tattoos for the first time. The people on the islands had tattoos on their shoulders, chest, backs, and legs. Often the tattoos were of animals or natural features like a river or a mountain. The European sailors liked them and made their own tattoos, so the idea traveled to Europe. Tattoos in Polynesia are still important today. They show information about a person's history, their island, or their job.

So is there a connection between traditional tattoos and fashionable tattoos? And can you call tattoos a fashion? Chris Rainier of National Geographic is an expert in tattoos and his book *Ancient Marks* has photos of tattoos from all over the world. He thinks people in modern societies often have tattoos because they are a connection to the traditional world. But tattoos aren't a fashion like clothes or a haircut because you can't put them on and take them off again like a jacket or a hat. They are permanent and for life.

TATTOOS
in fashion
and for life

Polynesian man with tattoos

8d The photos of Reinier Gerritsen

Real life talking about pictures and photos

1 Do you like looking at paintings and photos? Who is your favorite artist or photographer?

2 Look at the photo by Reinier Gerritsen. How do those people feel? Is it an interesting photograph? Why or why not?

3 🔊 **43** Listen and answer the questions.

1 Why does the person like Gerritsen's photos?
2 Where are the people in this photo?
3 Name the people the speaker talks about first, second, third, fourth, and fifth.

4 🔊 **43** Listen again and match the sentence beginnings (1–8) with the endings.

1 They often show	a	people in their everyday life.
2 On the right	b	the man and woman are talking.
3 The woman in the middle	c	is watching her.
4 In front of her, the woman with blonde	d	a little sad.
5 Then the other blonde woman on the left	e	is reading her book.
	f	I don't normally look at people very closely.
6 She looks	g	hair is listening to music.
7 Look at the other woman	h	at the back.
8 I like it because		

> ▶ **TALKING ABOUT PICTURES AND PHOTOS**
>
> **Introduce the photo**
> This photo shows …, I can see …
>
> **Location**
> On the left/right, in the middle, at the front/back
>
> **The people (appearance and actions)**
> She looks sad. He is reading.
>
> **Your opinion**
> I think …, I like it because …

5 Pronunciation silent letters

🔊 **44** Listen to these words. Which letter is silent? Then listen again and repeat.

interesting	sometimes	everyday
listening	blonde	closely

6 Work in pairs. Discuss another photo by Reinier Gerritsen on page 156.

7 Choose a picture or photo you like. Show it to your partner and talk about it.

8e How R U? ☺ tks

Speaking and reading

1 Read the text and discuss the questions.

1 How are emoticons different in the Eastern and Western Hemispheres?
2 Do you use emoticons in your texts and online messages?
3 Which emoticons from the article do you use? Do you use others?

Writing texts and online messages

2 Read these messages between two people. How does each person feel in items 2–4?

1 How R U?

2 Gr8 :-) Shopping 4 clothes. u wan 2 come?

3 Sry. Got English exam. :(

4 :0 Didn't know it's 2day. Call me after?

5 Thx C U l8r

3 Writing skill textspeak

a The messages in Exercise 2 use "textspeak." Compare them to the full version in normal English below.

A: How are you?
B: I'm great. I'm shopping for clothes. Do you want to come?
A: Sorry, but I've got an English exam today.
B: I didn't know it's today. Can you call me afterwards?
A: Thanks. See you later.

CULTURE

EASTERN HEMISPHERE		WESTERN HEMISPHERE
(^_^)	happy	:-)
(;_;)	sad	:-(
(*o*)	surprised	:O
(^_~)	winking	;-)
(^o^)	laughing	:D

The whole world uses emoticons in their texts and online messages. But emoticons around the world are not the same. In Eastern Hemisphere countries, the eyes are very important in emoticons. But with Western emoticons, the mouth is more important, and you turn your head to the left to read them.

b Textspeak makes English shorter. Find examples in Exercise 2 of the following:

1 The writer uses numbers with the same sound as a word.
2 The writer uses a letter with the same sound as a word.
3 The writer leaves out words: pronouns, auxiliary verbs, etc.
4 The writer leaves out letters when the word is obvious.
5 The writer use imperatives, not polite forms.

c Write this textspeak conversation using full sentences.

A: R U in town? _____
B: Am l8ter 2day. _____
A: Wan2 meet? _____
B: OK. @ 3? _____

d Write these full sentences using textspeak.

1 Thanks for the message.
2 Please meet me at the station.
3 Sorry I'm late.
4 See you on Monday at six.

4 Work in pairs. Arrange to meet this week. Write a text message to your partner. Swap your messages and write a reply. Continue until you agree on the day, the time, and the place.

An elephant at a festival in Jaipur, India

Before you watch

1 Work in pairs. Look at the photo and read the caption. Discuss the questions.

1 Where do you think the elephant in the photo is? Why are there colors on its face? Discuss with a partner.
2 Do you have animals at festivals in your country? Tell the class.

2 Match these words to the pictures (1–7).

> mask costume jewelry trumpet
> fireworks clown gloves

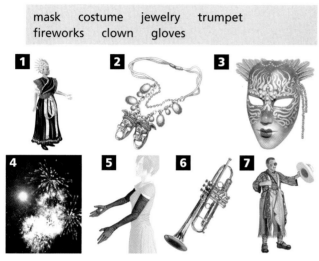

3 Answer these questions about the objects in Exercise 2.

1 Which can you see in your country?
2 When do you see them (e.g., at festivals, at special events)?

While you watch

4 Watch the video. There are five photos in the video and each one shows a festival or a special event. Mark the words you can see in each photo.

1 Fire Festival: makeup ☐ costume ☐ fireworks ☐
2 Rodeo: makeup ☐ jewelry ☐ clown ☐
3 Wedding: mask ☐ trumpet ☐ fireworks ☐
4 Elephant festival: makeup ☐ gloves ☐ mask ☐
5 Carnival: mask ☐ gloves ☐ jewelry ☐

5 Watch the video again. Answer these questions.

Photo 1
1 Where does the Beltane Fire Festival take place?
2 Does the narrator like the woman's costume?

Photo 2
3 Where is the clown from?
4 Is he making the audience laugh?

Photo 3
5 Where is the wedding?
6 What kind of music are the musicians playing?

Photo 4
7 Where is this photo?
8 What colors can you see on the elephant?

Photo 5
9 Where is the woman?
10 How often is the carnival?

6 Look at these sentences from the video. Are the underlined words very positive or very negative? Practice reading the sentences. Stress the underlined words.

She's wearing an <u>amazing</u> costume!
You can see some <u>fantastic</u> fireworks.
Those gloves are <u>wonderful</u>!
The colors are <u>incredible</u>.

7 **Fluency practice** **describing the photos**

Work in pairs. Play the video again with NO SOUND. Take turns being the narrator. Describe each photo when it is on the screen:

• where it is
• what you see
• what you like about it

After you watch

8 Read this email. Which event in the video is this person writing about?

> Hi!
> We're having a great time in Scotland! Last night, we went to a festival. There were lots of people and they were wearing interesting costumes and white makeup. One woman had a white dress and an amazing tall hat. Everyone carried fire! I've attached a photograph for you to look at.
> Bye for now!

9 Choose another festival or event in the video. Imagine you went to it. Write an email to a friend describing it. Then swap your email with a partner. Can you guess which festival or event they described?

UNIT 8 REVIEW

Grammar

1 Complete the sentences with the correct verb.

1 Penelope _____ blue eyes. (+)
2 I _____ a moustache. (not)
3 The two sisters _____ very smart. (+)
4 He _____ a black hat. (not)
5 Maciej and Ania _____ long hair. (not)
6 The dancer _____ very talented. (+)

2 Complete the sentences with the simple present or present continuous form of the verbs.

1 At the moment, they _____ (work) in Japan.
2 He _____ (always / start) work at nine.
3 What _____ (you / do) now?
4 Currently, she _____ (write) a book about fashion.
5 We _____ (live) in Los Angeles.
6 _____ (you / like) this dress?
7 Why _____ (you / wear) those shoes this evening? They're ugly!
8 A: Where are Pedro and David? They're late.
   B: They _____ (drive) here now.

I CAN	
use *be* and *have* to talk about appearance	
talk about actions now or at the time of speaking	

Vocabulary

3 Delete the incorrect word in each group.

1 APPEARANCE
  beautiful ~~forehead~~ ugly handsome
2 HEIGHT
  short tall ugly average
3 HAIR
  straight tall blond long
4 CLOTHES
  pants hat T-shirt lips
5 FACE
  neck eyebrows nose chin
6 ON YOUR BODY
  tattoo makeup dark clothes

4 Match the clothes with the parts of the body.

1 hands   a hat
2 feet   b socks
3 legs   c tie
4 head   d pants
5 neck   e gloves

5 Write some sentences about the people in this photo. Use words from Exercise 3.

New York City

They're …   They're wearing …
They have …

I CAN	
talk about clothes and appearance	
talk about the face and parts of the body	

Real life

6 Choose the correct option to complete these sentences about the photo in Exercise 5.

1 This photograph *shows / takes* a group of women in New York City.
2 The woman *on the right / in the middle* is looking at the photographer.
3 She *looks / has* happy.
4 Everyone is wearing a black and white *sweater / T-shirt*.
5 The women have got colorful *hair / makeup*.
6 Some women are wearing black *hats / belts*.
7 I *like / am liking* the photo.
8 The photo is *interesting / interested*.

I CAN	
describe a picture or photo	

7 Work in pairs. Look at photos of people in a magazine or on the Internet. Describe the photos.

Speaking

8 Work in pairs. Describe a member of your family. Talk about his/her appearance. Are you like him or her? Why? / Why not?

Unit 9 Film and the arts

Sydney Harbor, Australia
Photo by Annie Griffiths

FEATURES

1 Read about the photo and choose the correct ending (a or b) to complete the sentences. In one sentence, both endings are possible.

For visitors to Sydney, it's a strange sight: the huge face of a sleeping woman over the harbor next to the famous opera house. But for the locals, this outdoor movie theater is popular on warm summer evenings. The screen is the size of a large building and sits over the water. Moviegoers can watch their favorite stars from the beach or their cars.

1   The woman is ....
    a   on an ad   b   in a movie
2   The outdoor movie screen is ....
    a   on a building
    b   above the water
3   The audience watch their favorite actors ....
    a   on the beach   b   in their cars

2 Complete these sentences about yourself. Then tell your partner.

*   I go to the movies… (once a week? once a month?)
*   I usually watch movies on… (TV? DVD? the Internet?)
*   I like watching movies… (with friends? on my own?)
*   The last movie I saw in a theater was… (title?)

▶ **SEE OR *WATCH*?**

You **see** movies (at a theater).
You **watch** movies (on TV, on DVD, etc.).

9a Lights, Camera, Action! Film Festival

Vocabulary types of movies

1 Match these kinds of movies with the pictures (a–g).

> action movie   animation   comedy
> documentary   horror movie
> romantic comedy   science-fiction movie

2 Discuss these questions as a class.

1 Can you think of one movie for each type in Exercise 1?
2 What kinds of movies do you like? Which do you never watch?

Reading

3 Read the first paragraph of the article. What kinds of movies can you watch at this film festival?

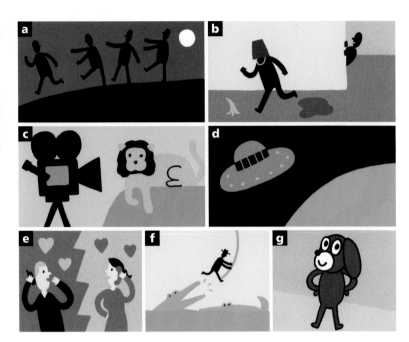

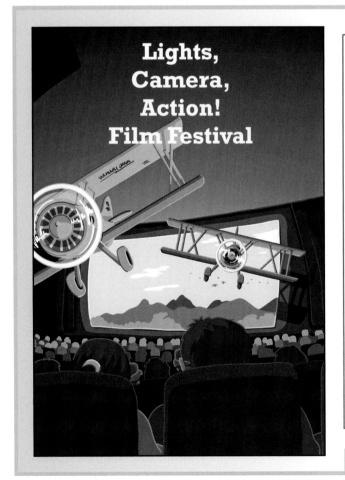

Come to the Lights, Camera, Action! Film Festival. Our festival isn't like the Oscars and Bollywood because you don't see lots of famous movie stars. We feature films by directors and actors from many different countries and cultures. You can see many kinds of movies including comedies, documentaries, and animation. Here are some of the films we are featuring this year.

My Wedding… and My Family
In this romantic comedy about an Indian family in Toronto, a daughter falls in love with a local man… and then the problems begin.

The Winning Number
This short film by director Rene Roy is about a young woman with a hard life… until everything changes forever.

A Desert Journey
This documentary by the director Mohammed Robertson is about the life of the nomadic people of Morocco.

For a complete schedule of events, visit **lcafilmfestival.org**.

4 Read the article and mark the statements true (T) or false (F).

1 The film festival is every year.
2 Lots of famous people come.
3 It shows one kind of movie.
4 This year you can see a movie about Russia.
5 *My Wedding… and My Family* is a comedy in China.
6 *The Winning Number* is a story about an old woman.

Listening

5 🔊 **45** Listen and write the missing verbs.

C = Carlos, B = Beata

C: Hey, Beata! Stop!
B: Oh, hi Carlos! Sorry, but I'm going to ¹ _____ a ticket for the next movie. It starts in five minutes. Are you going to ² _____ a movie too?
C: No, I'm not, but what are you ³ _____ afterwards? José, Monica, and I are going to ⁴ _____ dinner at a Japanese restaurant. Do you want to come?
B: No, thanks. I'm not going to ⁵ _____ out late tonight. I'm tired.
C: That's OK.
B: Got to go. Bye.
C: Bye. See you later.

Grammar *going to* (for plans)

6 Look at the conversation in Exercise 5. Underline four examples of *going to* and one example of the present continuous. Then answer the questions.

1 Do the underlined verbs talk about the present or the future?
2 How do you form the negative and question forms of *going to*?

▶ **GOING TO (FOR PLANS)**

I'm he's/she's/it's you're/we're/they're	going to + verb

I'm not/She isn't/They aren't going to have dinner.
What are you going to see?
Are you going to see a movie? Yes, I am. / No, I'm not.

going to go = going to (present continuous)
When we say *going to go* we usually use the present continuous form of *go*: *I'm going to go home. = I'm going home.*

For more information and practice, see page 166.

---

7 Make sentences with *going to* or the present continuous form.

1 we / see a movie at the new theater
2 I / not watch / this DVD
3 you / buy the tickets online or at the movie theater?
4 what time / they / go / the movie theater?
5 I / not sit / at the front of the movie theater
6 where / you / sit?
7 they / meet us after the movie?
8 I / never / watch a movie by that director again!

8 Pronunciation /tə/

🔊 **46** Listen to the sentences in Exercise 7. Notice the weak vowel sound in *to* is /tə/. Listen again and repeat.

Speaking

9 Imagine you are going to a film festival. Choose three movies you want to watch and plan your day.

In cinema 1	In cinema 2	In cinema 3
2–3:30 *Flight* – a wildlife documentary	2–3:40 *Big Love* – a romantic comedy	2–4 *The Road* – an action movie with fast cars
3:55–5:25 *Life on Mars* – a Hollywood science-fiction movie	4:10–5:30 *Animation festival* – short animation films by young filmmakers	4:15–5:35 *Historical Horror* – a documentary about the history of horror movies
5:40–7:15 *The Boy from Mumbai* – music, dance, and color from Bollywood	5:45–6:45 *Everest* – a powerful documentary about the mountain and its climbers	5:45–8:15 *Macbeth* – a new movie version of Shakespeare's famous play

10 Work in groups. You are going to the festival with the people in your group. Discuss and plan the movies you are going to see.

What are you going to see at two o'clock?

The Road because I love action movies.

9b People in film and the arts

Vocabulary art and entertainment

1 Work in pairs. Number these activities (1–6) in your order of preference (1 = first choice).

.... watch a movie on TV at home
.... see a movie in a theater
.... go to the theater to see a play
.... go to an art gallery
.... listen to live music at a concert hall
.... read a book at home

2 Complete the table with these words.

> art and paintings
> artist or painter   in a book
> in a movie theater
> in a concert hall
> director, actors, actresses (x2)
> music   a play or a musical

What?	Where?	Who?
movie		
	at the theater	
	in an art gallery	
novel		writer
		musicians

3 Talk about some of your favorite directors, actors, artists, writers, and musicians. Why do you like them?

> ▶ **WORDBUILDING suffixes (2)**
>
> We make nouns from verbs + suffix to describe people's jobs and occupations:
> *act – actor, direct – director,*
> *paint – painter, write – writer.*

Reading

4 Choose the correct words (a, b, or c) to complete the gaps (1–8) in the article.

	a	b	c
1	actor	director	artist
2	actors	directors	writers
3	does	has	makes
4	watching	seeing	going to
5	directors	explorers	painters
6	started	made	became
7	video	camera	theater
8	action films	comedies	documentaries

Making movies in the wild

Jack Gazzolo is a movie ¹ .... But in his movies, the animals are the ² .... and the scenery is some of the most beautiful and remote parts of the world. Jack ³ .... wildlife documentaries about his expeditions and posts them online.

As a child, he wanted to live in the jungle and he kept lots of plants in his bedroom. He loved ⁴ .... TV shows about the natural world with famous ⁵ ....

Before he ⁶ .... a filmmaker, he studied film and lighting and worked on movie sets. He made his first film in 2006 and bought his first movie ⁷ ....

Today, he films ⁸ .... in jungles, mountains, and rainforests all over the world.

Listening

5 🔊 **47** Listen to an interview with Jack. Number the topics (a–c) in the order he talks about them.

a   planning a movie
b   the subject of his next movie
c   the number of people in the movie crew

6 🔊 **47** Listen again. Answer the questions with *Yes, No,* or *Doesn't say.*

1   Does Jack plan his trips?
2   Does he use more than one camera?
3   Does a movie always have a director and camera person?
4   Is Jack going to film in the winter?
5   Is he going to take a year to make the movie?
6   Is his next movie for movie theaters?
7   Is the movie about an explorer?
8   Is it going to be a long movie?
9   Does he plan to take a vacation?

7 Discuss these questions as a class.

1   Would you like a job like Jack's?
2   Do you ever make movies or videos?

The Amazon River in Brazil

Grammar infinitive of purpose

8 Look at the two parts of the sentence from the interview with Jack.

$$\overset{1}{\underbrace{\text{I'm going to Brazil}}}\overset{2}{\underbrace{\text{to make a movie.}}}$$

Which part of the sentence describes the speaker's plan and which part describes why the speaker does something?

> ▶ **INFINITIVE OF PURPOSE**
>
> You use the infinitive of purpose to say why you are going to do something:
> *I'm going to a café* **to meet some friends.**
> *I'm going to London* **to see a musical.**
>
> For more information and practice, see page 166.

9 Work in pairs. Match 1–3 with a–c and make sentences starting with *I'm going to …*

1   buy this book about Martin Scorsese
2   art school
3   the theater

a   to read about his life
b   to see a play by Shakespeare
c   to study painting

10 Think about your plans. Tell your partner where, when, and why you are going. Use the time expressions and some of the places.

the movie theater	tomorrow
the theater	on Friday
a concert	on the weekend
an art gallery	next week
a museum	next month
another place?	

I'm going to the movies this weekend to see Johnny Depp's new movie.

Speaking

11 Work in pairs. Write down three of your future plans. Take turns to tell each other your plans. Ask your partner for the reason or more details.

I'm going downtown tomorrow.

Why are you going?

To meet some friends.

9c Nature in art

1

Vocabulary nature

1 Look at the five pieces of art about nature (1–5). Answer the questions.

1 Are they modern or traditional?
2 Do you know which country or period in history they are from?
3 What can you see in each piece of art? Use these words.

birds	butterflies	flowers	fruit
grass	trees	kangaroos	leaves
mountains	rocks	sea	sky

2 Do you have paintings or photos in your home? What kinds of pictures are they? What do they show (e.g. people, animals, places)?

Reading

3 Read about the five artists on page 111. Match them with their works (1–5).

4 Mark what is true for each artist, according to the article.

		Stanislaw Witkiewicz	Ginger Riley Munduwalawala	Andō Hiroshige	Damien Hirst	Vincent Van Gogh
1	paints and uses nature in art	✓	✓	✓	✓	✓
2	living now					
3	one painting costs millions					
4	people disagree about this artist					
5	died poor					
6	art is similar to ancient paintings					

Critical thinking the writer's preferences

5 Compare the verbs *like* and *prefer* in this sentence about the first artist. Does *prefer* mean like or like one thing more than another?

Many people like Stanislaw Witkiewicz's paintings of people's faces, but I prefer his paintings of landscapes.

6 According to the article, which of the five artists does the writer like? Which of their paintings does she prefer?

Speaking

7 Work in pairs. Compare two of the paintings on these pages and say which you prefer, and why. Which one do you like the most? Why?

> *Which do you prefer?*

> *I prefer this one because …*

> *This is my favorite painting because …*

Nature in art

Many artists paint and use nature in their work, but the results are very different. Art critic Liz Searle-Barnes looks at five of them.

Stanislaw Witkiewicz Stanislaw Witkiewicz was born in 1885 in Zakopane, Poland. He died in 1939, but you can see his paintings in art galleries all over Poland. Many people like Witkiewicz's paintings of people's faces, but I prefer his paintings of nature and landscapes. He painted this one in 1907. It shows the Hinczow Lakes in southern Poland. There are the green fields and the white rocks and I like this painting because the water in the lakes is so blue.

Ginger Riley Munduwalawala In the past, Aboriginal people painted pictures of nature on rocks. In parts of Australia, their rock art is 30,000 years old. Modern aboriginal artists also paint nature. This colorful painting by Ginger Riley Munduwalawala (1937–2002) shows hills, rivers, birds, and kangaroos.

Andō Hiroshige Japanese art is famous for landscape paintings. You can often see the sea and sky, the mountains, and trees. Andō Hiroshige, one of Japan's most famous artists, worked in the 19th century and he's one of Japan's most famous artists. He made and sold thousands of beautiful prints in his lifetime, but he died poor.

Damien Hirst Damien Hirst is the richest artist in England. He is a painter, but he is more famous for art with animals (living and dead), including a cow, a sheep, and a shark. In one room of a gallery, he put lots of fruit and real butterflies. They flew around the visitors. Some people say he's a genius, others disagree. Personally, I like his work, but I prefer his early paintings.

Vincent Van Gogh Van Gogh made eleven paintings of sunflowers. They were his favorites because he loved the color yellow. I prefer his other paintings, but many people love his sunflower paintings. They are everywhere: on cards, postcards, and T-shirts. Van Gogh died with no money, but in 1987 someone bought the last sunflower painting for $49 million.

art critic (n) /ˈɑrt ˌkrɪtɪk/ a person who studies and writes about art
landscape (n) /ˈlændˌskeɪp/ a painting of an area outside (with trees, rivers, mountains, etc.)

9d Making arrangements

Listening

1 Look at the photo of some theaters on Broadway in New York. Is there a theater district in your town or city? What was the last show you saw? What was it about?

2 🎧 **48** Listen to two phone conversations and answer the questions.

Conversation 1
1 Which show in the photo are they talking about?
2 When is the show?
3 Why isn't Adriana free?

Conversation 2
4 Can Adriana leave work early?
5 What time does the show start?
6 What time are they going to meet?

Real life inviting and making arrangements

3 🎧 **48** Complete the expressions for inviting and making arrangements with these words. Then listen again and check.

free	great	like	'd love	meet
see	'm sorry	time	want	

> ▶ **INVITING AND MAKING ARRANGEMENTS**
>
> **Inviting**
> Would you ¹ _____ to come?
> Are you ² _____ ?
> Do you ³ _____ to go?
> **Respond to the invitation**
> Thanks. I ⁴ _____ to.
> I ⁵ _____ , but I'm working late tonight.
> That's ⁶ _____ .
> **Making arrangements**
> What ⁷ _____ does it start?
> Let's ⁸ _____ at seven.
> ⁹ _____ you at seven.

4 Pronunciation showing enthusiasm

🎧 **49** Listen to these phrases for responding to invitations. Underline the word with the most stress. Then listen again and repeat.

1 I'd love to!
2 I'd really like to!
3 That's great!
4 That sounds fantastic!

5 Grammar present continuous for future reference

Look at the sentences in the grammar box. Do they refer to the present or the future?

> ▶ **PRESENT CONTINUOUS FOR FUTURE REFERENCE**
>
> I'm going to the theater tonight.
> I'm sorry, but I'm working late tonight.
>
> For more information, see page 166.

6 Work in pairs. Practice these telephone conversations.

Student A: You've got tickets for the musical *Jersey Boys* tomorrow night. It starts at 8 p.m. Call Student B and invite him/her.

Student B: Answer the phone. You are at work. Listen to Student A's invitation and say yes. Arrange to meet.

Then change roles and practice the same conversation for the musical *Wicked*. It starts at 8:30 p.m.

9e It looks amazing!

Writing reviews and comments

1 People often write reviews and comments on websites. Do you ever read them? Which ones?

2 Match these extracts from reviews and comments (1–5) with these categories.

> an art exhibition   a movie   music   perfume
> a restaurant

1 I loved their first album so I was excited about their second. Some of the songs are good, but it sounds very slow. Overall, it's a little disappointing.

2 We had dinner at this new place downtown. I had the tomato soup and it tasted great. Dessert was only OK, but in general I liked it.

3 One room in the gallery has paintings by Picasso when he was very young. They look amazing!

4 I felt scared at the beginning because it starts in the middle of the night with two people going to a house where a strange man opens the door. But after that it's very funny. I laughed for two hours.

5 I bought this because it has the name of my favorite actress on it, but it smells awful!

3 Which reviews in Exercise 2 are positive? Which are negative?

4 Writing skills giving your opinion with sense verbs

a Sense verbs are *look, feel, sound, taste, smell*. We often use sense verbs + adjectives in reviews. Underline five sense verbs + adjectives in Exercise 1.

b Work in pairs. Which sense verbs could you use to write about these items? You can choose more than one for each item.

> a musical at the theater   a very long book
> a gym   a new type of chocolate
> a new type of sports car   a computer game

c Which of these adjectives can you use with the verbs *look, feel, sound, taste, smell*? You can use the adjectives more than once.

> angry   beautiful   bored   delicious   loud
> interesting   nice   soft   terrible   tired

5 Choose two of the topics in Exercise 4b. Write a short review or comment for a website about them. Use sense verbs and adjectives.

6 Work in pairs. Exchange reviews and answer these questions:

- Is the review positive or negative?
- Did he/she use sense verbs and adjectives?
- Are you interested in the item reviewed?

A "camera trap" took this photograph of an ocelot.

Before you watch

1 Look at the photo. Why do you think this animal is difficult to photograph?

2 Read the text about a camera trap. It took the photo of the ocelot. Answer the questions.

1 How does it take a photo?
2 Why do wildlife conservationists use camera traps?
3 Why do camera traps take photos with no animals?
4 Where do you need to put the camera?

A camera trap is a special kind of camera. When something moves in front of it, it takes a photo. Wildlife conservationists use this technology because they can get a lot of information about animals during the day and also at night. Sometimes, camera traps take photos of animals you rarely see.
There are also disadvantages to camera traps. They sometimes take photos when a plant moves in the wind but no animal is present. It's also difficult to put them in the right place, where animals spend time. Usually this isn't easy.

wildlife conservationist (n) /'waɪld‚laɪf ‚kɑnsər'veɪʃənɪst/ person who protects animals in natural areas
wild (animals) (adj) /waɪld/ animals in natural areas

3 You are going to watch a video about the filmmaker Adrian Seymour. Answer the questions.

1 What can you guess about him?
2 Why do you think he uses camera traps?

While you watch

4 Watch the video with NO SOUND. Number Adrian's actions in the order he does them (1–9).

a He's getting up.
b He's going to bed.
c He's walking through the rainforest.
d He's putting a camera trap in a tree.
e He's taking a camera trap off a tree.
f He's looking for animals in the photos.
g He's taking a bath.
h He's watching an animal on his computer.
i He's climbing up a tree.

5 Watch the video again WITH SOUND. Choose the correct answer to the questions.

1 Where is the rainforest?
  a in Guatemala
  b in Costa Rica
  c in Honduras
2 Where do a lot of the animals live?
  a in rivers
  b in trees
  c under the ground
3 How many camera traps does he put in the trees?
  a six
  b sixteen
  c sixty
4 How long does Adrian wait before he looks at his camera traps?
  a four hours
  b four days
  c four weeks
5 When Adrian looks at the first photos, what does he think?
  a He is glad to see an ocelot.
  b He doesn't think there are any animals.
  c He thinks the camera is broken.
6 He sees a kinkajou in the pictures. Which three facts are true about kinkajous?
  a They come out at night.
  b They live in rainforests.
  c They also live in the desert.
  d They eat meat and fruit.

After you watch

6 Role play an interview with Adrian Seymour

Work in pairs.

Student A: You are Adrian Seymour. A reporter is going to interview you about your filmmaking in Honduras. Think about what you are going to say.

Student B: You are a reporter. You are writing an article about Adrian Seymour. Prepare some questions about Adrian's filmmaking and his work with camera traps in Honduras.

When you finish, change roles and repeat the interview.

UNIT 9 REVIEW

Grammar

1 Complete the sentences with the *going to* form of these verbs.

buy	not drive	take	meet	play	watch

1 We _____ a movie on TV tonight.
2 Matt and Raul _____ tennis.
3 I _____ friends for dinner.
4 They _____ here because there's a problem with their car.
5 _____ you _____ a vacation this year?
6 Rachel _____ the tickets online.

2 Make five sentences with *going to* and an infinitive of purpose.

I'm going to	the theater a concert hall an art gallery a café the mall	to have to see to listen to to look at to buy	coffee. a musical. music. clothes. paintings.

3 Read these present continuous sentences. Do they talk about the present (P) or the future (F)?

1 I'm making a documentary about butterflies at the moment.
2 I'm sorry, but I'm working late tonight.
3 Why are they waiting outside the movie theater?
4 Where are you going after work?
5 They aren't leaving tomorrow.
6 Chen and Li aren't coming, so let's start.

I CAN	
talk about future plans with *be going to*	
talk about the purpose and reason for a plan or action	
use the present continuous for future arrangements	

Vocabulary

4 Match these kinds of movies with the comments (1–6).

action	animation	comedy	documentary
horror	science fiction		

1 It's a story about space aliens.
2 It was very funny and I laughed a lot.
3 It's all about polar bears and how they live.
4 I couldn't watch the movie. It was too scary!
5 There are fast cars and the hero always wins.
6 The "actors" are all drawn by computers.

5 Complete the missing words in these sentences.

1 Actors work in TV, movies, and in the t_____ .
2 You look at paintings in an a_____ g_____ .
3 I play the guitar with a group of m_____ .
4 Steven Spielberg is a famous movie d_____ .
5 We listened to the music in a c_____ h_____ .

6 Complete the table with these words.

birds	butterflies	flowers	grass	kangaroos
mountains	sea	sky	trees	

landscape	plants	animals

I CAN	
talk about kinds of movies	
talk about art and entertainment	
talk about nature	

Real life

7 Put the conversation in order (1–8).

1 Would you like to go to the movies?
Sorry, but I'm working late.
When are you going?
OK. I'd love to come at nine.
The movie is also playing at nine.
Great. Let's meet outside the movie theater at quarter to nine.
At six.
8 Good. See you there. Bye.

I CAN	
invite someone	
make an arrangement	

8 Work in pairs. Role play a phone call. Arrange to meet next week. Then change partners and make another arrangement for a different day next week.

Speaking

9 Work in groups. Tell the others about your favorite musician, writer, actor, and artist. Say why you like them.

Unit 10 Science

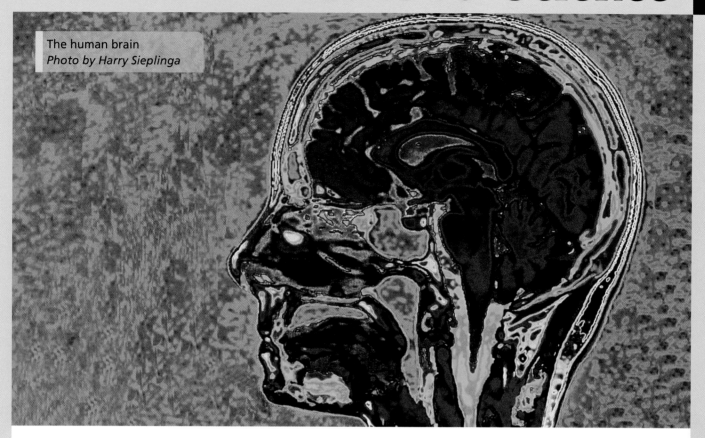

The human brain
Photo by Harry Sieplinga

1 Look at the photo of a human brain. Which is more intelligent: a human brain or a computer? Give reasons for your answer.

2 Look at the list. Which is true for a human brain (B)? Which is true for a computer (C)? Some sentences are true for both.

1 It needs energy. *B, C*
2 It uses chemicals.
3 It stores information.
4 It's usually easy to fix.
5 We don't know everything about it.
6 You can turn it off.

3 Neuroscience is the science of the brain. Match these other sciences (1–6) with their subjects (a–f).

1	astronomy	a	heat, light, energy
2	zoology	b	new machines
3	physics	c	planets and outer space
4	chemistry	d	living things
5	biology	e	chemicals
6	technology	f	animals

4 Which sciences did you study at school? Which do you like reading about in magazines or watching on TV? Why?

10a Technology has changed our lives

Vocabulary everyday technology

1 Look at the photo in the article. What is the boy doing? Do you ever use one of these? Why? / Why not?

2 Look at these pairs of words. Which do you use most? Which do you never use?

email / letter   music download / CD
search engine / library   book / ebook
map / GPS   online video / DVD
podcast / radio   text message / postcard

3 Think about people in these age groups: *teenagers, young adults, middle-aged people, sixties,* and *over sixties.* Discuss these questions.

1 Which do they use the most in Exercise 2?
2 How important is technology to each group?

Reading and listening

4 Read the article. Are these sentences true (T) or false (F) according to the article?

1 On average, there are four computers in many houses.
2 Over half the population think their life is better with technology.
3 Lots of people use pay phones.
4 Young people still write letters by hand.

5 As a class, discuss how many computers you have at home, and whether technology makes life better. Why or why not?

6 💿 **50** Listen to part of the survey from Exercise 4. The researcher interviews someone under the age of thirty. Mark the six activities in the article that she asks about.

Technology HAS changed our lives

a pay phone

People love technology. In a recent survey, researchers found:

- there are four computers in the average household.
- six out of ten people say their life is better with technology.

The researchers also say that new technology, particularly in communications, has changed our world forever. For example, have you ever used a pay phone or written a letter by hand? Many people haven't done these things or they don't do them anymore. In particular, the survey found that young people have never done the following activities because of modern technology:

- Called a movie theater for the movie times.
- Booked a vacation with a travel agent.
- Used a pay phone.
- Bought tickets for a concert over the phone.
- Had film developed into photos.
- Bought a CD.
- Written a letter by hand.
- Used an address or phone book.
- Used a paper map for a car trip.
- Paid by check.
- Watched programs at the time they are on TV.
- Sent a letter in an envelope.

7 🔘 **50** Listen again. Choose the correct ending (a, b, or c) for the sentences. Sometimes two endings are correct.

1 He always books vacations _____ .
   a with a travel agent   b online
   c by phone
2 He bought his father a CD because he
   _____ .
   a is poor   b had a birthday
   c can't download music
3 A GPS is _____ .
   a good for his job   b fast
   c not expensive
4 He pays with _____ .
   a credit card   b cash
   c online banking
5 He watches programs on _____ .
   a TV   b DVD
   c YouTube
6 He sends _____ .
   a texts   b postcards
   c emails

Grammar present perfect

8 Look at this question and answer from the interview, then answer the questions.

A: Have you ever booked a vacation with a travel agent?
B: Yes, I have, but it was a long time ago.

1 Are they talking about an experience in the past or present?
2 Do we know exactly when the action happened?

▶ **PRESENT PERFECT**

Use the present perfect to talk about an experience in the past. We don't say exactly when it happened.

	have	past participle
I/you/we/they	have (haven't)	booked a ticket. called the movie theater.
He/she/it	has (hasn't)	

Questions (with *ever*)

With the present perfect, we often use *ever* in questions and *never* in negative answers:
Have you ever downloaded music?
Yes, I have. / No, I haven't. I've never downloaded music.

For more information and practice, see page 167.

---

9 Complete the interview with the present perfect form of the verbs or *have/haven't*.

A: Have you ever bought a CD?
B: Actually, yes, I ¹_____ (buy) a CD.

A: And before a car trip, have you ever used a map?
B: Yes, I ²_____ .

A: Have you ever paid for something by check?
B: No, because I ³_____ (never / have) a checkbook.

A: So you never watch TV programs online?
B: Oh, I see what you mean. Well, I ⁴_____ (watch) videos on YouTube.

A: OK. And finally, ⁵_____ (you / ever / send) a letter in an envelope?
B: No, I ⁶_____ .

10 Pronunciation 've/'s

🔘 **51** Listen to eight sentences. Do you hear the full form or the contracted form?

1	have	've	5	have	've
2	has	's	6	has	's
3	have not	haven't	7	have not	haven't
4	has not	hasn't	8	has not	hasn't

Speaking

11 Work in pairs. Ask each other *Have you ever …?* questions about the fifteen activities in the article.

Have you ever developed film?

Yes, I have.

Have you ever used a phone book?

No, I haven't. I've never …

12 Think of other technology words. Ask your partner about other technology he/she has or hasn't used. Then work with another pair. Tell them what your partner has done or hasn't done.

He's read an ebook.

She's never downloaded a podcast.

10b How good is your memory?

This violinist reads the music and then she memorizes every note afterwards.

Speaking and reading

1 Do you have a good memory? Which of these are easy for you to remember? What do you do to remember them?

- names and faces
- addresses
- phone numbers
- dates and facts
- shopping lists
- English words

2 Work in groups of three. Read a short paragraph on the page marked in the chart, then memorize the important information and write notes in this table.

	Student A, p. 154	Student B, p. 155	Student C, p. 156
What was the topic of the article?			
What techniques did it describe?			

3 In your group, tell each other about the information in your article. When you listen to the other students, write notes in the table.

4 Afterwards, read the three articles again and compare your notes. Discuss these questions.

1 How much information did each of you remember?
2 Which of the memory techniques do you use?

Vocabulary memory and learning

5 Look at these groups of verbs. Two words have a similar meaning. Cross out the word with an opposite or different meaning.

1 study learn teach
2 know understand test
3 remember forget memorize
4 train relax practice

> ▶ **WORDBUILDING synonyms and antonyms**
>
> Synonyms are words with similar meanings: learn = study
> Antonyms are words with opposite meanings: remember ≠ forget

6 Work in pairs. Ask and answer these questions.

1 How often do you study English at home?
2 How many new words in English do you learn a week?
3 How do you memorize new words (in sentences, with pictures, writing them down)?
4 Do you ever test yourself? How?

Listening

7 Look at the photos and the headline. Answer the questions.

   1 Who is the man in the first photo?
   2 What has he won? Has he ever won it before?

NEWS

Nelson Dellis wins USA Memory Championship again!

Nelson Dellis and "memory athletes" at the USA Memory Championship

8 🔊 **52** Listen, then number the topics in the order you hear them.

   a the USA Memory Championships
   b what Nelson can remember
   c Nelson's memory techniques

9 🔊 **52** Listen again and answer the questions.

   1 How many new names and faces can Nelson memorize?
   2 How many numbers can he hear and repeat?
   3 What did he study in 2010?
   4 How much did he practice?
   5 Who does he teach his techniques to?

Grammar present perfect and simple past

10 Compare the verbs in these two sentences.

> Nelson **has won** the USA Memory Championship twice. He **won** the competition in 2011 and again in 2012.

   1 What are the two tenses?
   2 Which tense do we use when we know the exact time? And when we don't?

▶ **PRESENT PERFECT AND SIMPLE PAST**

We use the present perfect when we talk about something in the past, but we don't say (or know) exactly when it happened:
He's studied memory techniques.

We also use it to talk about something that started in the past and continues into the present.
He's taught his techniques to people.

We use the simple past when we talk about something in the past and we say exactly when it happened (with a time expression):
In 2010, he studied memory techniques.
We also use it for events that started and ended in the past.
*He won a memory competition **last year**.*

For more information and practice, see page 167.

---

11 Work in pairs. We often start a conversation with a question in the present perfect and then continue with simple past questions.

> *Have you ever studied in another country?*

> *Yes, I've studied in Mexico.*

> *When did you study there?*

> *I studied in Mexico in 1993.*

Write four similar conversations. Make questions with the words and write answers.

   1 Have / take / an English test?
     When / take it?
   2 Have / study / science? Where / study?
   3 Have / teach / a subject? What / teach?
   4 Have / learn / another language?
     What / learn?

Speaking

12 Ask your partner more questions about something he or she has learned.

> *Have you ever learned …?*

> *When / What / Where did you …?*

10c Why haven't scientists invented it?

Vocabulary science and invention

1 Look at these scientific inventions. Categorize them into groups a, b, or c and tell the class why.

  a   I need it every day.
  b   I sometimes need it.
  c   I never need it.

an iPod or MP3 player
a wheel   a vacuum cleaner
electricity   a knife   fire
scotch tape   the Internet

Reading

2 Look at the pictures (A–D) on page 123 and match them with the paragraphs.

3 Read the article about four types of scientific invention. Answer the questions.

  1   Which two haven't scientists invented?
  2   Which two have scientists invented, but we don't have them in our everyday life?

4 Match the words (1–5) with the definitions (a–e).

  1   invent
  2   discover
  3   test
  4   break down
  5   prototype

  a   the first of its kind
  b   make something that's never been made before
  c   find for the first time
  d   stop working
  e   find out if something works

5 Read the article again. Are the sentences true (T) or false (F)?

  1   The invisibility coat and the car used cameras.
  2   The car was 100% invisible.
  3   Flying cars are very popular.
  4   Teleporting doesn't use existing forms of transportation.
  5   Scientists can't move atoms across distances.
  6   Robots for the home cost a lot of money.

6 Discuss with a partner. Which invention from the article would you most like to have? Why?

Critical thinking the main argument and supporting information

7 In this article, the writer uses a main argument and supporting information. Look at these sentences:

Main argument: Many scientists have tried to invent invisible objects, but they haven't done it yet.

Supporting information: But as you can see in the photo, the wheels aren't invisible.

Now read these sentences from the article. Which are the main argument (M) and which are supporting information (S)?

  1   With all the cars on the road and the traffic problems, why don't we have flying cars?
  2   One reason is that cars are very heavy.
  3   Cities have roads for cars, but they don't have runways.
  4   A human being is made of trillions of atoms, so scientists don't know how to do it yet.
  5   Scientists have invented robots, so why don't we all have them?
  6   Probably because the technology is very expensive and the robots often break down.

Writing

8 Work in groups. Discuss one of these questions and write down two or three reasons. Then write a paragraph with the main argument (the question) and two or three supporting sentences.

  1   There are lots of people on Earth, so why haven't we built cities under the ocean?
  2   There are about 7,000 different languages on Earth, so why haven't we invented one language for everyone?
  3   We have elevators in tall buildings, so why haven't we invented an elevator into space?

WHY HAVEN'T SCIENTISTS
invented it yet?

Scientists have discovered and invented many things: computers, space travel, mobile communications. But there are a lot more things they haven't invented—or have, but we don't use them in our everyday life.

invisible (n) /ɪnˈvɪzəbəl/ you can't see an object
runway (n) /ˈrʌnˌweɪ/ road where an airplane takes off and lands (at an airport)
atom (n) /ˈætəm/ the smallest part of a chemical element
servant (n) /ˈsɜrvənt/ a person who works in another person's home

1 Invisible objects

Many scientists have tried to invent invisible objects, but they haven't done it yet. One scientist at Tokyo University put cameras on a coat. The cameras filmed objects behind the coat and showed them on the front. Unfortunately, the coat wasn't very comfortable! The car manufacturer Mercedes also tried this with a car. They put the camera on one side of the car and showed the image on the other side. But as you can see in the photo, the wheels aren't invisible.

2 Flying car

With all the cars on the road and the traffic problems, why don't we have flying cars? One reason is that cars are very heavy. Also, cities have roads for cars, but they don't have runways. And we have so many problems on our roads, do we really want them in the sky?

3 Teleporting

Teleporting is moving something from one place to another by reducing it to atoms and putting it back together again almost instantly. Teleporting is a very fast way to travel, but scientists haven't discovered how to do it. Solid objects are made of atoms, and with teleporting you have to move each atom one by one. A human being is made of trillions of atoms, so scientists don't know how to do it yet.

4 Robot servants

Scientists have already invented robots, so why don't we all have one? Probably because the technology is very expensive and the robots often break down. But many companies in Japan have made prototype robots for homes. They wash clothes, turn on the TV, turn off the lights, and change the music. Many scientists think we can all have a robot servant in our home in about ten years.

10d Problems with technology

Listening

1 Look at the photo and discuss the questions.

  1 How does the man feel? What do you think has happened?
  2 Has your cell phone or Internet connection ever stopped working? How did you feel?

2 ◆ **53** Listen and answer the questions.

  1 Where is Oscar?
  2 What time is it?
  3 What isn't working?
  4 What is the name of the hotel?
  5 What is the number?
  6 Where has Richard put the designs?

Real life checking and clarifying

3 ◆ **53** Look at these expressions for checking and clarifying. Then match the responses (a–f) with the expressions. Listen again and check.

▶ CHECKING AND CLARIFYING	
Is that three in the morning?	1 ____
Was that the Encasa Hotel?	2 ____
The number is 603 2169 2266.	3 ____
Is there anything else?	4 ____
Did you call our colleagues?	5 ____
Did you email me all the designs?	6 ____

  a So that's 603 2169 2266?
  b No, in the afternoon.
  c Yes, I did.
  d Yes, one thing.
  e No, the Ancasa Hotel. A for apple.
  f No, I didn't.

4 Pronunciation contrastive stress

  ◆ **54** Listen and underline the stressed word in the responses. Then listen again and repeat the response.

  1 A: Is that three in the morning?
     B: No, in the afternoon.
  2 A: Was that the Encasa Hotel?
     B: No, the Ancasa Hotel.
  3 A: Is that E for England?
     B: No, it's A for apple.

5a Work in pairs. Practice similar telephone conversations.

Student A
- You are working abroad, but your cell phone isn't working.
- Call Student B from the Hotel Innsbruck. Your number is 790 856 7211.
- Check that Student B emailed your presentation for tomorrow's meeting.

Student B
- Student A is abroad. Answer his / her call.
- Write down the hotel's name and number.
- You haven't emailed the presentation because Student A's email isn't working.

b Now reverse roles.

Student B
Call Student A from the Embassy hotel (number 800 779 0210).

Student A
Answer the call. Write down the hotel name and number and explain why you haven't emailed the presentation.

10e Please leave a message after the tone

Vocabulary email addresses and websites

1 Can you say these email addresses and websites? Check your answers with your instructor.

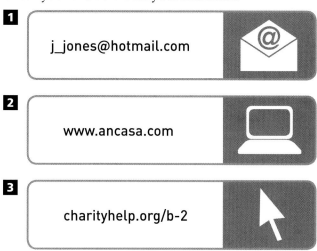

1 j_jones@hotmail.com

2 www.ancasa.com

3 charityhelp.org/b-2

2 Work in pairs. Take turns to say and write down your email address and your favorite website.

Writing a telephone message

3 🎵 **55** Listen to the voicemail and correct the four mistakes in the message.

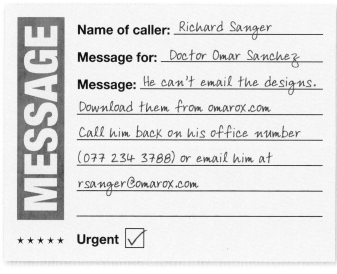

MESSAGE

Name of caller: _Richard Sanger_

Message for: _Doctor Omar Sanchez_

Message: _He can't email the designs._
Download them from omarox.com
Call him back on his office number
(077 234 3788) or email him at
rsanger@omarox.com
_____

★ ★ ★ ★ ★ **Urgent** ☑

4 Writing skill imperatives

a When we write messages, we often change the speaker's words and use imperatives. Look at this example.

> *Can he download them from this website?* →

Download them from this website.

b Read these five sentences from voicemails. Change them to imperatives.

1 Can you call Jim back?
2 I'd like you to email me the date of the meeting.
3 Can you meet me at the airport?
4 Would you book the hotel for two nights?
5 Can you send me Juan's number?

5 Prepare a message for a hotel voicemail. Include your name, number, and email address. Ask a colleague at the hotel to do something.

6 Work in pairs. Read your messages in Exercise 5 to each other. Fill in the form.

MESSAGE

Name of caller: _____

Message for: _____

Message: _____
_____
_____
_____
_____
_____

★ ★ ★ ★ ★ **Urgent** ☐

7 Check your partner's phone message. Is it clear? Is everything correct (the spelling, phone numbers, the email address)?

Baby Math

Babies naturally hold their breath under water.

Before you watch

1 Look at the photo and read the caption. Does that information surprise you? Discuss in pairs.

2 Look at the word box below. Listen and repeat the words after your instructor.

3 In the video, you will learn about human babies' reflexes and instincts. Read the list. With a partner, discuss what you think you will see the babies do.

eat	swim underwater
suck on a finger	sleep
grasp a finger	take steps
run	cry
smile	watch a computer screen
look at toys	laugh
hold a ball	

While you watch

4 As you watch the video, circle the items in Exercise 3 that you see.

5 Watch the video again. What reflexes do human babies share with other species? For each animal, write the human reflex. One answer will be used twice.

startle	add and subtract
hold breath underwater	grasp

6 Are these statements true or false? Correct the false information.

1 Human babies learn reflexes that help them survive.
2 Psychologist Karen Wynn does tests to see how bees can add and subtract.
3 In Wynn's tests, she uses toys to show babies simple math problems.
4 In the tests, babies look longer at outcomes that are expected.
5 Human babies, bees, and pigeons share an instinct: they can count.

After you watch

7 What have we learned from Karen Wynn's experiments? In small groups, talk about what her tests have and haven't shown us.

The tests have shown us that babies can …

We have learned that …

The tests haven't explained how …

We haven't seen …

8 Go online to research another experiment about babies or animals. Find out what the experiment was about, who took part in the testing, how the testing was done, and what the outcome was. Make a poster showing what you learned. Present your poster to the class.

> **add** (v) /æd/ to put numbers together
> **grasp** (v) /græsp/ to hold tightly
> **instinct** (n) /ˈɪnstɪŋkt/ something you know without learning it
> **outcome** (n) /ˈaʊtˌkʌm/ a result
> **reflex** (n) /ˈriˌfleks/ an action of the body that happens automatically
> **species** (n) /ˈspiʃiz/ group of animals that are similar
> **startle** (v) /ˈstɑrt(ə)l/ to move suddenly because of fear or surprise
> **subtract** (v) /səbˈtrækt/ to take away a number

UNIT 10 REVIEW

Grammar

1 Write *Have you ever ...?* questions with the prompts.

1 see / Angkor Wat?
Have you ever seen Angkor Wat?
2 ride / a motorcycle?
3 learned to play / a musical instrument?
4 meet / a famous person?
5 make / a movie?

2 Match these answers with the questions in Exercise 1.

a Yes, I have. I made a movie about my family for a college project.
b Yes, I have. I rode across the US on a Harley-Davidson last summer.
c No, I haven't, but my friend has met some.
d No, I haven't, but I'm going to Cambodia next year.
e No, I haven't, but I'd like to learn the guitar.

3 Work in pairs. Take turns to ask and answer the questions in Exercise 1.

4 Complete the conversation with the present perfect or simple past form of the verbs.

A: ¹ _____ (you / ever / visit) Rome?
B: Yes, I have. I was a student at the university.
A: Really? What ² _____ (you / study)?
B: Art. I also ³ _____ (work) in a museum for three months.
A: When ⁴ _____ (you / do) that?
B: In 2005.
A: ⁵ _____ (you / learn) Italian?
B: No, I didn't, because my parents are Italian so I ⁶ _____ (speak) Italian all my life.

I CAN

talk about past experiences with the present perfect ☐

talk about the past with the present perfect and simple past ☐

Vocabulary

5 Replace the old technology words in bold with these modern technology words.

| emails | GPS | podcast |
| search engine | | text message |

1 Have you ever written **letters**? *emails*
2 My son sent me a **postcard**.
3 Find the town on the **map**.
4 I'm listening to a **radio program** in English.
5 This **library** gives you lots of information.

6 Choose the correct option to complete the sentences.

1 I *study / understand* English every day for an hour.
2 Can you *know / remember* the address?
3 I always *memorize / forget* what this word means!
4 We can *practice / know* English together by only speaking English.
5 I need to *test / learn* myself before the exam.

7 Complete this sentence about yourself. Then compare with your partner.

This week in my English lessons, I've learned ...

I CAN

talk about everyday technology ☐

talk about learning English ☐

Real life

8 Put the words in the correct order to make questions for checking and clarifying.

1 Africa? / as / in / A / is / that
_____

2 thirteen / that / thirty? / or / was
_____

3 675-6475? / number / the / is
_____

4 there / anything / is / else?
_____

5 have / sent / the / email? / you
_____

I CAN

check and clarify information ☐

Speaking

9 Work in pairs. Discuss your favorite school subject and why you liked it.

Unit 11 Tourism

The desert in Jordan

FEATURES

1 Look at the photo. Why do you think the table is in the desert?

2 Read about this man's vacation in Jordan. Why was the table in the desert? What happened?

When I was nineteen, I went backpacking around the world. My favorite memory is when I was traveling in the desert in Jordan and I met some local people. They were called Bedouin and they lived in tents in the desert. They were very friendly and invited me for tea. It was a hot afternoon, but they put the table outside and made hot tea. We all sat in the middle of the desert, drank tea, and watched the sun go down. It was wonderful!

3 Which vacation did the man in Exercise 2 take?

a camping trip	backpacking around the world
a sightseeing tour	a vacation package by the beach
hiking in the mountains	

4 Work in groups. Discuss which vacations from Exercise 3:

- do you prefer?
- have you done in the past?
- are you going to do in the future?

I prefer vacation packages because I like to relax.

I've never been camping. But I am going backpacking next summer!

11a Going on vacation

Reading and vocabulary tourism

1 Read the quiz and find the words that match the definitions (1–7).

1 you buy this ticket to go somewhere and come back
  round-trip
2 you buy this ticket to go somewhere
3 you carry this bag onto the airplane
4 to reserve a hotel room before you arrive
5 special objects you buy on vacation
6 to give your bag to the airline before getting on the plane
7 looking at famous and interesting places

2 Work in pairs. Answer the quiz and read your answers. Are you Tourist A, Tourist B, or both? Tell the class.

> ▶ **WORDBUILDING word forms (1)**
>
> One word often has other forms. For example: *to tour* (verb) – *tourism* (noun) – *tourist* (person) – *tour guide* (noun + noun collocation).

Listening

3 Look at the website on page 131. What kind of tourist is it for? What does Jan Lanting talk about in the podcast?

4 🔘 **56** Listen to the podcast and answer the questions.

1 What month is it?
2 Why is it a good time to go to Malaysia?
3 Does everyone in Malaysia speak English?
4 In the Malaysian jungle, why is a local guide important?
5 When is a good time to go to the Arctic?
6 How can you travel to the Arctic?

5 Which place would you like to go to? Why?

What kind of **TOURIST** are you?

Answer the questions for Tourist A and Tourist B.

Tourist A Do you ...	(mark)
always buy a round-trip ticket?	☐
check more than one bag?	☐
book the hotel in advance?	☐
rent a car?	☐
buy souvenirs?	☐
use a tour guide?	☐
like sightseeing?	☐

Tourist B Do you ...	(mark)
often buy a one-way ticket?	☐
only take a carry-on bag?	☐
find a hotel after you arrive?	☐
use public transportation?	☐
buy local food at markets?	☐
learn some phrases in the local language?	☐
meet local people?	☐

Did you mark more questions for Tourist A or Tourist B? Turn to page 153.

WWW.INDIETRAVELINFO.COM

Travel information for people who like traveling on their own.

This month, we look at some of the top destinations for independent tourists. Click here to download a podcast of our interview with travel writer Jan Lanting. Listen to her top suggestions for this time of year.

The jungles of Malaysia

The Arctic Circle

Word focus *take*

6 We use the verb *take* with different types of nouns. Match these words to the three types.

> a taxi   an umbrella   a break

1 *take* + an object
2 *take* + time when you don't work
3 *take* + type of transportation

7 Find some more examples of *take* + noun in the audioscript on page 174.

Grammar *should/shouldn't*

8 Look at the verb *should* in these sentences. Answer the questions.

a You shouldn't go in the winter because it's very cold and very dark.
b Should I go on my own or with a tour?

1 What form is the verb after *should* and *shouldn't*?
2 How do you make a question with *should*? Do you use the auxiliary *do/does*?

> ▶ **SHOULD/SHOULDN'T**
>
> I/you/he/she/we/they should rent a car.
> I/you/he/she/we/they shouldn't take a taxi.
>
> Should I buy my ticket at the station?
> Yes, you should. / No, you shouldn't.
>
> For more information and practice, see page 168.

9 Work in pairs. Read the sentences (1–6). Then use the words in the table to give advice for each situation.

1 I'm so tired.
2 The sun is shining and it's hot.
3 I can't speak the local language.
4 Public transportation is slow.
5 This store is expensive.
6 Venice is a beautiful city.

You	should	take a vacation. go sightseeing. learn some words.
	shouldn't	buy your souvenirs here. take the bus. wear sunscreen.

Speaking

10 Work in pairs. Choose a country and prepare advice for a tourist. Include these topics:

- weather
- famous sites
- local food
- transportation
- language
- shopping

11 Work with another pair. Take turns giving advice and asking each other questions.

> *You should go to the beaches because they're beautiful in this country.*

> *Should I bring sunscreen?*

11b Planning a vacation

Reading

1 Work in groups. Discuss what you need to do before going on vacation. Make a list then compare your list with the class.

2 Read the leaflet below. Match these sub-headings with the sections in the leaflet (1–6).

> Road travel   Weather   Money and currency
> Safety and emergencies   Visas and immigration   Language

Information for tourists and visitors in Australia

1 _____
- You have to get a visa from the Australian Embassy before you leave.
- Tourists and visitors can stay for a maximum of six months.
- You cannot work in Australia without a work visa from the Australian Embassy in your country.

2 _____
- The currency is Australian dollars.
- Most stores, hotels, and banks in large cities accept credit cards.
- In smaller towns, you should always carry cash.

3 _____
- Australia is a multicultural country so there are many different languages.
- Most people speak or understand English.

4 _____
- There are three time zones. Temperature and climate is different from region to region.
- Summers are very hot. Always use sunscreen and wear a hat.

5 _____
- In the cities, you should stay with friends and not carry lots of cash.
- Dial 000 for Police, Fire, and Ambulance.

6 _____
- Tourists don't have to get a new driving license, but after a year, you have to take a new driving test.

> **hitchhiking** (n) /'hɪtʃˌhaɪkɪŋ/ getting a free ride in someone's car

3 Read the comments (a–f) from tourists in Australia. Mark yes (Y) or no (N) if they have read the leaflet.

a I've been a tourist here for seven months now.
b I got a work visa before I left home.
c Can I use US dollars here?
d Is English the only language?
e I've brought sunscreen.
f I dialed 999, but the police never answered.

Vocabulary **in another country**

4 Complete the information for visitors to Canada with these words.

> climate   currency   side   illegal
> license   multicultural   time zones
> visa

- For employment in Canada, most people need a work [1] _____ .
- The Canadian dollar is the national [2] _____ .
- There are six [3] _____ in Canada.
- Canada is a [4] _____ country with two official languages, French and English. Eighteen percent of the population has a different first language.
- Canada's [5] _____ is very different from season to season. It can snow in the winter, but in the summer the temperature can be very high.
- Drive on the right [6] _____ of the road.
- You have to carry your driver's [7] _____ when you drive.
- Hitchhiking is [8] _____ on highways, but you can hitchhike on local roads.

5 How similar is the information about Australia and Canada?

6 Work in groups. Discuss these questions about your country or countries. How many answers do you know? Afterwards, compare your answers with the class.

1 Do tourists need a visa?
2 How many time zones are there?
3 Is the climate different in different areas?
4 Which side of the road do you drive on?
5 Do you always carry your driver's license?
6 Is hitchhiking legal or illegal?

Grammar *have to / don't have to, can/can't*

7 Look at these sentences and match the meaning of the highlighted verbs with the words in the box.

> necessary   not necessary   possible
> not possible

1 You **have to** get a tourist visa from the Australian Embassy.
2 Tourists and visitors **can** stay for a maximum of six months.
3 You **cannot** work in Australia without a work visa.
4 Tourists **don't have to** get a new driver's license.

▶ **HAVE TO / DON'T HAVE TO, CAN/CAN'T**

You **have to** show your passport to passport control. (necessary)

You **don't have to** show a passport for travel in your own country. (not necessary)

All passengers **can** take one carry-on bag onto the plane. (possible)

You **can't** check in luggage over 50 pounds. (not possible)

For more information and practice, see page 168.

---

8 Look at the signs and notices for tourists in the next column. Choose the correct verbs.

1 You *have to / can* drive on the left-hand side.
2 Tourists *can't / don't have to* take photos here.

3 Guests *have to / don't have to* leave their room before 11 a.m.
4 Airline passengers with an online boarding pass *have to / don't have to* go to the check-in desk.

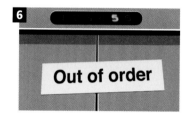

5 You *can / can't* smoke in this area.
6 You *can / can't* use the hotel elevator.

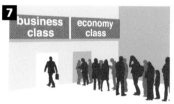

7 Business class passengers *cannot / don't have to* wait.
8 All passengers *have to / can* check in online.

9 **Pronunciation** /ˈhæftə/

🔊 **57** Listen to the sentences and repeat.

Writing and speaking

10 Work in pairs. Choose one situation below and complete the sentences (1–4).

- visiting another country as a tourist
- studying at your language school
- working for your company

1 You have to …   3 You can …
2 You don't have to …   4 You can't …

11 Work with another pair. Don't say the situation, but read your sentences. The other pair guesses the situation.

11c Should I go there?

Reading

1 Look at the photo on page 135 of tourists on a ship in Antarctica. Why do you think tourists go there? What do you think they can see? Would you like to go? Why? / Why not?

2 Read the article. Which paragraph (1–5) is about:

  a why Antarctica is a good vacation destination?
  b the writer's problem?
  c what type of vacation the writer likes?
  d changes in Antarctica?
  e the number of tourists in Antarctica?

3 Work in pairs and answer the questions.

  1 What does the writer want to do on his next vacation?
  2 What types of trips does he write about?
  3 What is his problem? Why?

4 Do you agree with the writer about other tourists? Why? / Why not?

Critical thinking arguments for and against

5 Work in pairs. List the writer's reasons (1) for and (2) against a vacation in Antarctica.

6 Work with another pair. Compare your lists. Then discuss the question in the last line of the article.

Grammar *everywhere, somewhere, nowhere, anywhere*

7 Which of these highlighted words refer to people or places? An object or event?

There are other tourists everywhere these days.
Nobody lives there.
I'd like to do something exciting.
Is there anywhere in the world without people?

> **► EVERYWHERE, SOMEWHERE, NOWHERE, ANYWHERE**
>
> | everywhere | somewhere | nowhere | anywhere |
> |---|---|---|---|
> | everybody | somebody | nobody | anybody |
> | everything | something | nothing | anything |
>
> Use *any-* in negative sentences and questions.
>
> For more information and practice, see page 169.

8 Choose the correct words to complete the text.

You should visit Nikko!

Is there [1] *everywhere / anywhere* in the world like Nikko, Japan? Of course, there are beautiful cities [2] *everywhere / somewhere* in Japan. But [3] *anywhere / nowhere* like Nikko. It's a great place to see [4] *everything / nothing* Japan has to offer: historical sites from the Edo period, beautiful nature, and local culture. There's always [5] *anything / something* to see. If you get lost, ask [6] *somebody / something* for directions. The local people are very friendly! And after a long day, sit in a hot spring and do [7] *nothing / everything*! Relax and watch the monkeys walking past.

Writing

9 Work in pairs. Choose a tourist destination and write a paragraph with the title "You should visit [name of your destination]!"

10 Put your paragraphs around the classroom. Read about the different vacation destinations. Tell the class which you would like to go to.

SHOULD I GO THERE?

Travel writer Carlos Gomm is planning his next vacation. But **should he go there?**

I don't like vacations with hotels, beaches, and swimming pools, and I'm not interested in sightseeing in old cities. I'd like to do something exciting, and nowadays lots of vacations offer excitement: backpacking over the Andes of South America or safaris in Africa. I could visit Australia and swim with dolphins.

But when I choose a vacation I always have the same problem: I don't want to go somewhere and see lots of other tourists. I want to be the only person there. The problem is that there are other tourists everywhere these days. Is there anywhere in the world without people?

What about Antarctica? It's a huge, beautiful continent. Between 1,000 and 5,000 scientists work there, but nobody lives there. There are no cities so there's no pollution or traffic, and it has lots of nature and wildlife. It sounds perfect!

Actually, there are also tourists in Antarctica. Tourism there began in the late 1950s. About 500 people a year visited from Chile and Argentina. Nowadays, about 50,000 tourists from all over the world cruise there every year, and the number is increasing.

So, like everywhere else with tourists, Antarctica is changing. You can't stay overnight, but you can visit wildlife areas. Some people think the numbers of wild animals and birds are decreasing as a result. However, there is also some positive news. Many cruise ships are members of the International Association of Antarctica Tour Operators (IAATO). They teach their passengers about Antarctica and its wildlife. The cruise companies also give money to environmental organizations in the region. These organizations want to help the nature and wildlife of Antarctica so it doesn't change in the future.

So what should I do? Go to Antarctica, go somewhere else, or stay at home?

safari (n) /səˈfɑri/ a type of vacation in Africa to look at animals
environmental organization (n) /ɪnˌvaɪrənˈment(ə)l ˌɔrɡənəˈzeɪʃən/ a group of people who want to help the natural world

11d A vacation in South America

Listening

1 How do you choose your vacation? Which of these do you use?

- travel books
- a travel website
- videos about places
- advice from family and friends
- a vacation brochure

2 🔊 **58** Listen and answer the questions.

1 What are the friends looking at?
2 Which countries in South America do they mention?
3 What type of vacation does the other person suggest at the end?

Real life making suggestions

3 🔊 **58** Work in pairs. Listen again and follow the instructions. Then compare answers.

Student A: Match the two halves of the sentences for suggesting.

Student B: Match the two halves of the sentences for responding.

> ▶ **MAKING SUGGESTIONS**
>
> **Suggesting**
> 1 You should   a suggestion?
> 2 How about   travel on your own.
> 3 Can I make   go on a tour?
> 4 Why don't you   go on that.
> 5 You could   visiting the Andes?
>
> **Responding**
> 6 Yes, but   you're right.
> 7 But the disadvantage good idea.
>   is that   there are lots of other
> 8 But the advantage   people with a bus tour.
>   is that   I'm interested in the wildlife.
> 9 Maybe   you see more with a tour
> 10 That's a really   guide.

4 Pronunciation /ʌ/, /ʊ/, **or** /u/

a 🔊 **59** Listen to and repeat these vowel sounds: /ʌ/, /ʊ/, and /u/.

b Match these words with the sounds in part a. Check your answers with your teacher.

could	cruise	bus	you	should
but	love	book	food	

5 Work in pairs. Discuss the best type of vacation for each of these people.

1 Wei has two weeks' vacation to take. He loves traveling, but he doesn't like crowded cities.
2 Alicia is a student. She has three months in the summer, but she doesn't have much money.
3 Pari and Arjun are in their sixties and don't work anymore. They have lots of free time. They've never traveled before.

6 Work in pairs. Role play a conversation. Choose a traveler from Exercise 5.

Student A: You're the traveler. Listen to Student B's suggestions and respond.
Student B: Suggest a vacation for Student A.

Then change roles, choose a different traveler, and repeat the role play.

11e Your feedback

Speaking

1a What is most important to you in a hotel? Put this list in order of importance (1 = most important, 6 = not important).

- a good restaurant
- near the airport and public transportation
- comfortable rooms with Internet or WiFi
- friendly staff
- a gym and swimming pool
- near the beach or downtown area

b Work in groups and compare your answers.

> I think a good restaurant is more important than a gym.

> I don't agree.

Writing a feedback form

2 Look at the feedback form and answer the questions.

1. Which parts of the hotel does it ask about?
2. How positive or negative was the feedback?

3 Writing skill questions

a Feedback forms and questionnaires often use a mixture of yes/no (closed) questions and open questions. We answer yes/no to closed questions and give longer answers to open questions. Read these questions from vacation feedback forms. Are they closed (C) or open questions (O)?

1. How was your bus tour? *O*
2. Did the tour guide answer all your questions? *C*
3. Were all our staff polite and helpful?
4. Did you book your vacation online?
5. How easy to use was our website?
6. Did you use the hotel swimming pool and gym?
7. Would you recommend this vacation to your friends?
8. What other suggestions can you make to improve our service?

b How does the form in Exercise 2 ask for more feedback after a closed question?

4 Work in pairs. Write a feedback form for passengers at an airport, customers at a restaurant, or visitors at a sports center.

5 Swap your feedback form with another pair.

- Write answers on their questionnaire.
- Give them feedback on their form.

GOLDEN BEACH HOTEL

Thank you for visiting our hotel. We hope you enjoyed your stay. Please spend a few minutes to complete this form. Your feedback and suggestions are very important to us.

How was your room?

___ very comfortable   ✓ quite comfortable
___ comfortable   ___ not very comfortable

How helpful were the staff?

___ very helpful   ___ quite helpful
___ helpful   ✓ not very helpful

Comment: *One day I called reception and nobody answered. I called three times!*

Did you use the gym? Yes / (No)

If "yes," please comment: _____

Did you eat in the hotel restaurant? (Yes) / No

If "yes," please comment: *The waiter wasn't very polite, but fortunately, the food was very good.* ☺

Overall, did you enjoy your stay? Yes / No

Please comment: *Yes and no. Overall, the room and the facilities were very good, but the staff weren't very friendly. They need to be more helpful and polite.*

Muslim pilgrims walk around the Kaaba in Mecca

Before you watch

1 Work in pairs. Look at the photo and read the caption. Answer the questions.

1 What religion are the pilgrims?
2 Where are they walking?

2 Match the religious people (1–3) to their religious holidays (a–c).

1 Muslims   2 Christians   3 Jews

a Christmas is on December 25.
b Hanukkah is a festival of light.
c Eid al-Fitr is a holiday at the end of Ramadan.

3 Which days are religious holidays in your country?

While you watch

4 Watch the video. Complete the sentences with these words.

| Arafat | Kaaba | Masjid al-Haram | Mecca |
| Mina | the Hajj | | |

1 _____ is a city in Saudi Arabia.
2 _____ is a religious journey or "pilgrimage."
3 _____ is the mosque in the middle of Mecca.
4 The _____ is in the middle of the mosque.
5 _____ is a tent city for pilgrims on the Hajj.
6 _____ is a religious place for Muslims. It is east of Mina.

5 Watch the video again. Choose the correct answer.

1 In which direction do Muslims pray?
  a towards Mecca   b towards Mina
  c towards Arafat
2 How many times in their lives should Muslims visit the Kaaba?
  a at least once   b twice
  c ten times
3 The pilgrims walk _____ the Kaaba.
  a around   b inside
  c under
4 Where do the pilgrims stay?
  a in Mecca   b in Mina
  c at Arafat
5 How long do they spend at Arafat?
  a a day   b a week
  c a month
6 When can the pilgrims return to Mina?
  a when the sun rises b at noon
  c when the sun goes down
7 At the end of the journey, what are women pilgrims called?
  a Hajji   b Hajjah
  c The video doesn't say.

After you watch

6 Complete the text about another religious pilgrimage with these words.

| cathedral | Christianity | pilgrimage |
| pilgrims | pray | religious |

The cathedral at Santiago de Compostela

Santiago de Compostela is a ¹ _____ city in northwestern Spain. In the center there is a famous ² _____ . Thousands of people come here to ³ _____ . Their religion is ⁴ _____ and a lot of them make a ⁵ _____ that lasts weeks or even months. The Christian ⁶ _____ start their journey in France or Portugal and follow a lot of different routes to Santiago de Compostela. About 200,000 pilgrims walk there every year.

7 Group discussion planning a short documentary video

Work in groups to plan a short (2–3 minutes) documentary video about a religious or public holiday in your country:

1 Choose a holiday.
2 Say when it takes place.
3 Describe what happens.
4 Decide on what you need to film.

8 Give a short presentation to the class of your plan for the documentary.

pilgrim (n) /ˈpɪlgrɪm/ religious traveler
pilgrimage (n) /ˈpɪlgrɪmɪdʒ/ a religious journey
pray (v) /preɪ/ to speak to God at a religious event or privately

UNIT 11 REVIEW

Grammar

1 Choose the correct option to complete the sentences.

1 We *should / shouldn't* stay if it's terrible.
2 She *should / shouldn't* study Italian before she goes to Italy.
3 You *should / shouldn't* rent an unsafe car.
4 Sometimes the hotels get full, so we *should / shouldn't* book a room in advance.

2 Complete the sentences about a tour guide's job with *have to, don't have to, can,* or *can't*.

1 I *have to* wear nice clothes, but I *don't have to* wear a uniform.
2 The tourists _____ smoke on the tour bus, but they can outside.
3 At lunchtime, I _____ eat with the tourists, but I don't have to.
4 I _____ know everything about the city because the tourists ask a lot of questions.

3 Write four sentences about your job or studies. Use *should, shouldn't, have to, don't have to, can,* or *can't*. Then compare your sentences with a partner.

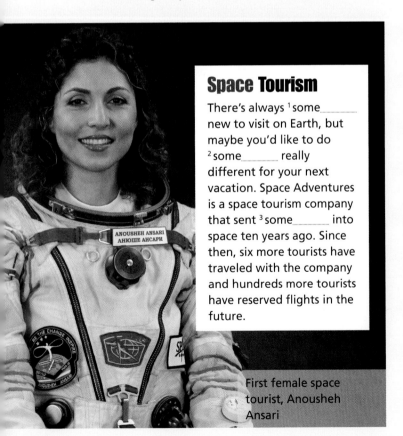

Space Tourism

There's always [1]some_____ new to visit on Earth, but maybe you'd like to do [2]some_____ really different for your next vacation. Space Adventures is a space tourism company that sent [3]some_____ into space ten years ago. Since then, six more tourists have traveled with the company and hundreds more tourists have reserved flights in the future.

First female space tourist, Anousheh Ansari

4 Complete the article with *body, thing,* or *where*.

I CAN	
give advice with *should* or *shouldn't*	☐
talk about necessity and possibility	☐
talk about places, people, and things	☐

Vocabulary

5 Complete the categories with these words.

camping	hiking	round-trip	sightseeing
one-way	souvenir	tour guide	tourist

1 Type of vacation: _____, _____, _____
2 Type of ticket: _____, _____
3 Something you buy on vacation: _____
4 Other people on a vacation: _____, _____

6 Match two words from each box to complete the sentences.

driver's	time	work

license	visa	zones

1 My country has three different _____ _____.
2 You need a _____ _____ to get a job.
3 You can get a _____ _____ when you pass the test.

I CAN	
talk about tourism	☐
talk about visiting another country	☐

Real life

7 Match the suggestions (1–4) with the responses (a–d).

1 How about going camping?
2 You should visit the beach.
3 Can I make a suggestion?
4 Why don't you go hiking in the mountains?

a That's a really good idea. I need some exercise.
b No, I prefer sleeping in a hotel.
c Yes, but it's crowded in the summer.
d Sure. What is it?

Speaking

8 Work in pairs. Talk about your last vacation. Consider these questions:

- Where did you go?
- What did you do?
- How was the accommodation?
- Would you recommend it?

Unit 12 The Earth

An Inuit man in the Arctic Circle
Photo by Ira Block

FEATURES

1 Work in pairs. Compare the two photos. How are the places in each one different?

2 This photo shows a man in the Arctic Circle holding a photo of South Carolina in the US. Fifty-six million years ago, the Arctic Circle looked like the photo of South Carolina. With a partner, answer these questions.

1 What do you know about climate change in the past?
2 What do you know about climate change today?

3 Work in groups. Answer these questions.

1 Is your country nearer to the Arctic Circle, the Antarctic Circle, or the Equator?
2 Where is it spring or summer at the moment? In the northern or southern hemisphere?
3 Have you ever traveled across the Equator to the other hemisphere? Where did you go?

12a Climate change

Vocabulary measurements

1 Match these abbreviations with their definitions.

Abbreviation	Meaning	It measures ...
1 %	square meters / feet	temperature
2 °C / F	kilometers / miles	area
3 km / mi	percentage	distance
4 l / gal.	kilograms / pounds	weight
5 m² / ft²	liters / gallons	quantity of water (or liquid)
6 kg / lb(s)	degrees Celsius / Fahrenheit	an amount out of 100

2 Complete these facts about the Earth with the correct abbreviation from Exercise 1.

Earth Fact File

1 The temperature at Earth's center is about 7,500 _____ / 1,300°F.
2 The North Pole is over 20,000km / 12,000 _____ from the South Pole.
3 70 _____ of the Earth's surface is water.
4 1,489,940,000,000km² / 57,000,000 _____ of the Earth is land.
5 A weight of 100kg / 220 _____ on Earth is only 16.5 _____ / 36lbs on the Moon.

one trillion = one million million 1,000,000,000,000

3 Which measurement do you look at when you ...

- buy a carton of orange juice?
- watch the weather on TV?
- go on a long journey?
- buy fruit or vegetables from the market?
- pay taxes?
- build a new house?

> ▶ WORDBUILDING word forms (2)
>
> Words about measurements often have more than one form:
> *long* (adj) – *length* (n), *high* (adj) – *height* (n), *weigh* (v) – *weight* (n)

Reading

4 What is the climate in your country (hot, cold, warm)? Has the climate in your country changed? How?

5 Look at the two maps on page 143 and read the article. Answer these questions for each map.

1 What does the map show?
2 How many years is it for?
3 How does it show the change?

6 Look at the maps again. Are these sentences true (T) or false (F)?

Map 1
1 The temperature in the Arctic Circle has decreased by 4°C.
2 The temperature change in the northern hemisphere is higher than in the southern hemisphere.
3 The temperature in some parts of Antarctica has decreased by 2°C.

Map 2
4 Rainfall has increased in western Australia and it has decreased in eastern Australia.
5 Rainfall has increased in all of Europe.
6 Rainfall has decreased in parts of Africa by 15%.

7 What do the maps show about your country? Is the information similar to your answers in Exercise 4?

CLIMATE CHANGE

Climate scientists have measured the temperature and rainfall on every part of the Earth over many years. They look at the changes and predict the future with the information. The first map shows the temperature over 30 years. In most parts of the world, the temperature has increased by a few degrees and scientists think it will increase in the future.

The second map shows rainfall on the Earth over 30 years. The amount of rain is very different from region to region. Rainfall has increased in some countries and scientists think it will increase in the future. But rainfall has also decreased in other parts and, in these regions, it won't increase. It will decrease.

In conclusion, the changes in climate will continue in the next century. The Earth will feel hotter and rainfall will be higher for some places, but lower for others.

Grammar *will/won't*

8 Look at the sentence with *will* and *won't (will not)*. Choose the correct option in the rules (1–3).

Scientists think it *will* change soon, but it *won't* happen here.

1 We use *will / won't* to talk about the *past / present / future*.
2 We *add / don't add* -s to *will* with *he / she / it*.
3 The verb after *will is / isn't* in the infinitive.

> ▶ **WILL/WON'T**
>
> Use *will* to talk about what we think or know about the future:
> *I/you/he/she/it/we/they'll (will) feel hotter.*
> *I/you/he/she/it/we/they won't (will not) feel colder.*
> *Will I/you/he/she/it/we/they feel colder?*
>
> **I (don't) think + will**
> We often use *will* with *I think*. For example: *I (don't) think it will snow.*
>
> For more information and practice, see page 169.

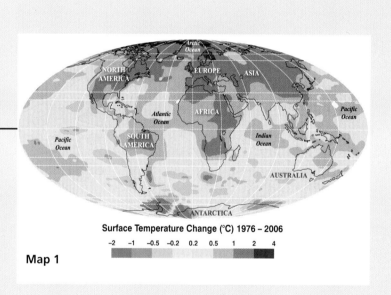

Surface Temperature Change (°C) 1976 – 2006

−2 −1 −0.5 −0.2 0.2 0.5 1 2 4

Map 1

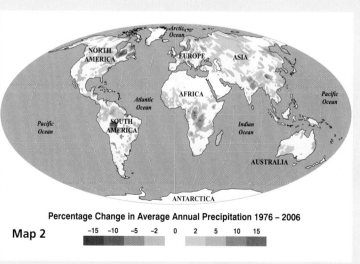

Percentage Change in Average Annual Precipitation 1976 – 2006

−15 −10 −5 −2 0 2 5 10 15

Map 2

9 Reorder the words to make sentences about the future.

1 it / be / hotter in my country / in the future / 'll
2 increase / the temperature in this country / in the future / won't
3 visit / one day / I'll / Antarctica / I think
4 be / less ice / will / in the Arctic Circle / there
5 the percentage of people living in cities / decrease / will
6 English / everyone / speak / will
7 more cars / won't / people / buy
8 I don't think / increase / the number of dry deserts / will

10 Work in pairs. Make the sentences in Exercise 9 into questions. Ask your partner for his/her opinion.

> *Will it be hotter in your country in the future?*

11 Pronunciation *'ll*

🔊 **60** Listen to six sentences. Do you hear *will* or *'ll*? Listen again and repeat.

1 will 'll   4 will 'll
2 will 'll   5 will 'll
3 will 'll   6 will 'll

Writing and speaking

12 Think about your partner's future. Write four sentences about:

• his/her future job
• his/her future travel
• his/her future home
• finances

13 Tell your partner your sentences. Does your partner think they will come true?

> *I think you'll become a musician.*

> *I don't think I will. I can't play a musical instrument!*

12b Exploring the Earth

Reading and vocabulary land and water

1 Which is your favorite place on Earth? Why? Tell the class.

2 Read the article. Answer the questions.

1 Which unexplored places are in water and which on land?
2 Which place would you like to explore? Why?

3 Complete this table with words from the article.

areas of water	areas of land
sea	desert
o...............	i...............
l...............	f...............
r...............	m...............

4 Work in pairs. Discuss the questions.

1 How many of these geographic places from Exercise 3 are in (or near) your country?
2 Which have you visited?

Grammar definite *the* or no article + names

5 Sometimes we use *the* + names of places. Find these examples in the article:

1 a group of islands (or countries)
   the Bahamas
2 the name of an ocean
3 a group of mountains
4 the name of a river

6 We can also use no article before some names of places. Find examples of no article + these names of places.

1 the name of a mountain
2 the name of a lake
3 the name of a country
4 the name of a continent

7 Work in groups. Think of one more example from other places on Earth for each category in Exercises 5 and 6. Compare your new lists with the class.

EXPLORING THE EARTH

We think humans have traveled everywhere on Earth. But here are five places where no human has ever been.

The Black Hole of Andros is on an island in the Bahamas in the Atlantic Ocean. The hole is 154 feet (47m) deep, and the water is 36 °C and very black. Nobody has ever swum in it.

Mount Dinpernalason is east of the Himalayan mountains. It isn't the highest mountain (Mount Everest is), but nobody has ever climbed it.

Lake Vostok in Antarctica is 25 million years old and covers 5,405 square miles (14,000k²). Unfortunately, you can't see the lake because it's frozen under a glacier.

The Merume Mountains are at the end of the Mazaruni River in Guyana. The journey by boat is dangerous so nobody has explored many of these mountains.

The Foja Mountains in Papua New Guinea are covered in tropical forest. Nobody has ever made a map of the region.

> ▶ **DEFINITE *THE* OR NO ARTICLE + NAMES**
>
> Use *the* with the names of:
> * deserts, seas, oceans, and rivers: *the Gobi desert, the North Sea, the Pacific Ocean, the River Amazon.*
> * plural names or groups of places: *the Alps, the United States of America, the Maldives.*
>
> Use no article with the names of continents, countries, lakes, or a single mountain: *Asia, Brazil, Lake Titicaca, Mount Fuji.*
>
> For more information and practice, see page 169.

EXPLORING THE DEEPEST
PLACE ON EARTH

¹ *The* Mariana Trench is in ² _____ Pacific Ocean. It's east of ³ _____ Mariana Islands and near ⁴ _____ Japan. It's the deepest place on Earth. In 2012, the film director James Cameron traveled down the Mariana Trench in a one-man submarine. He usually works in Hollywood in ⁵ _____ United States. Many of his films are famous, including *Titanic* (1997) and *Avatar* (2009). But Cameron is also a National Geographic explorer and has made a documentary about ⁶ _____ Sea of Cortez between California and ⁷ _____ Mexico. More recently, he has traveled down the Mariana Trench in a one-man submarine with 3D cameras.

James Cameron

8 Complete the text above with *the* or Ø (no article).

Listening

9 🔊 **61** Listen, then number these topics in the order you hear them.

a   the size of the submarine
b   the distance and time to reach the bottom of the Mariana Trench
c   another explorer
d   filming the Mariana Trench
e   the cost

10 🔊 **61** Listen to the interview again. Answer the questions.

1   How many miles is it to the bottom of the Mariana Trench?
2   How long did the journey take?
3   How big was the submarine?
4   How could James Cameron see at the bottom of the trench?
5   Who is Don Walsh?
6   How could Cameron afford to explore the Mariana Trench?

Word focus *how*

11 We often ask questions with *How …?* Match these questions (1–6) with their uses (a–f).

1   How big is it?
2   How well could he see?
3   How old is he?
4   How long did the journey take?
5   How much did he spend?
6   How did he travel there?

a   ask about quantity and price
b   ask about period of time
c   ask about ability
d   ask about age
e   ask how something happens
f   ask about size

Speaking

12 Write down the names of three famous places you have visited on Earth. Use these categories.

Category A: a mountain, forest, jungle, desert, or island
Category B: an ocean, sea, river, or lake
Category C: a city, country, or continent

13 Work in pairs. Tell each other the category but not the place and take turns asking questions with *How* to get the answer.

How far/near is it from here?

How do you travel there?

12c A new Earth

Speaking

1 Work in groups. In the future, do you think humans will live in these places? Answer A (Yes, definitely!), B (Possibly.) or C (No, never!). Give reasons.

| under the ocean | on the Moon |
| in the sky | near the Sun |

2 Do you think we will live anywhere else in the future?

Reading

3 Read the article on page 147. Add the sentences (a–d) to the end of each paragraph.

  a As a result, they are too hot and gassy or too cold and icy for human life.

  b With current space technology, humans will take 766,000 years to travel there.

  c And what will a new Earth look like?

  d So if water isn't on the surface, it's sometimes under rocks.

Vocabulary the Earth and other planets

4 Match each word in the pairs to the correct definition (a or b).

1 astronomer / explorer
  a someone who travels to and studies new places
  b someone who studies new places in space
2 planet / star
  a large round space object made of burning gas
  b large round space object made of rock and metal or gas
3 to travel / to orbit
  a to go around a planet or star
  b to go from one place to another
4 surface / rock
  a the outside or top part of something
  b solid part of the Earth or a planet

Critical thinking structuring an argument

5 Writers use these words and phrases (1–5) to structure their arguments. Find them in the article, then match them with their purpose (a–e).

1 First	a add information
2 More importantly	b introduce bad news
3 Unfortunately	c give a reason
4 However	d introduce your first point
5 (That's) because	e introduce an opposite idea

Speaking

6 What's your opinion about finding a new Earth? Is it important? Is life on the Earth and on other planets too different? Complete these sentences, then tell your partner.

In my opinion …
I think …
I don't think …

7 Write a short paragraph about your opinion in Exercise 6. Use some of the words and phrases in Exercise 5 to structure your argument. Begin your paragraph with: *Scientists are looking for a new Earth. In my opinion …*

LOOKING FOR A NEW EARTH

For thousands of years, humans have explored the Earth. Nowadays, we are exploring space. Astronomers are the modern-day explorers. Currently, many astronomers are looking for new planets and new places for humans to live in the future. But where do astronomers start looking?

First, astronomers look for a star. That's because our own Earth orbits a star (the Sun). More importantly, it is the correct distance from the Sun for heat and light. So when astronomers have found a star, they look at the planets around it. In recent years, astronomers have found nearly 400 new planets with stars. Unfortunately, many of these planets are either too near to the star or too far away.

However, if the planet is in a good position, astronomers look for three key things: water, air, and rock. Water is important because all life needs water. Humans drink it and grow plants with it. But plants need air to breathe. So life on other planets will need water and air. Rock is also important because there is often water under it.

After many years of looking, astronomers have found a planet that is similar to Earth. It's Gliese 581g and it's near a star. The astronomers think it has water and rock and the average temperature is cold, but not colder than Antarctica or the Arctic Circle, for example. Gliese 581g is bigger than the Earth and a year there lasts only 37 Earth days instead of 365. But astronomers do not think these are big differences, and some of them think Gliese 581g will be a new Earth. However, Gliese 581g is twenty light years from Earth—a distance of 11 trillion miles (18 trillion km).

12d Earth Day

Reading

1 Read about Earth Day. Answer the questions.

1 What do people do on Earth Day?
2 When and where did it begin?
3 Why did people go to it?

Real life making a presentation

2 🔊 **62** Listen and choose the correct answer. In two sentences, both answers are correct.

1 Davi is from ....
   a Brazil
   b the US
2 He talks about Earth Day in the ....
   a past
   b present
3 People in China planted 600,000 ....
   a flowers
   b trees
4 In Brazil, people picked up trash in the

   ....
   a cities
   b countryside
5 Davi thinks Earth Day is ....
   a important
   b fun

3 🔊 **62** Listen again. Complete these sentences from the presentation.

> ▶ **MAKING A PRESENTATION**
>
> Good morning, and ¹ .... for coming.
> My name's Davi, and ² .... Brazil.
> Today, ³ .... to talk about an important day.
> ⁴ .... , Earth Day began on April 22nd in 1970.
> ⁵ .... , more than 175 countries have an Earth Day.
> And ⁶ .... , in my country lots of people picked up trash.
> ⁷ .... , I really think Earth Day is important.
> Thank you very much ⁸ ....

Friends at Earth Day in Washington, DC

April 22nd is Earth Day. For one day every year, people in different countries help the Earth. For example, they clean parks, pick up trash, or plant trees. The first Earth Day was on April 22, 1970, in the US. Over 20 million people went to an Earth Day in their city. There were politicians, teachers, artists, and musicians. As one person said, "We had fun, but we also wanted to help the Earth and the environment."

4 Pronunciation pausing for commas

🔊 **63** Listen to and repeat these sentences from a presentation. Notice how the speaker pauses on commas.

1 Today, I'd like to talk about my company.
2 First, we started the company in 1999.
3 In conclusion, I think it's very important.

5 Prepare a short presentation. Choose one of these topics and follow the instructions (1–4).

• your local club or organization
• an important day in the year
• your company or place of study
• something (a club or organization) you think is important

1 introduce yourself and your subject
2 talk about its history
3 talk about now
4 say why you like it or why you think it's important

6 Work in groups and give your presentations.

12e Planning an event

Writing a poster

1 Look at the poster for Earth Day. Where do people normally put posters? What are the best places so people can see a poster?

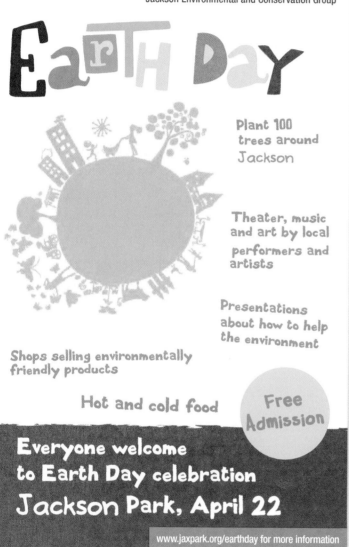

Jackson Environmental and Conservation Group

EARTH DAY

Plant 100 trees around Jackson

Theater, music and art by local performers and artists

Presentations about how to help the environment

Shops selling environmentally friendly products

Hot and cold food

Free Admission

Everyone welcome to Earth Day celebration Jackson Park, April 22

www.jaxpark.org/earthday for more information

2 Look at the poster. Which questions does it answer?

1 Who is organizing it?
2 What is it and what is it for?
3 What date is it on?
4 What activities are there?
5 Is there a parking lot or transportation?
6 Where is it?
7 What time does it start and end?
8 How much does it cost?
9 What can you buy (food, drink, anything else)?
10 Where can you get more information?

3 Writing skill **important words and information**

a We don't normally write full sentences on posters, notices, and ads. Look at the highlighted words in these sentences. Which words does the writer use on the poster? Which kind of words doesn't the writer use?

1 Everyone is welcome to our Earth Day celebration at Jackson Park on April 22.
2 We are going to plant 100 trees around Jackson.

b Underline the key words and information in these sentences. Then compare your ideas with the poster.

1 There will be presentations about how to help the environment.
2 Watch theater, listen to music, and look at art by local performers and artists.
3 Shops are going to be selling environmentally friendly products.
4 You can also buy hot and cold food.
5 Entrance to the event is free.
6 Visit our website at jaxpark.org/earthday for more information.

4 Work in groups to design a poster for an Earth Day in your town or city. Discuss this list of activities that many people do on Earth Day and choose one.

- plant lots of trees downtown
- pick up trash in the parks
- have a party in the park with local musicians
- sell energy efficient light bulbs
- visit local schools and talk to school children about Earth Day
- your own idea

5 Prepare and design a poster for your Earth Day. Include some or all of the information in Exercise 2. Use short sentences.

6 Put your posters on the wall in your classroom. Look at the posters by other groups. Do they include all the important information? Do they use short sentences?

Lava from a volcano

Before you watch

1 Work in pairs. Write three words to describe the volcano, then compare your words with other students in your class.

2 Discuss the questions as a class.

1 Are there any volcanoes in your country? Are they active?
2 Have you ever seen a volcano?

While you watch

3 Watch the video. Number these things in the order you see them.

a the Earth from space
b a map of the Ring of Fire
c a picture of Mount Vesuvius and Pompeii
d a diagram of the inside of a volcano
e an animal

4 Watch the video again. Match these names and words (1–6) with the descriptions (a–f).

1 the Ring of Fire   4 lava
2 tectonic plates   5 Kilauea
3 magma   6 Vesuvius

a the surface of the Earth is made of these large pieces of rock
b volcanoes around the Pacific Ocean
c a volcano in Hawaii
d a famous and dangerous volcano in history
e hot, melted rock under the ground
f magma at the surface of the Earth

5 Watch the video again. Are these sentences true (T) or false (F)?

1 Volcanoes are openings in the surface of the Earth.
2 There are 1,500 active volcanoes around the Pacific Ocean.
3 Tectonic plates are moving all the time.
4 Tourists cannot go near Kilauea because it's dangerous.
5 Two thousand people died in Pompeii.
6 Volcanoes always destroy life.

6 At the end of the video, the narrator says volcanoes are important for life. What are the reasons?

After you watch

7 Complete the text in the next column about Mount Vesuvius with these words.

active	eruption	lava
magma	tectonic plates	volcano

Mount Vesuvius is a famous ¹ _____ in southern Italy. Vesuvius was formed where the two ² _____ of Africa and Europe meet in this region. It's still an ³ _____ volcano, but there hasn't been an ⁴ _____ for many years. Visitors can see where the ⁵ _____ ran down the sides of the mountain in the past, but now trees and vineyards grow there. No one knows if it will erupt again, but there is still hot ⁶ _____ under the mountain so it's possible.

8 Group presentation **a presentation about volcanoes**

Work in groups to prepare a presentation about volcanoes. You can use information from the video and the Internet. Include the following:

1 The location of most volcanoes on Earth
2 The science of a volcano (why and how it's made)
3 Examples of active volcanoes you can visit
4 Why volcanoes are dangerous
5 Why we need volcanoes

9 Work with another group. Take turns giving your presentations.

- How similar or different were they?
- Did you learn something new about volcanoes from the other group?

> **active** (volcano) (adj) /ˈæktɪv/ a volcano that can erupt at any time
> **eruption** (n) /ɪˈrʌpʃən/ when lava comes out of a volcano

UNIT 12 REVIEW

Grammar

1 Complete the conversations with *'ll*, *will*, or *won't*.

A: I think we ¹_____ live in space someday.
B: No, we ²_____ . It's impossible.

A: In some parts of the world it ³_____ rain this year.
B: ⁴_____ deserts get larger?
A: Yes, they ⁵_____ .

2 Write *the* or Ø (no article) for these places.

1 _____ Polynesian Islands
2 _____ Michigan
3 _____ Atlas Mountains
4 _____ Africa
5 _____ Yangtze River
6 _____ United Arab Emirates
7 _____ Gobi Desert
8 _____ Iceland

3 In the future, where would you like to visit on the Earth? Write your top three destinations. Then compare your list with a partner.

I CAN	
make predictions with *will*	
use the definite article or no article with places	

Vocabulary

4 Complete the text with these abbreviations.

°F   ft   lbs   %   mi²

Easter Island is in the southeastern Pacific Ocean and its area is 63 ¹_____ . The climate is warm with an average temperature of about 68 ²_____ . The island is famous for 887 statues called *moai*. The largest moai weighs 164,000 ³_____ and is 32 ⁴_____ tall. Over 3,000 people live on the island and 60 ⁵_____ are Rapa Nui. Their Polynesian ancestors made the moai.

5 Complete the questions about Easter Island with these words. Then find the answers in the text.

tall   big   many   warm

1 How _____ is Easter Island?
2 How _____ is the climate?
3 How _____ is the largest moai?
4 How _____ people live on the island?

6 Choose the correct option to complete these sentences.

1 We spend the summer by the Baltic *Ocean / Sea*.
2 The Amazon *Lake / River* is in South America.
3 Madagascar is *a forest / an island*.
4 We all think they are cold places, but the Arctic and the Antarctic are also *deserts / mountains*.

7 Work in pairs. Which of the eight areas of land and water in Exercise 6 do you have in your country? Tell your partner.

I CAN	
use abbreviations	
talk about large areas of land and water	

Real life

8 Delete the extra word in each sentence from a presentation.

1 Good morning ~~you~~, and thank you for coming.
2 My name's Eva, and I'm from the Germany.
3 Today, I'm am going to talk about my company.
4 First, the company has began in 1965.
5 In conclusion, I think the company will to grow in the future.
6 Thank you very much for your listening.

I CAN	
make a presentation	

Speaking

9 You have reached the end of the book! Work in groups and prepare a quiz about facts in *Life*. Look at each unit and write one question about the information in it.

10 Work with another group and ask your twelve questions. Which group answered the most questions correctly?

UNIT 11a, Exercise 2, page 130

What do your answers mean?

Tourist A: You don't have much spare time so your vacations last a week or two weeks. Your favorite vacations are going on cruises or bus tours. You like taking lots of clothes and staying in comfortable hotels. You usually travel with groups of people.

Tourist B: You go on long vacations (a month or more) and you don't like planning them. Your favorite vacations are backpacking or hiking. You enjoy meeting local people, eating local food, and staying at small hotels or camping. You usually travel on your own or with a friend.

UNIT 6a, Exercise 8, page 71

Student A

1 Complete the questions about Arthur Honegger, who appears on the Swiss 20-franc bill, with *was* or *were*.

1 Where .... he born?
2 .... he French?
3 Where .... he from?
4 .... Arthur and his wife musicians?
5 How long .... they married?
6 When .... his music very popular?
7 Where .... there concerts of his music?

2 Ask your questions and complete the text.

Arthur Honegger was born in
¹ .... in 1892 but he wasn't ² .... He was from ³ .... Arthur and his wife were ⁴ .... He was a composer and she was a pianist. They were married for ⁵ .... At first, Honegger's music wasn't popular, but by ⁶ .... there were concerts of his music all over ⁷ ....

3 Answer Student B's questions about this person.

Ichiyo Higuchi was Japanese. She was born in 1872. There were five people in her family. Her father was a businessman, but they weren't rich. She was a writer and her books were very popular.

UNIT 3b, Exercise 12, page 37
Student A

1 Write questions about Joel with these prompts.

1 Who / work for?
2 Where / work?
3 Does / speak English?
4 What time / start work?

2 Ask Student B your questions and complete the fact file.

Name: Joel Sartore
Job: Photographer
Company: ¹ ....
Home: Lincoln, Nebraska
Place of work: ² ....
Children: He has three children.
Language: ³ ....
Normal working day: From ⁴ .... o'clock to six o'clock

3 Answer Student B's questions.

UNIT 5a, Exercise 4, page 58

pizza—Italy

ceviche—Peru

satay—Indonesia

kabsa—Saudi Arabia

pierogi—Poland

curry—India

UNIT 10b, Exercise 2, page 120

Student A

Memorizing names and faces

Do you often forget names and faces? When you meet someone for the first time, listen to them. Repeat their name and use it in the conversation. For example, "It's nice to meet you, Elaine." Look at their face and the clothes they wear. Introduce them to others and make conversation. With new colleagues, write down their name, job, and where you met them.

UNIT 2d, Exercise 6, page 28

Student A

1 You are the customer. You'd like a T-shirt. Ask for different colors and sizes. Ask about the price.

2 Now you are the salesperson. Small purses are $11.30 and the large ones are $19.70.

UNIT 3b, Exercise 12, page 37

Student B

1 Write questions about Joel with these prompts.

   1 What / do?
   2 Where / live?
   3 Does / have children?
   4 What time / finish work?

2 Answer Student A's questions.

> **Name:** Joel Sartore
> **Job:** [1] _____
> **Company:** *National Geographic* magazine
> **Home:** [2] _____
> **Place of work:** All over the world
> **Children:** [3] _____
> **Language:** English
> **Normal working day:** From nine o'clock to
> [4] _____ o'clock

3 Ask Student A your questions and complete the fact file.

UNIT 6a, Exercise 1, page 70

dollar – Canada
euro – France
peso – Mexico
pound – Egypt
renminbi – China

riyal – Saudi Arabia
rouble – Russia
rupee – Pakistan
yen – Japan

UNIT 5a, Exercise 11, page 59

Student A

You have a recipe for mushroom pizza.

You have:
• two tomatoes
• cheese
• flour
• pepper
• one potato

You need:
• an onion
• mushrooms
• salt
• another tomato
• olive oil

Find out what food you and your partner have and what you need to buy.

> *Do you have an onion?*   *Yes, I do. I have six.*

UNIT 1c, Exercise 7, page 14

Student A

How many people (live/work/have/speak/use) ...?	Spain	The US
population	47 million	_____
Spanish	_____	12%
a service industry (hotels, banks, etc.)	70%	_____
cell phones	_____	Everyone
the Internet	30 million	_____

UNIT 2b, Exercise 10, page 25

Draw six items of furniture in the first room and describe it to your partner. Draw your partner's room below it. Afterwards, compare your rooms.

UNIT 6a, Exercise 8, page 71

Student B

1 Complete the questions about Ichiyo Higuchi, who appears on the 5,000-yen bill, with *was* or *were*.

1 What nationality _____ she?
2 When _____ she born?
3 How many people _____ in her family?
4 What _____ her father's job?
5 _____ they rich?
6 What _____ her job?
7 _____ her books popular?

2 Answer Student A's questions about this person.

Arthur Honegger was born in Paris in 1892, but he wasn't French. He was from Switzerland. Arthur and his wife were musicians. He was a composer and she was a pianist. They were married for 29 years. At first, Honegger's music wasn't popular, but by the nineteen twenties there were concerts of his music all over Europe.

3 Ask your questions and complete the text.

Ichiyo Higuchi was ¹ _____ . She was born in ² _____ . There were ³ _____ people in her family. Her father was a ⁴ _____ , but they ⁵ _____ rich. She was a ⁶ _____ and her books ⁷ _____ very popular.

UNIT 2d, Exercise 6, page 28

Student B

1 You are the salesperson. The T-shirts are all medium or large. There aren't any small ones. There are lots of different colors. The price is $7.50 (medium) and $8.50 (large).

2 Now you are the customer. You'd like a purse. Ask for different colors and sizes. Ask about the price.

UNIT 7c, Exercise 9, page 86

1 Mercury
2 Venus
3 Neptune
4 Earth
5 Venus

UNIT 7a, Exercise 11, page 83

Student A

Read about the trip. Make questions in the simple past with the question words. Then take turns asking the questions and completing the text.

Peter McBride, Mark Rebholz, and John LaNoue are modern pilots. They flew from England to Cape Town in ¹ _____ (when?). Their airplane was from the 1920s and very similar to the *Silver Queen*. They took off from England. They arrived in ³ _____ (where?) three weeks later. They couldn't fly over parts of Africa so they flew over ⁵ _____ (which sea?) and they arrived in Saudi Arabia. Their plane had mechanical problems at Mount Kilimanjaro because of ⁷ _____ (why?). But they fixed the plane and they landed in Cape Town. They flew 3,500 miles, just to relive the past!

UNIT 7d, Exercise 7, page 88

UNIT 10b, Exercise 2, page 120

Student B

Memorizing numbers

Do you often forget phone or house numbers, or PINs? Some people "see" the whole number in their brain. Maybe the numbers are in color or they see the numbers like a picture. You can also repeat the whole number a few times, or learn the numbers in groups: the first two might be your age, your age, and the next three the house number of a friend. We remember better when we make it personal.

UNIT 1c, Exercise 7, page 14

Student B

How many people (live/work/ have/speak/use) …?	Spain	The US
population		300 million
Spanish	100%	
a service industry (hotels, banks, etc.)		55%
cell phones	Everyone	
the Internet		250 million

UNIT 5a, Exercise 11, page 59

Student B

You have a recipe for pierogi.

You have:
- six onions
- salt
- some tomatoes
- meat
- olive oil

You need:
- a potato
- flour
- mushrooms
- butter
- cheese

Find out what food you and your partner have and what you need to buy.

> *Do you have any butter?*   *No, I don't.*

UNIT 7a, Exercise 10, page 83

Student B
Read about the trip. Make questions in the simple past with the question words. Then take turns asking the questions and completing the text.

Peter McBride, Mark Rebholz, and John LaNoue are modern pilots. They flew from England to Cape Town in 1999. Their airplane was from the 1920s and very similar to the *Silver Queen*. They took off from ² _____ (where?). They arrived in Egypt ⁴ _____ (when?). They couldn't fly over parts of Africa so they flew over the Red Sea and arrived in Saudi Arabia. Their plane had mechanical problems at ⁶ _____ (where?) because of the strong wind. But they fixed the plane and they landed in Cape Town. They flew ⁸ _____ (how many miles?) just to relive the past!

UNIT 10b, Exercise 2, page 120

Student C
Memorizing directions and addresses
Taxi drivers learn hundreds of roads and addresses. How do they do it? Some people see the directions in their head. They see a picture of the roads or the buildings. Other people repeat the names of the roads, or the directions. You can also draw the directions on paper. When you draw, use different colors: the brain remembers more when it sees color.

UNIT 6d, Exercise 1, page 76

World Wildlife Fund: It helps animals in the wild and works on conservation and environmental projects.

Save the Children: It helps children around the world in both emergency situations and in long-term relief.

The Red Cross and the Red Crescent: It gives food and medicine to people in wars.

UNIT 8d, Exercise 6, page 100

Discuss these things.
- The subject of the photo
- Location of people and things
- The people (their appearance and what they are doing or wearing)
- Your opinion of the photo

UNIT 1

be (am/is/are)
Form

Affirmative	Negative
I **am** (I'm) 32.	I **am not** (I'm not) Sam.
You/we/they **are** (you're/we're/they're) Mexican.	You/we/they **are not** (aren't) married.
He/she/it **is** (he's/she's/it's) from China.	He/she/it **is not** (isn't) from the US.

Questions	Short answers
Am I in this class?	Yes, I **am**. / No, I'm **not**.
Are you/we/they the same age?	Yes, you/we/they **are**. / No, you/we/they **aren't**.
Is he/she/it from Canada?	Yes, he/she/it **is**. / No, he/she/it **isn't**.

Use

We use short forms (*I'm, He's, They aren't*) in everyday English (speaking and informal writing). We use full forms (*I am, He is, They are not*) in formal writing.

We can also use the negative contracted forms *'s not* and *'re not*.
He isn't a student. → *He's not a student.*
They aren't Turkish. → *They're not Turkish.*

We use full forms in questions and in affirmative short answers.
A: **Is** *he from the Netherlands?*
B: *Yes, he* **is**. (not ~~Yes, he's.~~)

Practice

1 Complete the conversations with the correct form of the verb *be*.

1 A: ___*Are*___ you Anne?
  B: No, I _____ . My name _____ Karine.
2 A: _____ you Chinese?
  B: Yes, we _____ . I _____ from Hong Kong and he _____ from Shanghai.
3 A: _____ Jaime from Bolivia?
  B: Yes, he _____ .
4 A: How old _____ Leo?
  B: He _____ eighteen.
5 A: _____ you students?
  B: Yes, we _____ .
6 A: _____ Pam married?
  B: No, she _____ . She _____ single.
7 A: What _____ your job?
  B: I _____ a scientist.
8 A: Ranulph Fiennes _____ an American explorer.
  B: No, he _____ . He _____ British.

Possessive 's
Form

We add *'s* to a person to talk about relatives and possessions.
Simon's brother (not ~~the brother of Simon~~)
Laura and Ben's parents
Ricardo's last name
Olga's teacher

Practice

2 Add *'s* to the correct word in the sentences about the explorer, Ranulph Fiennes.

1 Ranulph's last name is Fiennes.
2 His second wife name is Louise.
3 Louise son is Alexander.
4 Alexander is Ranulph stepson.
5 Ranulph daughter is Elizabeth.
6 The actors Joseph and Ralph are Ranulph distant cousins.

Possessive adjectives
Form and use

We also use possessive adjectives (*my, your, their*, etc.) to talk about relatives and possessions.

Subject pronoun	Possessive adjective	
I	**my**	**My** wife is Thai.
you	**your**	What's **your** address?
he	**his**	**His** name is David.
she	**her**	What's **her** last name?
it	**its**	France is famous for **its** cheese.
we	**our**	**Our** daughter's a teacher.
you	**your**	Where is **your** farm?
they	**their**	**Their** parents are Chilean.

There is only one form for singular and plural.
our parents (not ~~ours parents~~)

His means "of a man" and *her* means "of a woman."
Peter and his wife (not ~~Peter and her wife~~)
Sarah and her stepfather (not ~~Sarah and his stepfather~~)

Don't confuse *its* (possessive) and *it's* (it is).
It's a big farm. Its name is Wood Farm.

Practice

3 Complete the sentences.

1 _____ name's Tatiana. She's from Ecuador.
2 He's a scientist and _____ wife is a photographer.
3 You're in room 6 and _____ teacher is Stewart.
4 We're Australian, but _____ parents are Vietnamese.
5 I'm Megan and this is _____ husband, Jim.
6 My parents are Spanish. _____ names are Clara and Pedro.

UNIT 2

Plural nouns

Form

Singular	Plural	Spelling rule
chair shoe	chairs shoes	add -s
bus class	buses classes	add -es to nouns ending in -ch,- sh, -s,- ss, and -x
country	countries	change nouns ending in consonant + -y to -ies
shelf	shelves	change nouns ending in -f to -ves

Some nouns have irregular plurals:

man → men   person → people
woman → women   child → children

Use

We normally add -s to make plural nouns:
*It's a map.   They're map**s**.*

We don't use *a* or *an* with plural nouns.
They're climbers. (not ~~They're a climbers~~.)

Practice

1 Write the plurals.

1 room   *rooms*
2 plant   _____
3 family   _____
4 address   _____
5 brother   _____
6 city   _____
7 box   _____
8 glove   _____

this, that, these, those

Form

Singular	Plural
this	these
that	those

Use

We use *this* and *these* to talk about things and people that are near us.
We use *that* and *those* to talk about things and people that are not near us.
We can use *this, that, these,* and *those* with or without nouns.
This coffee is cold.
These gloves are very small.
That's Mount Everest in the distance.
Are those your boots over there?

Practice

2 Complete the sentences with *this* or *these*.

1 ____This____ camera is Japanese.
2 Are _____ your keys?
3 _____ map's not very good.
4 _____ photos are incredible!
5 Is _____ your cell phone?

3 Complete the sentences with *that* or *those*.

1 What's _____?
2 _____ are our bags over there.
3 Are _____ boots new?
4 Is _____ a pen?
5 _____ people are from China.

there is / there are

Form

	Singular	Plural
Affirmative	**There is ('s)** a rug.	**There are** two pictures.
Negative	**There is** no table.	**There are no (aren't)** any beds.
Question	**Is there** a TV?	**Are there** any books?
Short answers	Yes, **there is.** / No, **there isn't.**	Yes, **there are.** / No, **there aren't.**

Use

We use *there is / there are* to say that something exists. We often use them to describe places.
There are two sofas in my living room.

We use *there's, there isn't,* and *there aren't* in everyday English (speaking and informal writing).

We use *any* before a plural noun in negative sentences and questions.
There aren't any pictures on the walls.

Don't confuse *There is* and *There are* with *It is* and *They are.*
There's a rug on the floor. It's Persian.

Practice

4 Complete the conversations with *is*, *'s*, *are*, *isn't*, or *aren't*.

1 A: _Are_ there any plants in the living room?
    B: Yes, there _____ a big one in front of the window.
2 A: _____ there a flashlight in your bag?
    B: No, there _____ , but there _____ a flashlight app on my cell phone.
3 A: _____ there any pictures on the wall?
    B: Yes, there _____ two or three. There _____ a very nice Picasso.
4 A: _____ there a desk in the bedroom?
    B: No, sorry, there _____ .
5 A: _____ there any carpets in the living room?
    B: No, there _____ , but there _____ a big rug.

Prepositions of place

Form

*The computer is **on** the desk.*
*The book is **under** the bed.*

in   on   next to   above   under   in front of   between

behind   on the left   in the middle   on the right   opposite

Use

We use prepositions of place to describe where people and things are.
Where's the umbrella? It's next to the door.

Practice

5 Complete the sentences with these prepositions.

| on (x2)   in   opposite   behind   to |
| between   of |

1 My backpack is _behind_ the door.
2 There's a desk in front _____ me.
3 The first-aid kit is _____ the drawer.
4 There's a bus stop _____ the store.
5 Your gloves are _____ the table.
6 The bathroom is _____ the right.
7 There's a picture _____ the window and the door.
8 The keys are next _____ the phone.

UNIT 3

Simple present (*I/you/we/they*)

Form

Affirmative	Negative
I **live** here.	I **don't** (do not) **live** here.
You **live** here.	You **don't** (do not) **live** here.
We **live** here.	We **don't** (do not) **live** here.
They **live** here.	They **don't** (do not) **live** here.

don't = do + not

Questions	Short answers
Do I **like** city life?	Yes, I **do**. / No, I **don't**.
Do you **like** city life?	Yes, you **do**. / No, you **don't**.
Do we **like** city life?	Yes, we **do**. / No, we **don't**.
Do they **like** city life?	Yes, they **do**. / No, they **don't**.

***Wh*- questions**

Question word	do	Subject	Infinitive
Where	**do**	I/you/we/they	**live**?

In short answers, we use *do* or *don't*. We don't use the full verb.
Do you live downtown? Yes, I do. (not *Yes, I live.*)

Wh- questions start with a question word like *Where, What, What time, Who.*

Use

We use the simple present to talk about:
- permanent situations: *We live in Turkey.*
- general facts: *7,000,000 people live in Bogota.*
- routines: *I go to work by train.*

Practice

1 Complete the sentences with the simple present form of these verbs.

| go   eat   not have   not like   live   work |

1 My grandparents _go_ for a walk every day.
2 I _____ in an art gallery.
3 Many people in Amsterdam _____ a car. They go everywhere by bicycle.
4 We _____ next to a café where we often _____ .
5 I _____ shopping downtown. It's too crowded.

2 Put the words in order to make questions.

1 you / Do / downtown / work ?
Do you work downtown?

2 close / What time / the / stores / do ?

3 Do / work / the bus / take / to / you ?

4 do / What / do / in the evenings / people ?

5 your / friends / Where / do / meet / you ?

Simple present (*he/she/it*)
Form

Affirmative		Negative	
He/she/it	work**s**.	He/she/it	**doesn't** (does not) work.

Yes/No questions	Short answers
Does he work?	Yes, he **does**. / No, he **doesn't**.
Does she work?	Yes, she **does**. / No, she **doesn't**.
Does it work?	Yes, it **does**. / No, it **doesn't**.

Wh- questions

Question word	does	Subject	Infinitive
Where	**does**	he	work?
What	**does**	she	do?
Who	**does**	he	live with?

Spelling rules for simple present affirmative *he/she/it*
- Most verbs: *live → lives, work → works, start → starts*
- Verbs ending with *-s, -sh, -ch, -x: finish → finishes, relax → relaxes*
- Verbs ending with consonant + *-y: study → studies*

Irregular verbs
do → does   have → has   go → goes

Practice
3 Write affirmative (+) and negative (–) sentences, and questions (?).

1 She (work) on a boat (+)
She works on a boat.

2 He (have) children (–)

3 (your husband / work) in an office (?)

4 Sarah (study) archaeology in college (+)

5 Murad (teach) Arabic (–)

4 Complete the sentences with the simple present form of the verbs.

1 I ___*don't have*___ (not have) a job.
2 My son _____ (go) to school by bus.
3 This class _____ (end) at 7 p.m.
4 _____ your mother _____ (work)?
5 What _____ Barney _____ (do)?
6 Lola _____ (not speak) English.

UNIT 4
like/love + *-ing*
Use
After *like* and *love*, verbs are in the *-ing* form:
*They **like** cycling.*
*We **love** playing tennis.*
*I **don't like** singing.*

Form

Infinitive	Verb + *-ing*	Spelling rule
play	play**ing**	With most verbs, add *-ing*.
dance	danc**ing**	Verbs ending in *-e*, delete the *-e* and add *-ing*.
swim	swim**ming**	Verbs ending in a vowel + consonant, double the consonant and add *-ing*.

Practice
1 Complete the sentences with the *-ing* form of these verbs.

climb	dance	do	go	~~run~~	study	travel

1 They like ___*running*___ along the beach.
2 Tom doesn't like _____ to the gym.
3 He doesn't like _____ to rap music.
4 Do you like _____ languages?
5 She loves _____ mountains.
6 They love _____ to different countries.
7 I like _____ Tae Kwon Do.

Adverbs and expressions of frequency
Form

100%	always
	usually
	often
	sometimes
	not often
0%	never

Use

We use adverbs of frequency to talk about how often we do something.

Adverbs of frequency

- One-word adverbs usually go before the main verb or after the verb *be*.
  I sometimes go fishing.
  He's often on the Internet.
- *Sometimes* or *usually* can go at the beginning or end of a sentence.
  Sometimes we go out on Friday evenings. We go out on Friday evenings sometimes.
  Usually, I get up late on the weekend. I get up late on the weekend usually.

Expressions of frequency

When the adverb is a phrase (*every month, once a day, twice a month*) it goes at the end of the sentence.

Practice

2 Put the words in the correct order.
1 on vacation / Karla / books / always / reads

2 tennis / Luke / often / play / doesn't

3 go / the theater / We / to / often

4 boring / is / My / never / life

5 have / in the afternoon / I / a snack / usually

6 always / after work / watches / He / TV

7 usually / on Sundays / We / for a walk / go

8 go / to / my lunch break / I / art galleries / on / sometimes

can/can't

Form

Affirmative and negative		
I/you/he/she/it/we/they	**can** **can't (cannot)**	swim.

Yes/No questions	Short answers
Can I/you/he/she/it/we/they sing?	Yes, I **can**. / No, I **can't**. Yes, she **can**. / No, she **can't**. Yes, we **can**. / No, we **can't**. etc.

Use

We use *can* to talk about ability.
I can speak French. = I know how to speak French.

Can is a modal verb. This means:
- There is no *-s* in the third person singular.
  She can play the guitar. (not ~~She cans play the guitar.~~)
- We don't use *does* or *don't* in the negative.
  I can't drive. (not ~~I don't can drive.~~)
- We don't use *do* or *does* in questions.
  Can you ski? (Not ~~Do you can ski?~~)
- The next verb is the infinitive without *to*.
  He can speak Japanese. (not ~~He can to speak Japanese.~~)

Practice

3 Complete the sentences with *can* or *can't* and one of these verbs.

drive	play	~~run~~	see	sleep	speak	take

1 Slow down! I _can't run_ fast.
2 I'd like a job in Spain, but I _____ Spanish.
3 _____ you _____ tennis?
4 I _____ , but I don't have a car.
5 Where's my bicycle? I _____ it.
6 It's very noisy outside. I _____ .
7 She _____ great photos.

UNIT 5

Count and noncount nouns (*a*, *some*, and *any*)

Form and use

	Count nouns	Noncount nouns
Affirmative	I don't have **an** orange. We have **some** nuts.	It needs **some** salt.
Negative	We don't have **a** lemon. There aren't **any** nuts.	I don't want **any** pasta.
Questions	Do you have **a** banana? Are there **any** nuts?	Do you have **any** milk? Is there **any** bread?

Some nouns you can count. These **count** nouns have both a singular and a plural form. We use them with an indefinite article (*a/an*) or numbers: *an onion, two onions.*

Some nouns you can't count. These **noncount** nouns are singular and have no plural form. We use them with the definite article or no article. You cannot use them with *a/an* or numbers: *water* (~~two waters~~), *pasta* (~~two pastas~~)
I often have pasta for dinner.

some and any

We use *some* in affirmative sentences:
- with plural nouns: *There are some potatoes.*
- with noncount nouns: *There is some water.*

We use *any* with count and noncount nouns:
- in negative sentences: *We don't have any bananas. We don't have any bread.*
- in questions: *Are there any tomatoes? Is there any meat?*

We also use *some* in questions when we ask for or offer something.
Can I have some water?
Would you like some chips?

Practice

1 Complete the sentences with *a, an, some,* or *any.*

1 Are there ___any___ eggs?
2 She usually has _____ cookie with her coffee.
3 I'd like _____ bread, please.
4 There isn't _____ salt in this soup.
5 I often have _____ apple for breakfast.
6 Do you have _____ lentils?
7 There isn't _____ orange juice.
8 Would you like _____ nuts?

a lot of and not much / not many

Form

Affirmative	Negative	Questions
With count nouns: I eat **a lot of** fish.	I don't eat **many / a lot of** cakes.	Do you eat **many / a lot of** eggs?
With noncount nouns: I drink **a lot of** milk.	I don't eat **much / a lot of** salt.	Do you eat **much / a lot of** fruit?

Use

We use *a lot of, much, not much, many,* and *not many* to talk about quantity.

Count nouns
- We use *a lot of* in affirmative and negative sentences, and in questions.
- We use *many* in negative sentences and questions.
- We don't usually use *many* in affirmative sentences.

Noncount nouns
- We use *a lot of* in affirmative and negative sentences, and in questions.
- We use *much* in negative sentences and questions.
- We never use *much* in affirmative sentences.

Note: *a lot of = lots of* (there is no difference in meaning or use)

how much / how many

We use *how much* and *how many* to ask about quantities.
- *How much* + noncount nouns
  How much bread do you want?
- *How many* + count nouns
  How many supermarkets are there?

Practice

2 Choose the correct option to complete the sentences.

1 Do you drink (much) / many water?
2 He eats *much / a lot of* meat.
3 Do you need *much / many* onions?
4 They grow *a lot of / much* potatoes in Peru.
5 How *much / many* fruit do you eat in a week?
6 There isn't *much / many* cheese on this pizza.
7 I don't buy *much / many* food.
8 We don't have *much / many* good restaurants.

UNIT 6

was/were

Form

Was and *were* are the past of *am/is/are.*

Affirmative	Negative
I/he/she/it **was** old.	I/he/she/it **wasn't** old.
You/we/they **were** old.	You/we/they **weren't (were not)** old.

Yes/No questions	Short answers
Was I/he/she/it old?	Yes, I/he/she/it **was.** No, I/he/she/it **wasn't.**
Were you/we/they old?	Yes, you/we/they/**were.** No, you/we/they/**weren't.**

Use

We use *was* and *were* to talk about the past.

Practice

1 Complete the sentences with *was, were, wasn't,* or *weren't*.

1 Marie Curie's face ____was____ on Polish currency in the 1980s.
2 It _____ also on the last French 500 franc bills before the euro.
3 She _____ a scientist and winner of two Nobel prizes.
4 The prizes _____ for her work on radioactivity.
5 She was a French citizen, but she _____ French.
6 She _____ born in Poland.
7 In those days, there _____ any universities with woman students in Poland.
8 Marie and her French husband Pierre _____ married in 1895.
9 Their daughter and her husband _____ also Nobel prize-winners.

Simple past (affirmative): regular and irregular verbs
Form

Affirmative
Regular
I/you/he/she/it/we/they **worked**.
Irregular
I/you/he/she/it/we/they **went**.

Verbs only have one form in the simple past.

Regular verbs
We add *-ed* to regular verbs to form the simple past: *work → worked, walk → walked, play → played*.

Notice the spelling rules for other regular verbs:
- for verbs ending in *-e*, we add *-d*: *live → lived, decide → decided*.
- for two-syllable verbs ending in *-y*, we change the *-y* to *i* and add *-ed*: *study → studied*.
- for verbs ending in vowel + consonant (not *-l, -w, -x,* or *-y*), we double the consonant: *stop → stopped*.

Irregular verbs
Many common verbs have an irregular affirmative form in the simple past:
be → was/were, do → did, go → went, make → made, get → got, cost → cost

Use
We use the simple past to talk about finished actions and events in the past. We often use a time phrase (*yesterday, last week, ten years ago*) with the simple past.
They lived a thousand years ago.
He contacted the museum last week.

Practice

2 Complete the sentences with the simple past of the verbs.

1 They ____paid____ (pay) $5,000 for their car.
2 I _____ (have) a metal detector then.
3 We _____ (go) to Peru last year.
4 George Washington _____ (become) president in 1789.
5 Frida Kahlo _____ (live) in Mexico.
6 My grandfather _____ (work) in a bank.
7 Howard Carter _____ (discover) gold objects in Tutankhamen's tomb.
8 She _____ (make) a gold ring yesterday.

UNIT 7

Simple past: negatives, questions, and short answers
Form and use

Negatives
I/you/he/she/it/we/they **didn't travel** by train.

Questions
Did I/you/he/she/it/we/they **travel** by train?

Short answers
Yes, I/you/he/she/it/we/they **did**.
No, I/you/he/she/it/we/they **didn't**.

Wh- questions
Why/When **did** I/you/he/she/it/we/they **travel** by train?

We use the auxiliary verb *did/didn't* for negatives and questions.
Kate didn't take the train.
Did you use a map?

We also use *did/didn't* for short answers.
Did they drive? Yes, they did.

Remember, we use the infinitive form of the verb.
We didn't go. (not *We didn't went.*)

Practice

1 Complete the conversations with *did* or *didn't*.

1 A: _Did_ you bring a map?
   B: Yes, I _____ . It's here.
2 A: How much _____ the bus ticket cost?
   B: I don't know. I _____ pay.
3 A: _____ you have a good trip?
   B: Yes, we _____ . It was great.
4 A: Who _____ you travel with?
   B: Just my wife. My children _____ come.
5 A: What time _____ the plane take off?
   B: I'm not sure. I _____ look at my watch.
6 A: _____ the *Mayflower* sail to the New World?
   B: Yes, it _____ . Its first journey there was in 1620.
7 A: _____ you visit the transportation museum in Osaka?
   B: No, we _____ . We _____ have time.
8 A: _____ you take a bus to the airport?
   B: Yes, we _____ . It was very easy.

Comparative adjectives

Form

Adjective	Spelling rule	Example
one-syllable adjectives	+ -er + -r if the adjective ends in -e	warm → warmer safe → safer
adjectives ending in one vowel + one consonant	double the consonant + -er	big → bigger
adjectives with two or more syllables	more + adjective	boring → more boring interesting → more interesting
two-syllable adjectives ending in -y	change -y to -ier	easy → easier
irregular adjectives		good → better bad → worse far → farther

We use *than* after a comparative sentence.
*An airplane is faster **than** a ship.*

Use

We use comparative adjectives to compare two things or people.

Practice

2 Write sentences with comparative adjectives.

1 Travel by air / by road (safe)
   Travel by air is safer than by road.
2 My car / your car (old)
3 Trains / buses (expensive)
4 A bike / a car (slow)
5 Learning a language / learning a musical instrument (difficult)
6 Male elephants / females (big)
7 My trip to work / your trip to work (long)

Superlative adjectives

Form

Adjective	Spelling rule	Example
one-syllable adjectives	+ -est + -st if the adjective ends in -e	near → nearest large → largest
adjectives ending in one vowel + one consonant	double the consonant + -est	big → biggest
adjectives with two or more syllables	the most + adjective	the most amazing
two-syllable adjectives ending in -y	change -y to -iest	easy → easiest
irregular adjectives		good → the best bad → the worst far → the farthest

We use *the* before a superlative.
*Neptune is **the farthest planet from the sun.***

Use

We use the superlative form to compare something to other things (*the biggest, best,* etc.) in a group.

Practice

3 Complete the sentences with the superlative form of the adjectives.

1 The HSR (high-speed rail) is _the fastest_ (fast) train in the world.
2 Seoul's subway system is _____ (long) subway system in the world.
3 My car is _____ (small) car on the street.
4 Who's _____ (good) driver here?
5 Neil Armstrong is one of _____ (famous) astronauts in history.
6 Fridays and Sundays are _____ (expensive) days to travel by plane.
7 My trip to Patagonia was _____ (amazing) journey of my life.
8 Atlanta has _____ (busy) airport in the world.

UNIT 8

be vs *have*

We use *be* + adjective to describe appearance (inherent qualities).
She is pretty.
They are tall.
We are Vietnamese.

We use *have* + adjective + noun to describe specific attributes.
He has blue eyes.
I have long hair.
You have a great sense of humor!

In sentences that describe inherent qualities and specific attributes, we can also use *be* + adjective + *with* + noun.
He is tall and he has dark hair. / He is tall with dark hair.

Practice

1 Write sentences with the correct form.

1 Jake / black hair
  Jake has black hair.
2 I / not / Italian
3 Lily / curly hair?
4 Her parents / very smart
5 your car / new?
6 you / blue eyes?
7 Rob and Helen / not / married
8 My phone / expensive

Present continuous
Form

Affirmative	Negative	Question
I'm (am) working.	I'm not (am not) working.	Am I working?
You/we/they're (are) working.	You/we/they aren't (are not) working.	Are you/we/they working?
He/she/it's (is) working.	He/she/it isn't (is not) working.	Is he/she/it working?

We form the present continuous with the simple present of the verb *to be* + verb + *-ing*.

Use

We use the present continuous to talk about:
• things happening now. *I'm eating dinner.*
• things happening around now, but not necessarily at the moment. *She's walking to work a lot these days.*

We don't usually use stative verbs (*be, have, like, love,* etc.) in the present continuous.

Present continuous and simple present
We use the simple present (not the present continuous) to describe a habit or routine.
He usually wears sneakers, but today he's wearing boots.

We use different time expressions with the present continuous and the simple present:

Present continuous
now, these days, at the moment, today, this week/month/year

Simple present
usually, often, every day, once a week, never

Notes

Notice the spelling rules for the *-ing* form:

- for most verbs, add *-ing*: *walk → walking, play → playing, read → reading*
- for verbs ending in a consonant + vowel + consonant, double the last letter of the verb and add *-ing*: *sit → sitting, run → running, put → putting*
- for verbs ending in *-e*, delete the final *-e* and add *-ing*: *make → making, come → coming, write → writing*

Practice

2 Complete the sentences with the simple present or present continuous form of the verbs.

1 Why *are you wearing* (you wear) gloves? Are you cold?
2 I _____ (read) a good book now.
3 She _____ (not work) today.
4 _____ (you usually take) a shower in the morning or at night?
5 Who _____ (you wait) for?
6 He _____ (not like) wearing hats.
7 I can't talk, I'm _____ (make) dinner.
8 Our cousins _____ (stay) with us today and tomorrow.

UNIT 9

going to (for plans)

Form

Affirmative	Negative
I'm (am) going to see a movie.	I'm not (am not) going to see a movie.
You/we/they're (are) going to see a movie.	You/we/they aren't (are not) going to see a movie.
He/she/it's (is) going to see a movie.	He/she/it isn't (is not) going to see a movie.

Questions	Short answers
Am I going to see a movie?	Yes, I am. / No I'm not.
Are you/we/they going to see a movie?	Yes, you/we/they are. / No, you/we/they aren't.
Is he/she/it going to see a movie?	Yes, he/she/it is. / No, he/she/it isn't.

Use

We use *going to* to talk about our plans for the future. *We're going to watch a DVD this evening.*

With the verb *go* we can say *going to go* or *going*. *I'm going to go out tonight. = I'm going out tonight.*

We often use future time expressions with *going to* (e.g., *next week, tonight, tomorrow, this evening*). *We're moving next month.*

Practice

1 Complete the sentences with *going to* and these verbs.

come	~~meet~~	not have	not pay	see
study	visit	write		

1 We *'re going to meet* Abigail at the movies.
2 What movie _____ they _____?
3 _____ Flavia _____ to our party?
4 He _____ a novel next year.
5 _____ you _____ your cousin in Chile?
6 I _____ a vacation this summer.
7 He _____ math next year.
8 I _____ extra money to see the movie in 3D.

Infinitive of purpose

Form and use

We can use an infinitive to talk about why we do something. This is called an infinitive of purpose. *I'm going to Madrid to visit the Prado Museum.* (not *I'm going to Madrid for visit the Prado Museum.*)

We often use the infinitive of purpose to answer the question *Why?* *Why are you going to the store? To get a newspaper.*

Practice

2 Complete the answers to these questions with infinitives of purpose. Use these verbs.

get	invite	learn	make	see	~~take~~

1 Why are you going to get up early tomorrow? *To take* Ben to the airport.
2 Why is she going to Mexico? _____ Spanish.
3 Why are they going to the movies early? _____ good seats.
4 Why are you going to call Jim? _____ him to dinner.
5 Why are you going to buy apples? _____ a fruit salad.
6 Why are you going to the art gallery? _____ a photography exhibition.

Present continuous for future reference

We can use the present continuous to talk about the future and to make future arrangements with another person. *I'm meeting my friends at ten.* *He isn't working tomorrow.* *Where are you eating out tonight?*

UNIT 10
Present perfect
Form

Affirmative	Negative
I/you/we/they**'ve (have) called** several times.	I/you/we/they **haven't (have not) used** a public telephone.
He/she/it**'s (has) been** to Spain.	He/she/it **hasn't been** to Panama.

Questions	Short answers
Have I/you/we/they **seen** that movie?	**Yes,** I/you/we/they **have.** **No,** I/you/we/they **haven't.**
Has he/she/it **arrived?**	**Yes,** he/she/it **has.** **No,** he/she/it **hasn't.**

We form the present perfect with *have/has* + the past participle (*lived, sent*, etc.).

With regular verbs, past participles end in *-ed*. They are the same as the past simple: *book → booked, call → called, play → played*

Many verbs have irregular past participles. They are often, but not always, different from the past simple: *see → saw → seen, write → wrote → written, buy → bought → bought, be → was/were → been, go → went → gone*

Use

We use the present perfect to talk about experiences in the past. We don't say exactly when they happened.
I've made a CD.   I haven't bought DVDs.

With the present perfect we often use *ever* (= in your life) in questions and *never* (not in your life) in negative answers.
Have you ever been to Brazil?   He's never used a map.

We use the affirmative form with *never*.
I've never been to Greece. (not ~~I haven't never been to Greece.~~)

Practice

1 Complete the sentences with the present perfect form of the verbs.

1 I *'ve downloaded* (download) a lot of music.
2 My mother _____ (travel) to Tokyo.
3 My aunt _____ (never/use) a computer.
4 I _____ (not write) many letters by hand.
5 _____ you ever _____ (cook) Indian food?
6 She _____ (not read) any plays.
7 He _____ (never / buy) a CD.

Present perfect and simple past
Use
Present perfect
We use the present perfect when we talk about something in the past without saying exactly when it happened.
I've been to Costa Rica.
We often use words like *ever* and *never* because they do not give an exact time.
Have you ever learned a new language?

Simple past
We use the simple past when we talk about an action that started and ended in the past. We often say when it happened. We often use it with past time expressions like *last week, yesterday, in 2012.*
We went to Beijing in 2008. (not ~~We have been to Beijing in 2008.~~)

We use the simple past with the question *When ...?*
When did he win the competition? (not ~~When has he won the competition?~~)

Practice

2 Choose the correct option to complete the conversations.

1 A: *Have you ever been / Did you ever go* to Rome?
   B: Yes, I *have / did*. I *have worked / worked* there between 2005 and 2008.
2 A: *I've forgotten / forgot* his name.
   B: It's Roger. He *was / has been* in college with me last year.
3 A: *Have you seen / Did you see* Mark yesterday?
   B: Yes, I *did / have*. I *saw / have seen* him here.
4 A: What *have you done / did you do* last night?
   B: Some friends *have come / came* over.
5 A: What *have you learned / did you learn* in your guitar lesson last week?
   B: The teacher *taught / has taught* us chords.
6 A: *Have you ever studied / Did you ever study* a foreign language?
   B: Yes, I *have / did*. I *'ve learned / learned* Arabic last year.
7 A: Feng's *visited / visited* a lot of countries.
   B: *Have you ever traveled / Did you ever travel* with him?
8 A: *Have you won / Did you win* a prize in the dance competition last month?
   B: No, I *haven't / didn't*, but I *had / have had* fun.

UNIT 11

should/shouldn't
Form

Affirmative	Negative
I/you/he/she/it/we/they **should** take an umbrella.	I/you/he/she/it/we/they **shouldn't** take a lot of cash.

Questions	Short answers
Should I/you/he/she/it/we/they buy a ticket in advance?	**Yes,** I/you/he/she/it/we/they **should.** **No,** I/you/he/she/it/we/they **shouldn't.**

Should is a modal verb. Remember that this means:

- There is no third person *-s*.
  He should go. (not *He shoulds go.*)
- There is no *to* before the verb.
  You should do it. (not *You should to do it.*)
- The negative is with *not* (*n't*).
  You shouldn't do it. (not *You don't should do it.*)
- There is no auxiliary *do* in questions.
  Should I come? (not *Do I should come?*)

Use

We use *should* to give advice.
You should put sunscreen on. = I think it's a good idea.
You shouldn't go on your own. = I think it's a bad idea.

Practice

1 Complete the sentences with *should* or *shouldn't* and these verbs.

> ~~do~~   eat   get   go   learn   stay   watch   wear

1 He ___*should do*___ some exercise. He needs it!
2 You _____ gloves. It's very cold.
3 You _____ a tango show when you're in Buenos Aires.
4 I _____ some Italian phrases before I go to Sicily.
5 You _____ at that restaurant. The food's terrible.
6 I _____ a new job. This one's stressful.
7 They _____ at that hotel. It's noisy.
8 I _____ to bed late tonight. I've got an exam tomorrow.

have to / don't have to, can/can't
Form

Affirmative	Negative
I/you/we/they **have to** show a passport.	I/you/we/they **don't have to** show a passport.
He/she/it **has to** show a passport.	He/she/it **doesn't have to** show a passport.

Questions	Short answers
Do I/you/we/they **have to** buy a ticket?	**Yes,** I/you/we/they **do.** **No,** I/you/we/they **don't.**
Does he/she/it **have to** buy a ticket?	**Yes,** he/she/it **does.** **No,** he/she/it **doesn't.**

Affirmative	Negative
I/you/he/she/it/we/they **can** take one bag on the plane.	I/you/he/she/it/we/they **can't** smoke on the plane.

Use

We use *have to, don't have to, can,* and *can't* to talk about rules and possibilities.

- We use *have to* + infinitive to say that something is necessary.
  You have to turn off your cell phone on the plane.
- We use *don't have to* to say that something is not necessary.
  You don't have to show your passport.
- We use *can* to say that something is possible.
  You can check in online.
- We use *can't* to say that something is not possible.
  Passengers can't take knives in their carry-on bag.

Practice

2 Choose the correct option (a–c) to complete the sentences.

1 Passengers _____ check in online.
  a have to   b can't   © can
2 Pilots _____ wear a uniform.
  a have to   b can't   c can
3 We _____ check in. I did it online.
  a have to   b don't have to   c can
4 You _____ smoke on a plane.
  a can   b can't   c don't have to
5 You _____ pay for food on planes.
  a can often   b can't often   c often have to
6 You usually _____ book plane tickets before you fly.
  a have to   b don't have to   c can't
7 You _____ stand up when a plane is taking off.
  a have to   b can   c can't
8 Sometimes children _____ fly for free.
  a don't have to   b can   c can't

everywhere, somewhere, nowhere, anywhere

Form

	-where	-thing	-body
every-	everywhere	everything	everybody
some-	somewhere	something	somebody
no-	nowhere	nothing	nobody
any-	anywhere	anything	anybody

Use

- Use these words with singular verbs.
  Everybody likes traveling. (not ~~like~~)
- Use *any-* in negative sentences and questions.
  I didn't buy anything in the stores.
  Is there anywhere to stay in this town?

Practice

3 Write in the missing part of the word.

1 There are cafés every *where* in Paris.
2 He wants to buy some _____ here.
3 I called the airline, but no _____ answered.
4 Hello? Is any _____ there?
5 I think _____ body needs a vacation.
6 I put my sunglasses _____ where and I can't find them.
7 I'm bored. There's _____ thing to do!
8 I haven't been _____ where recently.

UNIT 12

will/won't

Form

Affirmative	Negative
I/you/he/she/it/we'll (will) change.	I/you/he/she/it/we won't (will not) change.

Question	Short answers
Will I/you/he/she/it/we/they live for a long time?	Yes, I/you/he/she/it/we/they will. No, I/you/he/she/it/we/they won't.

Will is a modal verb. This means:
- There is no third person *-s*.
  He will go. (not ~~He wills go.~~)
- There is no *to* before the verb.
  It will get hotter. (not ~~It will to get hotter.~~)
- The negative is with *not* (*n't*).
  It won't be cold. (not ~~It don't will be cold.~~)
- There is no auxiliary *do* in questions.
  Will they come? (not ~~Do they will come?~~)

Use

We use *will* and *won't* to make predictions.
The Earth will get warmer. / He won't buy a car.

We often use *think* or *don't think* before *will* when we make predictions.
I think it'll snow tomorrow. / I don't think we'll go to Peru.

We usually say *I don't think + will*, not *I think + won't*.

Practice

1 Complete the sentences with *will* (*'ll*) or *won't*.

1 We *won't* buy a car that's too expensive.
2 Do you think it _____ snow this weekend?
3 I don't think we _____ see him again.
4 It's a national holiday tomorrow so the shops _____ be open.
5 He's doing his homework now because he _____ have time this evening.
6 I'm going to the doctor's at 9 a.m. so I _____ miss the meeting. Sorry.

Definite *the* or no article before names

Form and use

the	no article
- deserts: the Sahara - seas: the Red Sea - oceans: the Atlantic - rivers: the Nile - plural names or groups of places: the United States/ the U.S., the Alps, the Philippines	- continents: Africa - countries: Mexico - states: California - towns and cities: Milan - places in towns and cities (streets, buildings, etc.): Hidalgo Street, Peking University, Shinjuku Station - lakes: Lake Tahoe - a single mountain: Mount Everest

Practice

2 Add *the* to the correct place (or places) in the sentences. If the sentence is correct, mark it (✓).

1 We went to Andes when we were in Argentina.
2 Africa is bigger than Europe.
3 Mississippi is the longest river in United States.
4 Mont Blanc is the highest mountain in Alps.
5 Would you like to go to Lanzarote in Canary Islands?
6 Have you ever swum in Atlantic Ocean?
7 I'd love to visit Atacama desert.

Unit 1

🔊 1

I: Hello. What's your name?
M: My name's Mike Burney.
I: Are you from Great Britain?
M: Yes, I'm from the UK, but I travel all the time.
I: And are you married?
M: Yes, I am. My wife's name is Sally. She isn't at home at the moment.
I: Why? What's her job?
M: She's also an explorer and we often travel together.
I: Is she from the UK too?
M: No, she isn't. She's from Canada.
I: Are you the same age?
M: No, we aren't. I'm thirty-six and Sally is thirty-five.

🔊 2

1 I'm thirty-one.
2 Are you from England?
3 No, I'm not.
4 Her name's Helena.
5 We aren't from the US.
6 We're from Canada.
7 No, he isn't.
8 Is he married?

🔊 3

1 they're / their
2 he's / his
3 its / it's
4 are / our
5 you're / your

🔊 4

A B C D E F G H I J K L M N O P Q R S T U V W X Y Z

🔊 5

1 R: Hello, can I help you?
G: Hi. Yes, I'm at this conference but I'm early.
R: Yes, you're the first! That's OK. What's your name?
G: Gary.
R: Hi Gary. My name's Rita. I'm the conference manager.
G: Nice to meet you, Rita.
R: Nice to meet you too. What's your last name, Gary?
G: Laurens.
W: Laurens? Are you on my list? Can you spell that?
G: Sure. It's L-A-U-R-E-N-S.
R: OK. There's another person with that name at this conference.
G: Really?
W: Yes, but her last name is Lawrence. L-A-W-R-E-N-C-E.

2 R: Oh! Here's someone else. Hello. My name's Rita and I'm the conference manager.
V: Hi, I'm Valerie.
R: That's a beautiful name. What's your surname Valerie?
V: Moreau. That's M-O-R-E-A-U.
R: M, M, M, Mason, Moore, Moreau! OK. Well, you're the second person here, so I'd like to introduce you to Gary. He's from the U.S.
G: Nice to meet you, Valerie.
V: Nice to meet you too.
G: Are you from France?
V: Actually no, I'm from an island in the Pacific Ocean.
G: New Caledonia?
V: That's right!
R: Well, I have to go. Nice talking to both of you.
G: Bye Rita. See you later.
V: Bye.

Unit 2

🔊 6

I: Hello. Today, I'm in the north of Scotland. We're at the bottom of a mountain. It's very beautiful but it's very cold and I'm here with Andy Torbet. Andy, are you from Scotland?
A: Yes, I am. I'm from Aberdeen.

I: Now Andy, you're a professional climber so you've got a backpack with you today. What's always in your backpack?
A: Well, this is my hat. It's good because it's cold today, but it's also important when it's hot because of the sun.
I: I see. And what's this?
A: It's a first-aid kit. It's always in my backpack.
I: Mm. Good idea. And what's that?
A: It's my camera. I take it everywhere. And these are my climbing boots.
I: Right. And over there. What are those?
A: My gloves.
I: Right, they ARE important today! OK. So we've got everything. Let's start climbing.
A: Sure. Let's go.

🔊 7

I: I see. And what's this?
A: It's a first-aid kit. It's always in my backpack.
I: Mm. Good idea. And what's that?
A: It's my camera. I take it everywhere. And these are my climbing boots.
I: Right. And over there. What are those?
A: My gloves.

🔊 8

1 this
2 these
3 keys
4 it
5 pink
6 green
7 big
8 read

🔊 9

1. Mexican
2. Chinese
3. Chilean
4. Egyptian
5. Spanish
6. Brazilian
7. Turkish
8. Portuguese

🔊 10

1 A: Hello, can I help you?
B: Yes, I'd like some coffee, please.
A: Large or small?
B: Large, please.
A: That's three fifty.

2 A: Hi, can I help you?
B: Yes. These purses are nice, but they're very small. Are there different sizes?
A: Yes, there are. … These are large.
B: Is there a medium size?
A: No. Only two sizes.
B: OK. And are there other colors?
A: Yes, these red ones.
B: Oh, those are nice! How much are they?
A: They're nineteen dollars and thirty-five cents.

3 A: Hi, can I help you?
B: Hi, I'd like a ball, please.
A: A soccer ball? A tennis ball?
B: Sorry, a soccer ball.
A: Well, the soccer balls are here.
B: Are they all black and white?
A: Umm, no. There are different colors for different teams. This one's red, white and blue for Team USA.
B: Is there one for Brazil?
A: No, there isn't … sorry.
B: Oh. OK, that one, please.
A: This one?
B: Yes, please. How much is it?
A: It's twenty-one dollars.

🔊 11

This ball is nice, but that one is horrible!

Unit 3

🔊 12

It's twelve o'clock at night and I'm in the Midnight Sun restaurant in the north of Norway. It's very busy and very popular with Norwegians and tourists because the food here is great. It's called the Midnight Sun restaurant because in the summer in Norway, the sun is always in the sky. There's light for twenty-four hours a day, and so this restaurant is open all day and all night.

🔊 13

1 It's six o'clock.
2 It's three thirty.
3 It's nine twenty-five.
4 It's quarter to four.
5 It's five minutes past two.
6 It's two minutes to twelve.

🔊 14

R: Do you have a car in New York?
S: No, I don't. I go everywhere by bike.
R: Really? Where do you live?
S: Downtown, in Manhattan.
R: Is it expensive?
S: Yes, it is. Well, the stores are expensive, but there are lots of free places like art galleries and museums.
R: Sounds great. Do you like art?
S: Yes, I do. And I like the theater. This city has great theaters!
R: I'm sure. And what do you do?
S: I'm a student and I work in a restaurant at lunchtime. It's popular with tourists so it's crowded every day.
R: So you're very busy! What time do you get off work?
S: At about three o'clock. After work I go home or I go to Central Park. I really like it. It's beautiful and quiet. I often meet friends there.

🔊 15

I: Today I'm with Frank Richards. Frank, what do you do exactly?
F: I'm a marine archaeologist. I work for a university and I study places under the sea.
I: Where do you work? In an office?
F: I have one, but I don't work in an office very often. I'm usually on a boat or underwater.
I: What time do you start work?
F: Well, it depends. On the boat, I get up at just after five o'clock. I work with a team of other marine biologists and I meet everyone for breakfast at about six. During breakfast, we talk about the day. After breakfast, I start work. It's a long day.
I: Do you work late?
F: On the boat, yes, but I don't finish late when I'm at home.
I: Do you have a family?
F: Yes, I live with my wife and my son. Sometimes my son goes to work with me. He loves the boats!

🔊 16

1. works
2. lives
3. finishes
4. studies
5. gets
6. meets
7. starts
8. loves
9. speaks
10. teaches
11. goes
12. travels

🔊 17

1 What does Frank do? He's a marine archaeologist.
2 Where does James come from? England.
3 When does Frank start work? After breakfast.
4 Does James have an office? Yes, he does.
5 Does Frank finish work early? No, he doesn't.

🔊 18

1 1, 3, 5, 7, 9, 11, 13
2 11, 21, 31, 41, 51, 61, 71
3 21st, 31st, 41st, 51st, 61st, 71st, 81st
4 1st, 2nd, 3rd, 4th, 5th, 6th, 7th

🔊 19

T: Hi, we'd like to go to the aquarium. Is it near here?
G: It's about fifteen minutes away, but you go past some interesting places on the way. Here's a map. Go straight on Decatur Street and continue on Marietta Street. Cross Spring Street and turn right on Centennial Olympic Park Drive. The park is on your left. It's very nice. Go left at the top of the park and on the right there's the World of Coca-Cola.
T: Oh, that sounds interesting.
G: Yes, it is. Go past it and the aquarium is opposite.
T: Great. Thanks a lot.

Unit 4

💿 20

1 Well, in my free time I go shopping. I go downtown every Saturday with friends. It's fun!
2 In my free time, I go fishing with my brother. We get up early in the morning and drive for about two hours. It's quiet and very relaxing.
3 After work, I go to the gym. I go about three times a week. After a long day with lots of other people, it's nice to go on your own and it's good for you, of course.

💿 21

playing   listening   singing   watching
going   doing   dancing   shopping

💿 22

Paul Nicklen is a nature photographer. He usually works in the Arctic, but he travels to other places too. His photos include bears in British Columbia and leopard seals in Antarctica. He goes to the Arctic at least once a year—between August and November, you can see polar bears every day. But he doesn't only work in cold places. Sometimes he goes to warm climates, like Florida, where he photographs manatees. When he is not traveling, you can find Paul at his home on Vancouver Island in Canada.

💿 23

1 I'm always late for work.
2 We don't often take breaks.
3 How often do you go there?
4 I go to the gym twice a week.

💿 24

T: Hello, Gap Year Volunteer Work. Can I help you?
S: Oh, hi! I'd like some information about your gap year jobs. I'm a student and I want to travel next year. Do you have any interesting volunteer jobs?
T: Sure. We have a job for English teachers. Are you good at teaching?
S: Umm, I don't know. I can speak English well, but what other jobs are there?
T: Can you write? There's an English newspaper in Bolivia. They need journalists. But it's for eighteen months.
S: No, I can't go for eighteen months. And I'm not very good at writing. Is there anything else?
T: Do you like animals?
S: Yes, I love them!
T: Well, we have a job in Zambia. It's with lion cubs.
S: Wow! That sounds interesting. What's the job exactly?

💿 25

1 Are you good at teaching?
2 I'm not very good at writing.
3 Can you write?
4 I can speak English well.
5 Do you like animals?
6 Yes, I love them!

Unit 5

💿 26

1 chicken
2 juice
3 cheese
4 orange

💿 27

1 This is kabsa. It's a popular dish in my country, Saudi Arabia, and in other countries like it. You need some chicken or some people make it with fish. Cook the chicken with an onion, some salt and pepper, and other seasonings. Some tomatoes are good with it as well. We eat it with rice. And I put some nuts and raisins on the top. It's delicious!
2 Ceviche is popular in Peru, but also in countries like Chile. It's easy to make. It's fish, but you don't cook it. You put lemon juice on the fish and this "cooks" it. Sometimes we eat it with onions and maybe a salad as well. You eat it cold.
3 Spaghetti Bolognese is a famous dish all over the world but the real Bolognese comes from my city of Bologna, in Italy. Our city's dish is pasta with Bolognese sauce. People put different things in the sauce and every Italian has his or her favorite recipe. For example, some people use carrots. I don't use any carrots but you always need some meat, onions, and tomatoes. You eat it hot but when we have some left, I eat it cold for lunch the next day.

💿 28

M: Hello, can I help you?
C: Yes. I'd like some bananas, please.
M: These are nice and fresh.
C: OK.
M: How many do you want?
C: Umm, they're quite big so six, please.
M: OK. Anything else?
C: Yes. Some rice, please.
M: How much do you want? A pound?
C: Yes, a pound.
M: Here you go. And what about some of this sauce. It's local.
C: Is it hot?
M: Yeah, it's hot, but it goes with anything.
C: OK.
M: How many do you want?
C: Just one bottle … oh actually, two. And I also need some bread. Do you sell any?
M: No, but there's a place on the other side of the market. So, that's six bananas, a pound of rice, and two bottles of sauce.

💿 29

1 A lot of people in Brazil eat fruit for breakfast.
2 I live in the United States of America.
3 I'd like a bottle of water, please.
4 A friend of mine is vegetarian.
5 I eat my main meal in the middle of the day.
6 There are many varieties of potato.

💿 30

A: This is a nice place.
B: Yes, it's one of my favorite restaurants. They have great pizzas.
C: Good afternoon. How are you today?
B: We're great, thanks.
C: Great. My name's Arthur and I'm your waiter today. So here is the menu. Can I get you anything to drink first?
A: Yes, I'd like a bottle of water, please. Sparkling.
B: Oh, good idea.
C: One bottle or two?
B: One for both of us, thanks.
C: OK.
B: Well, the garlic fries are really good.
A: Yes, they look good. But I don't want an appetizer. I'll have the seafood special.
B: Really? Are you sure?
A: Well, I'd also like dessert …
B: OK.
C: Hi. Here's your water. Are you ready to order?
A: Yes, I'd like the seafood special.
C: OK. Good choice.
B: And I'd like a four-cheese pizza.
C: OK. Any appetizers?
B: No, thanks. We're fine.
C: OK. So, one seafood special and one four-cheese pizza.
A: That was delicious.
B: Good. Are you ready for dessert?
A: Actually, I'm full.
C: Hi. How was everything?
B: Very good, thanks.
C: Can I get you anything else? Some dessert?
A: No, thanks. Could we have the check, please?
C: Oh, sure.

Unit 6

💿 32

Is there a popular shopping district in your city? That's usually a good place for street musicians to earn money. These mariachi often play in the street because people give them coins and small amounts of money. But after a few hours, that can add up to a lot of money. One of the best places on the street for street musicians is near a currency exchange office. Tourists go there and change their money. Then, when they come out, they often give their small coins to the musicians before they go shopping.

💿 33

1 A: Hello, I work for the museum and we'd like to interview visitors. Your answers can really help the museum in the future.
   B: Yeah, sure.
   A: Great! So, my first question is: Are you here to visit all of the museum or are you here to see one exhibition?
   B: Actually, I'm interested in the exhibition of Anglo-Saxon objects.
   A: Oh, that's good.
   B: Yeah, it's very exciting because I read a lot of history books about the Anglo-Saxons.
   A: OK. And how do you know about the exhibition?
   B: I read an article about it in the newspaper.
2 A: Excuse me, I work for the museum. Can I ask you some questions about your visit today?
   C: Umm, sure. What kind of questions?
   A: Well, my first question is this: Are you here to visit all of the museum or are you here to see one exhibition?
   C: I don't know, really. My children have a school project about archaeology and history so we came here. It's my first time in a museum.
   A: Really? Is it interesting?
   C: Not for me. I think history's boring but my children are excited.
   A: Oh. Well, are they interested in a special period of history?
   C: I don't know. I'll ask them. Kids! Kids!

🔊 34

1	live	lived
2	decide	decided
3	like	liked
4	want	wanted
5	start	started
6	play	played
7	visit	visited
8	travel	traveled

🔊 35

1 A: Hi? Hello? I'm collecting for a charity.
   B: Umm, what's it for exactly?
   A: It's for poor children in different countries. We use the money for food and hospitals and also for new schools. So could you give us something?
   B: OK. Here you are.
   A: Thank you!
   B: You're welcome.

2 A: Hey. Can I ask you something?
   B: Yes, of course. What is it?
   A: Well, I don't have any money until tomorrow. Could you lend me some money?
   B: I'm sorry, but I can't.
   A: Don't worry. I can ask someone else.
   B: OK. Sorry.

3 A: Oh no! It's two dollars for the parking lot. I only have a five-dollar bill.
   B: So what's the problem?
   A: The machine only takes coins. You can't use bills. Can I borrow some money?
   B: Actually, I don't have any coins. I only have a ten-dollar bill! But look! It takes credit cards.
   A: I don't have a credit card.
   B: Don't worry. I do.

🔊 36

Could you give us something?

Can I ask you something?

Could you lend me some money?

Can I borrow some money?

Unit 7

🔊 37

I: This week's program is about a famous journey nearly one hundred years ago. In 1920, an airplane called the *Silver Queen* traveled from England to Cape Town. It was the first airplane to travel on this journey. Here in the studio to tell us about this journey is travel historian Nigel Ross.
H: Hello.
I: So Nigel, in 1920, this was a small airplane and there weren't many airports in Africa at that time. How dangerous was this journey?
H: Oh, it was very dangerous for the two pilots.
I: Yes, the two pilots were Pierre Van Ryneveld and Quintin Brand. Did they have maps for this journey?
H: Yes, they did. Well, for some parts of the journey. For example, they had maps for Europe, Egypt and South Africa. But they didn't have maps for other parts of Africa.
I: And why did they go on this journey? Was it for the money?
H: All travelers and explorers go for different reasons. But Van Ryneveld and Brand didn't go for the money. I think they flew there because it was new. They wanted to be the first.

🔊 38

1 The saiga lives in Central Asia. In the spring, it walks to higher places. A male saiga can walk about 22 miles a day and it's faster than a female. The journey is more difficult for a female saiga because she has her calf in the spring.

2 Many turtles swim longer distances than other sea animals, but the loggerhead turtle has a longer journey than other turtles. It leaves the beach as a baby and it swims around 9,000 miles. Fifteen years later, the female turtle returns to the same beach and lays eggs.

3 Tree frogs go on shorter journeys than other animals, but for a small tree frog the journey isn't easier. Every spring it climbs down a tree. That's about 100 feet. It lays eggs in water and then returns up the tree. For a tree frog, that's a very long journey.

🔊 39

1 Africa is hotter than Europe.
2 Australia isn't colder than Antarctica.

🔊 40

1 C: Doctor Egan? Doctor Egan?
   E: Yes, are you Doctor Cunningham?
   C: That's right. Nice to meet you. But please, call me Sonia.
   E: Nice to meet you too, Sonia. I'm Charles.
   C: How was your flight?
   E: Not bad. A little tiring because we were delayed for ten hours.
   C: That's right. I got your message.
   E: Oh, that's good. But I had a good night's sleep at the airport hotel.
   C: Oh, was it comfortable?
   E: Yes, very. I feel fine now.
   C: Great! OK. My car is outside.
   E: Good. Let's go.

2 F: Hi, how was your trip?
   E: Very interesting. And I had some very useful meetings with Doctor Cunningham.
   F: Good. Did you try the local food?
   E: Yes, I did. It was delicious. I ate fresh seafood every night.
   F: And what was the weather like?
   E: Terrible! On the second day we couldn't travel anywhere.
   F: Why? What happened?
   E: There was a terrible storm. It rained for twenty-four hours and all the roads were closed.

🔊 41

1 How was your flight?
2 Was it comfortable?
3 Did you try the local food?
4 What was the weather like?
5 Why? What happened?

Unit 8

🔊 42

A: I've got some photographs here from my vacation in Spain.
B: Oh, let me see.
A: This one is from a town called Banyoles. It's in Catalonia.
B: What's this one?
A: This is of three children in masks. It was a special festival. They always have it in the summer. People come from all over for the food and music.
B: Why do they have those masks?
A: It's part of the festival. The masks are called *capgrossos* in the local language. I think they're a little ugly.
B: Oh no! I don't think so. He has an amazing white face. And look at those red cheeks!
A: Yeah, but he doesn't have any eyebrows.
B: Oh, that's right. Well, he has one. So are they brothers and sister?
A: Yes, that's right. I think this one's the oldest brother. He's tall, or maybe it's just the hat. And she's his little sister. She has these great big blue eyes.
B: She's similar to my daughter with that blonde hair and the red ribbon.
A: I hope she isn't!

🔊 43

Reinier Gerritsen is one of my favorite photographers. He's from the Netherlands, but you can often see his photos around the world, in magazines and sometimes in galleries. I've got some books by him as well. His photos are very interesting. They often show people in their everyday life. This one is on the New York subway. It's early morning so I think most of the people are traveling to work. They're all standing close together, but they aren't talking to each other. Well, on the right, the man and woman are talking, but the others aren't. The woman in the middle is reading her book. And in front of her, the woman with blonde hair is listening to music. Then the other blonde woman on the left is watching her. I'm not sure what she's thinking, but she looks a little sad. Oh, and look at the other woman at the back. She's looking straight at the photographer. I take the train to work every day, but I never think about the other people. I like it because I don't normally look at people very closely. But Gerritsen does.

🔊 44

interesting

sometimes

everyday

listening

blonde

closely

Unit 9

🔊 45

C: Hey, Beata! Stop!

B: Oh, hi Carlos! Sorry, but I'm going to buy a ticket for the next movie. It starts in five minutes. Are you going to see a movie too?

C: No, I'm not, but what are you doing afterwards? José, Monica, and I are going to have dinner at a Japanese restaurant. Do you want to come?

B: No, thanks. I'm not going to stay out late tonight. I'm tired.

C: That's OK.

B: Got to go. Bye.

C: Bye. See you later.

🔊 46

1 We're going to see a movie at the new theater.
2 I'm not going to watch this DVD.
3 Are you going to buy the tickets online or at the movie theater?
4 What time are they going to go to the movie theater?
5 I'm not going to sit at the front of the movie theater.
6 Where are you going to sit?
7 They're going to meet us after the movie?
8 I'm never going to watch a movie by that director again!

🔊 47

I: Jack Gazzolo is a movie director. He travels to different parts of the world to shoot animals in the wild. You can see his movies on television and on the Internet. Today I'm talking to Jack about his movies. So, Jack, how do you plan a movie?

J: At the beginning, there is a lot of planning for the trip. You have heavy camera equipment so it's expensive to travel. And you often need special visas to film in some countries.

I: How many people work on the movie?

J: It depends on the movie. But there's always a director and a camera person. On bigger movies, you need more people.

I: And how long does it take to make a movie?

J: Well, I'm planning a movie at the moment and we're going to shoot it in the summer. Then I'm going to edit it in the autumn. So in total, it takes about a year.

I: So tell us about your next film project. Where are you going?

J: To Brazil.

I: Why are you going there?

J: I'm going to Brazil to make a movie for television. It's about a tribe in the Amazon. After that, I'm going to Argentina for three weeks.

I: Why are you going there?

J: To take a vacation!

🔊 48

1 R: Hi Adriana. It's Rachel.

A: Hi. Sorry, but I'm at work. I can't talk now.

R: I know, but I'm going to the theater tonight. I've got two tickets for *Phantom of the Opera*. My friend works at the theater and sometimes he gets free tickets.

A: Great.

R: So would you like to come?

A: Thanks, I'd love to. When is it?

R: Tonight!

A: Tonight?

R: Yes, are you free?

A: I'm sorry, but I'm working late tonight.

R: Oh. Can't you ask your manager?

A: I can try.

R: OK. Bye.

2 R: Hello?

A: Hi Rachel. It's me again. Do you still have the extra ticket?

R: Yes, why? Do you want to go?

A: Yes, my manager said I can leave early. What time does it start?

R: At seven thirty, so let's meet at seven outside the theater.

A: That's great! See you at seven.

🔊 49

1 I'd love to!
2 I'd really like to!
3 That's great!
4 That sounds fantastic!

Unit 10

🔊 50

A: Hi, I'd like to ask you a few questions about how technology has changed your life.

B: Sure, go ahead.

A: So, have you ever booked a vacation with a travel agent?

B: Yes, I have but it was a long time ago. These days I do it online.

A: Thanks. Here's the next question. Have you ever bought a CD?

B: Actually, yes, I *have* bought a CD. Normally I download music, but last week I bought a CD for my father. It was his birthday and he doesn't know how to download music.

A: I see. And before a car trip, have you ever used a map?

B: Yes, I have. Well, I did in the past but now I use my GPS, because I drive a lot for my job.

A: OK. And what about money? Have you ever paid for something by check?

B: No, because I've never had a checkbook. I pay for everything with a credit card. Oh, and I also do online banking.

A: Interesting. And TV. Have you ever watched a program while it's on TV?

B: Yes, of course. I do that every night.

A: So you never watch TV programs online?

B: Oh, I see what you mean. Umm, well, I have watched videos on YouTube.

A: OK. And finally, have you ever sent a letter in an envelope?

B: I'm not sure. Let me think. Umm, no, I haven't because I send emails or texts.

🔊 51

1 Have you ever sent a letter?
2 Yes, he has.
3 I haven't called anyone from a pay phone.
4 No, she hasn't!
5 We've never written letters by hand.
6 She's bought a CD.

7 No, I haven't.
8 The computer hasn't printed your photo.

🔊 52

Do you always forget names and faces? All the time? And how many numbers like telephone numbers can you remember? Not many? Well, meet Nelson Dellis. Nelson can listen to 99 names and look at their faces. Then he can memorize every one of them. He can also hear 300 different numbers and then repeat them.

Because of his special memory, Nelson has won the USA Memory Championship twice. He won the competition in 2011 and again in 2012. The USA Memory Championships are like the Olympic Games, but the athletes train their brains and they take different memory tests.

So how does Nelson do it? He says he doesn't have a special memory. Like normal people, he's forgotten names, dates, and numbers, but in 2010 he studied memory techniques and he practiced for hours and hours every day. Since then, he's won competitions and he's taught his techniques to people all over the US.

🔊 53

R: Hello, Omarox Engineering.

O: Hello, Richard. This is Oscar.

R: Hello, Oscar. Where are you now?

O: I'm in Kuala Lumpur.

R: Great. What time is it there?

O: Umm, it's three o'clock.

R: Is that three in the morning?

O: No, in the afternoon. I just arrived but my cell isn't working. I'm calling from a telephone at the hotel.

R: I see.

O: So I want to give you the name of my hotel for the next two days. It's the Ancasa Hotel.

R: Just a minute. I need a pen. OK. Sorry, was that the Encasa Hotel?

O: No, the Ancasa Hotel. A for apple.

R: Oh, sorry. Ancasa.

O: And the number is six oh three, two one six nine, two two, six six.

R: So that's six zero three, two one six nine, two two, six six.

O: That's right.

R: Is there anything else?

O: Yes, one thing. Did you call our colleagues about tomorrow?

R: Yes, I did. They can meet you at three.

O: Good. And did you email me all the designs?

R: No, I didn't because your email wasn't working. The email came back three times this morning.

O: That's because my cell isn't receiving email. Can you put them on the company website so I can download them?

R: Done.

O: Oh, great. Thanks. Bye for now.

54

1 A: Is that three in the morning?
  B: No, in the afternoon.
2 A: Was that the Encasa Hotel?
  B: No, the Ancasa Hotel.
3 A: Is that E for England?
  B: No, it's A for apple.

55

V: Hello. This is the Ancasa Hotel. Please leave a message after the tone.
R: Hello. This is Richard Sanger calling. That's S-A-N-G-E-R. This is a message for Doctor Oscar Sanchez. Please tell him I can't email the designs so they are on a website. He can download them from this address. It's omarox—that's O-M-A-R-O-X—dot com slash a dash one, once again that's omarox dot com slash e dash one. And can he call me back on my home number? It's 077 234 3785. Or email me at rsanger@omarox.com. Please give him this message before he leaves this morning. It's urgent.

Unit 11

56

I: Hello and welcome to your weekly podcast from indietravelinfo.com. With me today is travel writer Jan Lanting with some more suggestions on vacations for the independent traveler. So Jan, today I want to start with your advice for travelers this month. It's the end of March. Can you give some suggestions for good places to visit?
J: OK. Well, Malaysia is good for this time of year. It's very hot.
I: Great, maybe I should take a vacation there. What about the language? Do people speak English?
J: Yes, a lot of people speak some English. But of course, when you travel you should take a phrase book and learn a few phrases in the local language as well.
I: And what about hotels?
J: In the big cities, hotels are often busy so you should book in advance. But in the countryside, it's no problem. You can always find a room. I also recommend a tour in the jungle.
I: The jungle?!
J: Sure! You can go walking through the jungle and see lots of amazing animals and plants.
I: Should I go on my own or with a tour guide?
J: You shouldn't go into the jungle on your own. Always go with a local guide because it can be dangerous.
I: OK. Now for our final destination. The Arctic?
J: That's right, the Arctic.
I: But it's very cold.
J: Yes, you shouldn't go in the winter because it's very cold and very dark. At the end of March, it's sunny and the days are longer so you should go then.
I: Yes, but how do you get there? Should I go on my own or with a tour?
J: It's very difficult on your own, but you can take a ship with a lot of travel companies now. They offer special tours. So it is possible. If you want more details, there are links on my blog at www …

57

1 You have to drive on the left-hand side.
2 Guests have to leave their room before 11 a.m.
3 Airline passengers with an online boarding pass don't have to go to the check-in desk.
4 Business class passengers don't have to wait.

58

A: That looks interesting.
B: It's a vacation brochure.
A: Oh really?
B: Yes, I've got a month in South America so I'm looking at places to go.
A: I went there last year. It's an amazing part of the world. I went on a cruise all the way from Brazil to Argentina. You should go on that.
B: Yes, but I'm interested in the wildlife.
A: How about visiting the Andes? That was part of my bus tour in Chile.
B: But the disadvantage is that there are lots of other people with a bus tour. I like traveling on my own.
A: But the advantage is that you see more with a tour guide. And you visit places other tourists don't normally go to.
B: Hmm. Maybe you're right.
A: Can I make a suggestion? If you have a month, why don't you go on a tour for two weeks and then you could travel on your own afterwards?
B: Actually, that's a really good idea.

59

/ʌ/, /ʊ/, /uː/

Unit 12

60

1 It'll rain here tonight.
2 I will visit space in my lifetime.
3 I think I'll learn Spanish.
4 Will you visit me one day?
5 The percentage of people in the countryside will decrease.
6 I don't think there'll be more snow this winter.

61

A: It's the deepest place on Earth and before now, nobody has ever been to the bottom. But the film director and National Geographic explorer James Cameron has traveled down to the bottom of the Mariana Trench. With me in the studio is our science expert Jenny Walters to tell us how he did it.
B: Good evening.
A: So Jenny. First of all, how deep is the Mariana Trench?
B: It's seven miles to the bottom. That's a long way down.
A: It sure is. How long did the journey take?
B: Cameron took over two hours to get to the bottom, and then he spent about four hours down there.
A: And how did he travel there? In some kind of submarine?
B: That's right. It was a special one-man submarine.
A: I see. How big is it exactly?
B: It's 23 feet long but it has a big engine so there isn't much room for a human.
A: So you're in a small space and it's dark down there. I couldn't do it. How well could he see?
B: It's very dark but the submarine has lights, of course. So Cameron could see small sea creatures. He described it as a "desert." He also had cameras on the submarine, and he plans to make a 3D movie about the adventure.
A: And of course he isn't the first explorer, is he? How many other explorers have been there?
B: There was one other. Don Walsh went down in 1960, but he didn't go to the bottom. In fact he was on the ship when Cameron went down.
A: Wow! How old is he now?
B: I think he's in his eighties.
A: That's amazing! And I have one last question that everyone wants to know the answer to. How much did James Cameron spend on this? Thousands? Millions?
B: I'm afraid I don't know, but films like *Titanic* and *Avatar* made a lot of money at the box office, so I think he could afford it.

62

Good morning, and thank you for coming. My name's Davi and I'm from Brazil. Today, I'd like to talk about an important day in my year called Earth Day.

First, Earth Day began on April 22nd in 1970. Over 20 million people went to Earth Day in different cities across the US. There were politicians, teachers, artists, and musicians. Since that day in 1970, Earth Day has become famous all over the world.

63

1 Today, I'd like to talk about my company.
2 First, we started the company in 1999.
3 In conclusion, I think it's very important.

Inside Photos: 9 t (STEPHEN ALVAREZ/National Geographic Creative), 11 b (Paul Gunning/Alamy), 12 b (KENNETH GARRETT/National Geographic Creative), 14 c (FRITZ HOFFMANN/National Geographic), 15 c (Bryan Christie Design), 16 t (i love images/business/Alamy), 17 tl (i love images/business/Alamy), 17 bl (©Junial Enterprises/Shutterstock.com), 18 (Martin Puddy/Corbis), 20 cl (© Erika Cross/Shutterstock.com), 21 t (Sarah Leen/National Geographic Creative), 22 tl (Andy Torbet), 22 bl (Andy Torbet), 22 (Andy Torbet), 22 bc (Andy Torbet), 22 tr (©bogdan ionescu/Shutterstock.com), 22 tc (©Elnur/Shutterstock.com), 22 tr (©joingate/Shutterstock.com), 22 cr (©Bill Fehr/Shutterstock.com), 22 cr (©Olga Kovalenko/Shutterstock.com), 22 cr (©George Dolgikh/Shutterstock.com), 22 cr (©Kletr/Shutterstock.com), 22 cr (©Maxx-Studio/Shutterstock.com), 22 cr (©Nadezhda Bolotina/Shutterstock.com), 22 cr (©Galcka/Shutterstock.com), 22 cr (©Nataliya Hora/Shutterstock.com), 22 br (©HomeStudio/Shutterstock.com), 24 tr (©Santiago Cornejo/Shutterstock.com), 24 cr (©Gorins/Shutterstock.com), 24 br (©yampi/Shutterstock.com), 24 cr (©yampi/Shutterstock.com), 24 br (©smena/Shutterstock.com), 25 tr (Matthew Hams), 27 b (Ignacio Ayestaran/National Geographic Creative), 28 t (RICHARD NOWITZ/National Geographic Creative), 30 (Andrew Parker/Alamy), 31 bl (ZEE/Alamy), 31 bc (Accent Alaska.com/Alamy), 31 br (© Denis Vrublevski/Shutterstock.com), 31 bl (LH Images/Alamy), 31 br (©Jonnystockphoto/Shutterstock.com), 32 bl (The Athenaeum) 33 b (Folio), 33 t (Marvin E. Newman/Photographer's Choice/Getty Images), 34 tr (Jon Hicks/Corbis), 34 cl (©Nadiia Gerbish/Shutterstock.com), 34 br (Tyrone Turner/National Geographic), 34 cr (©Rachel Lewis/Lonely Planet Images/Getty Images), 34 bl (Jon Hicks/Corbis), 36 b (G. Anker), 36 b (©PhotoSky/Shutterstock.com), 37 b (Joel Sartore/National Geographic Creative), 39 b (Hxdbzxy/Dreamstime.com), 40 t (©spirit of america/Shutterstock.com), 41 cl (©Julia Shepeleva/Shutterstock.com), 41 cr (Andrew Watson/Getty Images), 44 tr (©xe-pOr-ex/Shutterstock.com) 45 t (Mary Ellen McQuay/First Light/Getty Images), 46 tl (Helen and Morna Mulgray), 46 cl (Camille and Kennerly Kitt), 46 bl (Press Association Images), 47 bl (Kzenon/Alamy), 48 tl (paul nicklen/National Geographic Creative), 48 b (paul nicklen/National Geographic Creative), 51 br (Sylwia Duda/Getty Images), 51 tr (AFP/Getty Images), 51 bl (Caters News Agency Ltd), 52 bl (©wizdata/Shutterstock.com), 53 bl (©StockLite/Shutterstock.com), 53 br (©Konstantin Sutyagin/Shutterstock.com), 54 (meghimeg/Flickr/Getty Images), 55 cl (Folio), 55 cl (©Adrian Reynolds/Shutterstock.com), 55 bl (© kreatorex/Shutterstock.com), 56 tr (Alain Grosclaude/Agence Zoom/Stringer/Getty Images) 57 t (Photo Shelter), 58 tl (Oran Tantapakul/Fotolia), 58 tl (valery121283/Fotolia), 58 tc (Bianca/Fotolia), 58 tr (Peter Polak/Fotolia), 58 cl (Lorenzo Buttitta/Fotolia), 58 c (James Insogna/Fotolia), 58 c (ildar akhmerov/Fotolia), 58 cr (kamonrat/Fotolia), 58 cl (Vidady/Fotolia), 58 c (thongsee/Fotolia), 58 c (kritchanut/Fotolia), 58 cr (leftleg/Fotolia), 58 cl (studio_ms/Fotolia), 58 cl (Aaron Amat/Fotolia), 58 c (MediablitzImages/Fotolia), 58 cr (yakovlev/Fotolia), 58 bl (Larisa Siverina/Fotolia), 58 bc (Vidady/Fotolia), 58 bc (Natika/Fotolia), 58 br (danheighton/Fotolia), 59 tl (©marco mayer/Shutterstock.com), 59 cl (©Karen Grigoryan/Shutterstock.com), 59 b (Bon Appetit/Alamy), 61 bl (Ian Dagnall/Alamy), 62 bl (Corbis), 62 bl (Paul Nicklen/National Geographic Image Collection/Alamy), 63 bkgd (deadlyphoto.com/Alamy), 64 tl (Richard Nowitz/National Geographic Creative), 65 tr (©J. Helgason/Shutterstock.com), 65 bl (©AVAVA/Shutterstock.com), 65 bc (©Marcell Mizik/Shutterstock.com), 65 bl (©stockyimages/Shutterstock.com), 65 bl (©stefanolunardi/Shutterstock.com), 65 bc (©shutterstock), 65 br (©Tony Northrup/Shutterstock.com), 66 (Mike Behnken/Flickr/Getty Images), 68 tr (David Wootton/Alamy) 69 t (Alija/E+/Getty Images), 70 b (Peter Symes Images), 71 tr (©schankz/Shutterstock.com), 71 cl (©Nathalie Speliers Ufermann/Shutterstock.com), 71 cr (©Nathalie Speliers Ufermann/Shutterstock.com), 71 bl (Steve Stock/Alamy), 71 br (©MPanchenko/Shutterstock.com), 72 cl (Phil Wills/Alamy), 73 bl (Interfoto/Alamy), 73 tr (KENNETH GARRETT/National Geographic Creative), 75 t (Robert Harding Picture Library Ltd/Alamy), 76 tl (World Wildlife Fund), 76 tl (©Save the Children Federation, Inc.), 76 cl (International Federation of Red Cross and Red Crescent Societies), 78 (Kenneth Garrett/National Geographic Image Creative), 79 tl (National Geographic Creative), 79 tr (National Geographic Creative), 79 cl (National Geographic Creative), 79 br (National Geographic Creative), 80 bl (Ingram Publishing/Alamy) 82 c (Peter McBride), 84 cl (©Oleg Znamenskiy/Shutterstock.com), 85 tl (Ria Novosti/Alamy), 85 tc (©Amanda Nicholls/Shutterstock.com), 85 tr (©Heiko Kiera/Shutterstock.com), 86 b (©dedek/Shutterstock.com), 87 (NASA), 87 bl (NASA), 88 cl (Folio), 89 tl (Folio), 89 cl (Folio), 89br (Bus Stop/Alamy), 90 (Nasa/dpa/Corbis Wire/Corbis), 92 cl (North Wind Picture Archives/Alamy) 93 t (Mario Babiera/Alamy), 94 t (Tino Soriano/National Geographic Creative), 94 t (Tino Soriano/National Geographic Creative), 96 cr (Joel Sartore/National Geographic Creative), 96 b (Eyevine/National Geographic Creative), 98 cr (Folio), 99 (Mike Powell/Stone/Getty Images), 100 t (BEN HORTON/National Geographic Creative), 102 (Travel Pictures/Alamy), 104 tr (Sir Juan Pablo) 105 t (National Geographic Creative), 106 cl (National Geographic Society), 106 cr (South Pacific Pictures Limited), 106 bl (Aleksei Vakhrushev), 106 br (Merva Faddoul), 106 bl (Frank Ramspott/Vetta/Getty Images), 108 b (Adrian Seymour), 108 bl (©Dariush M/Shutterstock.com), 109 bl (Adrian Seymour), 109 bl (©AND Inc/Shutterstock.com), 110 tr (Art Directors & TRIP/Alamy), 111 cl (Limmen Bight River Country, 1992 (synthetic polymer paint on canvas), Munduwalawala, Ginger Riley (1937–2002)/Art Gallery of New South Wales, Sydney, Australia/Mollie Gowing Acquisition Fund for Contemporary Aboriginal/Art 1992/The Bridgeman Art Library), 111 cl (V&A Images/Alamy), 111 b (Oli Scarff/Getty Images) 112 tr (Kike Calvo/National Geographic Creative), 113 b (Peter Bennett/Ambient Images Inc./Alamy), 114 (Frans Lanting Studio/Alamy), 115 c (Mark Carwardine/Photolibrary/Getty Images), 117 t (Harry Sieplinga/HMS Images/The Image Bank/Getty Images), 118 tl (Raul Touzon/National Geographic Creative), 120 t (Maggie Steber/National Geographic Creative), 121 cl (Don Emmert/AFP/Getty Images), 121 tl (Nicole Glass), 123 t (Mercedes-Benz), 124 tr (Oliver Eltinger/Fancy/Corbis), 127 tl (Tom Dick + Debbie), 127 cl (Tom Dick + Debbie), 127 cl (Tom Dick + Debbie), 127 bl (Tom Dick + Debbie), 128 bl (©S.Borisov/Shutterstock.com) 129 t (Alexander Nesbitt/Aurora/Getty Images), 130 b (Folio), 131 tl (Thomas Marent/Rolf Nussbaumer Photography/Alamy), 131 bl (Borge Ousland/National Geographic Creative), 132 cr (©Brian Guest/Shutterstock.com), 132 bl (Adina Tovy/Lonely Planet Images/Getty Images), 134 r (Mike Lyvers/Flickr/Getty Images), 135 t (KEENPRESS/National Geographic Creative), 136 tr (Edward Parker/Alamy), 137 (©hackerkuper/Shutterstock.com), 138 (Kazuyoshi Nomachi/Terra/Corbis), 139 tr (Raul Touzon/National Geographic Creative), 140 bl (Gagarin Cosmonaut Training Center/CNP/Corbis News/Corbis) 141 t (Ira Block/National Geographic Image Collection), 143 cl (National Geographic Creative), 145 bl (Rex Features), 147 tl (©Photobank gallery/Shutterstock.com), 147 t (©Photobank gallery/Shutterstock.com), 147 tr (Lee Prince/Shutterstock.com), 148 tr (Todd Gipstein/National Geographic Creative), 149 cl (©Didou/Shutterstock.com), 150 (Jorge Santos/age fotostock/Getty Images), 151 tr (©Pasquale/Shutterstock.com), 152 bl (Thomas J. Abercrombie/National Geographic Creative)Communication Activities, 155 cr (Folio) Communication Activities, 156 br (Reinier Gerritsen).

Text: We are grateful to the following for permission to reproduce copyright material:
Louise Leakey for family details on 12. Reproduced with kind permission; Andy Torbet for details on 22 and interview on 170. Reproduced with kind permission; National Geographic for extracts on 27, 46, 89, 101, 106, 142, 143, 153.

Illustration: Beehive Illustration 61, 67, 103, 133, Bob Lea 123, 144, 146, David Russell 032, 40, 83, 143, Matthew Hams 31, 40, 106, 158, 159, Reinier Gerritsen 100.